THE STORY OF
EARLY INDIAN CIVILIZATION

THE STORY OF
EARLY INDIAN CIVILIZATION

GERTRUDE EMERSON SEN
Illustrated by Edith Emerson

GANESH
who blesses beginnings

ORIENT LONGMANS

BOMBAY - CALCUTTA - MADRAS - NEW DELHI

ORIENT LONGMANS LTD.

Registered Office : 17 CHITTARANJAN AVENUE, CALCUTTA 13
NICOL ROAD, BALLARD ESTATE, BOMBAY 1
36A MOUNT ROAD, MADRAS 2
1/24, ASAF ALI ROAD, NEW DELHI 1

LONGMANS, GREEN & CO. LTD.
48, GROSVENOR STREET, LONDON W. 1
RAILWAY CRESCENT, CROYDON, VICTORIA, AUSTRALIA

LONGMANS GREEN (FAR EAST) LTD.
443 LOCKHART ROAD, HONG KONG

LONGMANS OF MALAYSIA LTD.
44 JALAN AMPANG, KUALA LUMPUR

LONGMANS SOUTHERN AFRICA (PTY) LTD.
THIBAULT HOUSE, THIBAULT SQUARE, CAPE TOWN

LONGMANS CANADA LTD.
137 BOND STREET, TORONTO 2

First published, 1964

An abridged and revised version of THE PAGEANT OF INDIA'S HISTORY, Volume 1, originally published by Longmans, Green & Co., Inc., New York, 1948.

Price : Rs. 6·00

Printed
at The Jupiter Press Private Ltd., Madras-18.

CONTENTS

ILLUSTRATIONS

CHAPTER I

The Indian Map

BEFORE turning back the pages of the book of time to the
first fitful traces of human life in India, let us take a look
at the map of India before a part was cut away to form Pakistan.
Certain physical peculiarities stand out at once. To the west
lies the Arabian Sea, to the east, the Bay of Bengal, to the south,
the vast expanse of the Indian Ocean. On the north the land is
firmly welded to the great continent of Asia. Here the boundary
consists of a high mountain wall some sixteen hundred miles long,
the Himalaya, or "Abode of Snow." Mountain spurs descend
nearly to the coastlines at both ends of this giant barrier. Strewn
among its ranges are hundreds of peaks more than twenty
thousand feet high. Mount Everest, at the eastern end, is the
world's highest peak, which was finally climbed in 1953.

Shut in by an icy rampart on the north and by water on all
other sides, India at first appears to have been endowed by nature
with a very special geographical unity of its own. Yet if oceans
are a means of isolating and protecting a country, they also offer
an inviting pathway for adventurous sailors, and passes cleave
the Himalayan wall, both in the northwest and northeast. Through
these, from prehistoric times, traffic has continuously flowed in
both directions.

Millions of years ago, India presented a picture very different
from the one revealed by the modern map. The Himalayas did
not exist at all, but in their place was a great sea. As a result
of the uneven pressure of two great continental blocks, the
bottom of this sea was slowly squeezed upwards into gigantic
folds. The sea drained away and finally disappeared, leaving
only a string of lakes in mid-Asia — and behold, the mighty
Himalayas, rising nearly six miles into the air ! Fossils of deep-
sea salt-water mollusks scattered in large numbers over many of
the Himalayan passes and slopes, up to an altitude of twenty
thousand feet, mutely tell the story of how the rocks in which
they lie embedded, or from which they have been washed out by
the slow action of wind and ice, were once the ooze of some
dark and silent ocean floor.

No human beings were there to witness the giant upheaval, for
man had not yet emerged on earth. Yet as geologists measure

time, the Himalayas are really quite young mountains, a mere sixty odd million years old or so, compared with such really elderly mountains as the Appalachians, twice their age, or the Alps. Strangest of all, the Himalayas, are still growing ! Even within historic times, the slopes have been tilted more steeply upwards. Far down inside the earth under the Himalayan arc, mysterious pressures are still at work, recorded at the surface in the form of frequent and violent earthquakes. North India has not yet settled down to stable conditions. In south India, on the other hand, the ancient rock formations are among the oldest in the world, and earthquakes there are extremely rare.

Several of India's mighty rivers have their sources near together in the remote ice caves of the Himalayas. Thundering down through steep gorges, gathering volume from many tributaries as they go, the Indus and the Ganga wind their way in opposite directions, the one to merge itself in the Arabian Sea, the other in the Bay of Bengal. Both are about fifteen hundred miles long. The Jumna joins the Ganga at Allahabad. The Brahmaputra, or Tsang-po, the longest river of them all, also rises in the Himalayas, within a hundred miles of the headwaters of the Indus, but for the greater part of its length it flows in an easterly direction across southern Tibet. Then it twists suddenly around in a great crook and enters Assam, eventually pouring its brown torrents into the Bay of Bengal. Compared with these mighty streams, the rivers of the Deccan plateau and of south India, though beautiful and romantic, are less impressive. The Mahanadi, Godavari, Krishna and Cauveri all flow eastward into the Bay of Bengal. The only important rivers with a western outlet, apart from the Indus, are the Tapti and the Narbada.

Rivers have always played a vital part in Indian history. Along their banks the earliest settlements were made, the first great cities grew up. For thousands of years the teeming population has been cultivating their fertile valleys. Is it any wonder that from very early times India's life-giving rivers came to be regarded as sacred ?

To the Indus, India even owes its most familiar name. In Sanskrit, *sindhu* means river. To the people of the old settled regions of the northwest, there could naturally be only one " sindhu." The Iranians, first cousins of the ancient Sanskrit-speaking people of India, transformed *sindhu* into *hindhu* and named the country beyond, *Hindustan*. When trade and war brought the Greeks and Iranians into close touch with each other about 600 B.C., the Greeks for the first time learned of this distant river country in southern Asia, but to suit their own manner of speech they changed the Persian *hindhu* into *indos*. Later the Romans modified this into *indus*. The English, in their turn, called the river Indus, and the country India, or Hindustan. It is also called Bharat today, from the legendary founder of the line of Indian kings.

The whole of India lies north of the Equator, in about the same general latitude as North Africa and Central America. Though snow is unknown in the plains and the temperature always remains above freezing point, frosts sometimes occur, and in spite of bright sunshine by day, the winds that sweep down from the Himalayan heights in December and January can be bitterly cold. For the greater part of the country, the three seasons are a mildly cold winter from October to February, an intensely hot season from March to June, and a rainy season, from July to September.

It is upon the regularity and sufficiency of the rains that India chiefly depends for her agricultural prosperity. If it is late in arriving or weak in volume, if it brings excessive rain in its wake or fails altogether, then misery is in store for millions, and the gaunt spectre of famine haunts the land. Even granted a good monsoon, the annual rainfall is distributed very unevenly. It varies from an average of five inches or less in the Rajputana desert of western India to 100 inches or more along the Malabar coast and in parts of Assam. The small hill town of Cherra Punji, in Assam, claims the distinction of being the wettest place on earth.

The kind of cultivation practised in different parts of India naturally depends upon such factors as latitude, rainfall or irrigation facilities, and character of the soil. Rice is extensively grown in Bihar and in the torrid wet regions of Assam, Bengal, Orissa, Andhra and Madras. Wheat is the chief product of colder places like the Punjab and Uttar Pradesh. Cotton thrives in the Punjab and the Deccan. Sugar-cane is a major crop of Uttar Pradesh and Bihar, and is increasing in importance in Madras and the Deccan. Jute fibre is produced mainly in Assam and Bengal. Tea is confined to the hilly regions of Assam, Bengal and south India. Pepper is the monopoly of Kerala. Millet, the staple food of the poor, is widely grown on dry uplands. Such, then, is the Indian subcontinent, in physical outline.

It is often said that India is a living ethnographic museum. This is quite true. All human types are to be found in the land, from the most primitive of shy jungle folk, who hide in the forest, dress in bark, and shoot with poisoned arrows, to the ultramodern university-educated young men and women of Calcutta, Madras and Bombay, from the patient tillers of the soil, who bear the burden of providing the sustenance of life for the four hundred and forty million Indians on their scorched bent backs, to the saffron-robed holy men, who renounce the world of personal desires and happiness to seek " another something ", which can be defined only in terms of spirit.   Amid this medley of human types are many complicated race mixtures. Each group has its own peculiar historical reason for being what it is, and each has contributed something specially its own to the rich and varied pattern of Indian life — for Hindu India stands, and has always stood, for the tolerant fusion of many ways of living and many ways of thinking.   Already old before modern means of transport and communication had achieved a dull uniformity in life over wide areas of the earth, these overlapping cultures in India have persisted almost intact to the present day.

In out of the way corners of south India exist primitive tribes whose hair and features probably bespeak one or more waves of immigration, ages back, from Africa.   Other tribes in the north, almost as primitive in their level of culture, are Mongoloid, and their original homeland must have been Tibet or northeastern Asia.   Still others, in central and eastern India, are possibly the remnants of some vast mysterious prehistoric movement of peoples flowing between India and the islands of the Pacific and Indian Ocean.   In comparison with the total population these really primitive folk are not numerous today.   (The previous census lists twenty million tribal people.)   Up to now, they have had no system of writing, no books, no records of their own past, apart from tenacious legends.   But they are the experts of the jungle and the forest, and the whole of Indian art and literature is drenched with an intimate knowledge and love of animals and birds, of trees and flowers, which they have bequeathed.

The early and characteristic Indian civilization, as distinct from all the other great civilizations and cultures of the world, has Hindu thought for its background.   Nearly all the other great civilizations of the ancient world, Sumerian, Assyrian, Babylonian, Iranian, Egyptian, even Greek and Roman, lie buried in their ruined cities.   The diligent spade of the archaeologist now and then brings to light some noble fragment of the past, which seems to have little connection with the present.   In India, for untold centuries, the aspirations and ideas of the Hindus, expressed through religion, art, music, literature, manners and the peculiar structure of their society, have maintained creative vitality.   The link with the past has never been destroyed, in spite of all the vicissitudes of history.   Even the divergent faiths emerging on

Indian soil from time to time, such as Buddhism, Jainism and Sikhism, are offshoots sprung from the ancient stem. They are basically reform movements, rather than new religions.

In race, Hindus are mainly a blend, in varying degrees, of two great families of mankind, Dravidian and Aryan. The Dravidian-speaking stock already inhabited Dravida, the old name for south India, at the time when the curtain of history first rises on the Indian peninsula. There is no evidence that the Dravidians ever entered India from outside, though contacts between the Dravidians and Africa, or between the Dravidians and the Mediterranean people, may have existed from remote antiquity. About the Aryans, scholars still quarrel violently.

Did the Aryans, or Aryas, whose name originally meant " kinsmen " and later came to mean " noble ", enter India from the northwest, most probably around 2000 B.C., or did they spread outward, during an even earlier age, from northern India itself ? Did two branches of the same sturdy race migrate in opposite directions, one to the northwest and Europe, the other to the southeast and India, from some original homeland in Asia Minor, or southern Russia beyond the Caucasus, driven by the drying up of their pasture lands ? There are equally good arguments for both views, and it is not likely that any final answer will ever be found. All that is certain is that the Aryan-speaking people of India and Iran, and of Greece and Europe, however different they now seem, derive their speech from a common parent language, and still reflect, in many of their most profound ideas and firmly established customs, a remote common inspiration.

This significant discovery first came to light through the comparatively modern science of philology, the study of root words and syntax. Obviously, where these are unmistakably alike or similar, some kind of relationship exists. Philology has shown that all the languages and dialects of the world can really be reduced to eight or nine great families. These are Aryan, Semitic, Hamitic, Turanian, Tibetan-Chinese, Dravidian, Austric, Amerindian (American Indian), and a group of related African languages. To the great Aryan family belong more languages, living and dead, than to any other single group. English, Celtic, French, German, Spanish, Italian, Russian, Armenian, Latin, Greek, old and modern Persian, Sanskrit and the modern languages spoken in northern India today, are all affiliated, and one original source is the ancient Aryan tongue. One can see the relation at a glance between Sanskrit *pitri, matri,* Bengali *pita, mata,* Greek *pater, meter,* Latin *pater, mater,* French *père mère,* German *vater, mutter,* English *father, mother.*

According to their own account, the early Indo-Aryans waged a fierce war over a long period of time with the darker skinned people, presumably the Dravidians, whom they found already in possession of the land. Gradually they made themselves masters of the whole of north India. They did not attempt to advance by force of arms beyond the dividing line of the Vindhyas, but contented themselves with a gradual cultural conquest of the southern part of the peninsula. But this Aryan conquest of ancient India was not entirely one-sided. As time passed, Aryan and Dravidian inevitably intermingled, and the haughty Aryan was ultimately compelled to admit vast groups of non-Aryans into his exclusive society and to welcome popular Dravidian gods and goddesses to a place of honour beside his own *devas*, or " shining ones ". Out of the mingling and fusion of these two great distinctive civilizations, Hinduism emerged.

Throughout long centuries, many other streams of influence have entered India. From central and western Asia, time and again, invading hordes poured down into the Indian plains. A few came as refugees. Most were pushed by hunger, passion for plunder or lust for power. Persian, Greek, Parthian, Scythian, Hun, Turk, Afghan, Arab, Mongol, European, have appeared upon the scene and helped themselves to what they could. Some of the invaders returned swiftly whence they came, loaded with much booty. Some settled down and made India their home, contributing curious blendings of blood and the yeast of new ideas, creating new forms of art, introducing new customs, new fashions in dress, new religious beliefs. The hundred and forty million Muslims divided between India and Pakistan today are a permanent inheritance of more than a thousand years of such invasions from Asia, with their resulting conversions. In the seventh century, fleeing before some of those same Muslims, a little band of Persian fire worshippers, of the Zoroastrian faith, found a hospitable welcome in India. The Parsis of the West Coast are their direct descendants. Two small sects of Indian Jews and a very ancient sect of Syrian Christians still reside in Kerala. In the modern period, came the invasions of the white Europeans, by sea.

" Variety in unity " was perceived as the basic plan of life by the wise teacher-saints of ancient India. Variety is deeply inherent in Indian life. It is to be found in the extremes of the natural environment. It is in the very blood of the inhabitants. It expresses itself in a rich and imaginative art, in wide-ranging thought. Giving, taking, borrowing, assimilating, creating, India has come to be what she is, perhaps the most provocative and fascinating country in the world.

CHAPTER II

Dawn Over India

MANKIND'S earliest written records, with which history properly begins, do not go back more than about six thousand years. Yet hundreds of thousands of years before primitive man had the creative idea of drawing symbols to express what he wanted to say, he was living here on this earth. A universal Stone Age culture existed — so called from the material of the tools in use — and it is from their stones that we try to form some dim idea of how our remotest ancestors lived.

Stone Age man has left plenty of traces in India. Typical tools have been picked up in great quantities in many widely scattered places, mostly on the surface of the ground, but exploration for ancient remains of human life is comparatively recent in India, and the findings are still very incomplete and haphazard. The oldest Indian Stone Age tools are made of a light-coloured quartzite, a volcanic rock harder than flint. The commonest tool is a hand axe, flaked off on both sides. In the region of the Sabarmati River, in western India, layers bearing implements of the earlier and later periods of the Stone Age have been found to be separated by a gravel deposit of two hundred feet. This gives some idea of the length of time for the transition to be effected.

Neolithic, or New Stone Age, settlements in India show that the favourite instrument was then the celt, resembling a chisel, but many different kinds of tools were already being used. In this period dark-coloured volcanic traprock was the most common material, but smaller tools, such as those picked up in the Vindhya region and elsewhere, were often made of beautifully tinted or translucent stones like crystals, agate, chalcedony, jasper, carnelian and chert. A most interesting New Stone Age tool factory was unearthed not very long ago in Madras State. It contained tools in every stage of manufacture, including knives, scrapers, adzes, chisels, hammers, axes, arrowheads, spearheads, maceheads, mortars and pestles — everything, in fact, which primitive man had as yet devised to help him in his stern struggle with nature.

There are several cave sites in India where primitive rock paintings have also been discovered. They lie in Uttar Pradesh,

Bihar, Madhya Pradesh and Madras. It is not easy to fix a date for paintings of this type, but stone implements and bones of animals of both extinct and living species found in or near the Indian caves indicate high antiquity. The Indian paintings generally follow the style of similar prehistoric paintings in Spain and Africa. They depict in a most realistic way animals running or leaping, warriors in pursuit or fighting with one another, birds flying. The animals are the familiar elephants, buffaloes, goats, deer, horses, rhinoceroses and monkeys of present-day India.

In the usual order of things, India, like the rest of the ancient world, should have passed through a Copper and Bronze Age before reaching the Iron Age, and north India, indeed, seems to have done so. Stretching in a long line from Baluchistan and the Indus Valley all the way to Bengal are more than a hundred sites where primitive copper objects have been located. They consist of barbed harpoons, swords, chisels and spearheads. In one of these sites, Gungeria, in Madhya Pradesh, 424 hammered copper objects, equal in weight to 828 pounds, were unearthed, along with 102 thin silver plates. Old copper mines of the Chota Nagpur district, not far distant, were probably the chief source of the raw material for what must have been an extensive copper industry in north India in those early days. The ruined site of Mohenjo-daro in Sind, first excavated some four decades ago, now in Pakistan, has revealed that the inhabitants of this ancient Indian city, typical of the well-established Indus civilization of 3000 B.C., were perfectly familiar with copper and bronze, but not a single object of iron has been discovered there.

South India, on the other hand, presents a curious, unsolved archaeological puzzle. Primitive copper, bronze and iron objects have all been found lying promiscuously together in prehistoric sites, but iron objects far outnumber those of copper and bronze. Either south India passed directly from the Stone Age into the Iron Age, without any middle period at all, or independently and much earlier than the rest of India, south India had discovered iron for itself. Numerous iron deposits exist in the south, easily worked from the surface, and remains of primitive forges, forge tools and slag heaps are abundant. Remarkable skill in mining and metalwork was certainly highly developed in south India from remote times. A prehistoric gold mine exists at Maski, near Hyderabad, and the settlement close by appears to have been in continuous occupation from Neolithic times. Polished stone implements, black and red pottery, beads, shell ornaments, small terra-cotta figurines, the unique find of a tiny cobra head cut from amethyst, and many objects of metal have come from this fascinating spot.

In south India, primitive pottery and articles of polished stone and metal are most commonly found in the megalithic sites associated with prehistoric burials. Such ancient burial sites exist in many countries. Large unhewn stones, or monoliths, are laid or set in various patterns technically described as cairns, circles, menhirs, cromlechs, dolmens or barrows. The burial chambers are sometimes above ground, sometimes excavated in the rock beneath. So huge are some of the megalithic stones that it seems as if only a race of giants, now extinct, could have moved them. Possibly the tombstones of today are the last vestige of the practice of our Stone Age ancestors, who in this way sought to place an imperishable mark over their graves.

One of the most interesting of the prehistoric sites of south India is a great burial ground discovered in the Tinnevelly district of Madras, at the extremity of the peninsula. It covers an area of 114 acres. Funerary urns supported on rings and containing human skeletons or collections of human bones were found ranged in pits or chambers excavated from the solid rock, originally closed with stone slabs. Rice husks and decayed grain in the urns, or in smaller jars of polished black and red ware, show that food offerings were made to the dead at the time of burial. Household and personal articles, including bronze bowls, gold ornaments, iron swords, carnelian beads and small figures of water buffaloes and other animals have also been dug up at this place. Though urn burial seems to have been widely practised in south India, terra-cotta or stone sarcophagi with legs have also been discovered in certain places.

From the strikingly uniform megalithic remains of southern India, it is possible to gain some idea of the early culture which existed there at the dawn of Indian history. The cultivation of rice was certainly practised, no doubt carried on in prehistoric times as it still is in tropical Asia, with the help of the water buffalo. The presence of numerous terra-cotta spindles in the Indian grave chambers, taken with the fact that cotton is a native plant of the Deccan, indicates that the ancient inhabitants were familiar with spinning and undoubtedly made cotton cloth. They were also expert fishermen. On the coast close to the Tinnevelly burial ground are the remains of a very ancient pearl-fisheries establishment, and it is quite possible that even in neolithic times Dravidian traders went out from this pearl centre on long adventurous voyages. Shells were also extensively used in the making of ornaments. Shell remains in inland sites like Maski bear witness to the important shell trade carried on from earliest times.

Unfortunately, no great prehistoric towns or cities like those uncovered in northwestern India have as yet been discovered in southern India, though Aryan tradition credits the non-Aryan inhabitants with being architects and city builders of great skill, and makes specific mention of their " thirty iron towns " and " hundred stone forts." All the evidence points to the existence of a widespread and stable prehistoric culture throughout south India.

It is now generally believed that before the conflict with the Aryan-speaking people, Dravidians were in occupation of the greater part of India. The Gonds, a people dwelling in central India, speak a Dravidian dialect, and to this day there is a small unexplained " island " of Dravidian-speaking people living in Baluchistan, on the far side of the Indus. They bear no resemblance in racial qualities to the South Indians of today, nor are they known to have been in contact with any Dravidian culture within historical times. Yet their language, Brahui, belongs to the Dravidian family. The Indus Valley itself shelters in its dry sands the material evidence of an advanced pre-Aryan city civilization, dating back five thousand years. Some are convinced that it was essentially Dravidian in origin.

At least five thousand years ago, only a very short time after the Sphinx and the Pyramids rose in Egypt, and at the very same time when the great Sumerian civilization was flourishing at places like Kish and Tell-Asmar, and royal palaces and tombs were being built at Ur, in Mesopotamia, northwestern India, too, boasted an advanced and typical civilization of its own. The Indus civilization, as it is now officially called, was not confined to the Indus Valley. It extended over an area considerably greater than the contemporary Egypt or Sumer. It included not only Sind and the Punjab, but Baluchistan and Seistan on the west and Saurashtra on the south. Sites of the same civilization have been discovered in Gujarat, Rajputana and Himachal Pradesh, and a few recent finds indicate that it extended even to Delhi and eastward into the Gangetic Valley.

Before the twentieth century, the existence of the Indus civilization was not even guessed. In 1922, an Indian archaeologist, R. D. Banerji, began to investigate some second-century Buddhist ruins in Sind, at a spot locally known as Mohenjo-daro, " place of the dead." This lay on the old bank of the Indus, four miles from the present course of the river and some two hundred miles

north of Karachi. Mr. Banerji soon ascertained that the bricks
used for a structure crowning a low hill had been dug from the
ruins of an ancient city which lay directly beneath and around
the later Buddhist monument. The Archaeological Department
of India at once realized the importance of his discovery and took
over the task of making a thorough exploration.

Some fifty years earlier, certain small stone seals engraved with
a mysterious script, unlike any other seals then known in the
ancient world, had begun to turn up in the neighbourhood of
Harappa, in the Punjab, 450 miles north of Mohenjo-daro.
Harappa, now also transferred to Pakistan, is situated in the
vicinity of the old bed of the Ravi, a branch of the Indus. Unfortunately, it was long used by neighbouring villagers as a brick
quarry, and, worse still, it was subsequently made to supply
quantities of ballast for railway construction. As an archaeological site, therefore, it had been ruined. In the course of the new
excavations at Mohenjo-daro, hundreds of seals like those already
known from Harappa were unearthed. A few similar seals,
eighteen so far, have since come to light from the ancient Sumerian cities of Kish, Ur and Tell-Asmar. One, extracted from a
layer of debris at Kish, beneath a temple which could be definitely
dated as of the third millenium B.C., gave the first clue to the
genuine antiquity of Harappa and Mohenjo-daro.

Nor were these lonely cities of the time. Nal in Baluchistan,
Amri, Jhukar, Lohumjo-daro and Chanhu-daro, in Sind, Kotla
Nihang, in the Punjab, and many other allied sites, were all found
to belong to roughly the same period. The indefatigable explorer,
Sir Aurel Stein, traced an ancient caravan road strung with a
whole series of prehistoric settlements running from northwest
India and Baluchistan through the Makran desert to Iran and
Mesopotamia. It is now certain from a study of the pottery
remains, from beads of Mohenjo-daro and Ur incised with an
identical pattern, from the discovery of Indus seals far afield,
that a flourishing trade was once carried on between these ancient
centres. Confirmation is found in the discovery at Mohenjo-daro
of a pottery jar of a type which can be dated between 2800 and
2500 B.C., with a Sumero-Babylonian inscription in cuneiform
characters, the special nail-writing of ancient Mesopotamia.

The Indus civilization clearly belongs to the period following
the Neolithic and preceding the Iron Age, that is, to the latter
part of the third millenium B.C. Flint knives and articles of stone
were still in common use, and copper and bronze objects were
plentiful, but iron was not yet known. No outstandingly magnificent or valuable works of art, such as have given supreme

distinction to the ancient centres in Sumer, Egypt, Crete and Troy, have so far been discovered in the Indus Valley. Neither have any palaces or royal tombs, upon which the ancient artists of other lands lavished all their skill and ingenuity, and the State its wealth, come to light. On the other hand, the Indus cities reflect an extraordinarily high degree of comfort for ordinary people, and they are the oldest planned cities known.

The excavated area of Mohenjo-daro, the most important example of an Indus city of ancient times, covers more than 240 acres. Three different levels of occupation, one on top of another, have so far been uncovered. The city was continuously lived in for a period of at least six hundred years, from 3300 to 2700 B.C., after which it was apparently deserted. The solid foundations and walls of the lowest city extend down considerably below the present water level, making deeper digging impossible. The city of the lowest level, however, is the most solidly built and covers the largest area, and the pottery of the deeper layers is superior in workmanship to any found in the upper levels.

The streets were broad and straight, all running north and south, or east and west. The principal street was thirty-three feet wide. Both sides of the streets were flanked with houses substantially built of burnt bricks. They were provided with open courtyards, private wells and bathrooms. One of the most striking features of the ancient city is the excellent drainage system it maintained. Pottery pipes or well-constructed channels set in the outer walls carried the waste water and refuse from individual houses down to large street drains. These were made of stone, carefully cemented and waterproofed with asphalt. A large bathing tank, thirty-nine feet long, twenty-three feet wide and eight feet deep, has broad steps leading down at both ends to the paved floor. The lining of the tank is three to four feet thick and is made of bricks laid in gypsum backed by an inch of bitumen.

The houses of Mohenjo-daro are devoid of paintings or decorations of any sort. Perhaps the city was a busy river port, whose occupants were more concerned with trade and personal comfort than with art. The debris, however, has yielded thousands of articles of practical daily use, many showing that in the minor arts the Mohenjo-darians had attained masterly skill.

Although the greater part of the pottery is plain, there is a distinctive red and black painted ware polished like lacquer. Clay was easily procured from the banks of the river near by. It was turned on a fast wheel, given a slip of red ochre upon which designs were painted in black manganese and sometimes in other colours, and was then fired in well-made round ovens. Finally it was burnished. Typical Indus designs take the form of intersecting circles, triangles, trefoils, tree and vegetable patterns and ribbon borders. A few specimens have designs of animals, fish, birds and human beings. Among implements and tools, a bronze adze ten inches long, a portion of a ruler with divisions accurately marked, a saw with offset teeth and graded weights and scales are the most interesting. Chairs, spoons of tortoise shell, silver drinking cups and cosmetic boxes have also been collected.

The large population of Mohenjo-daro could scarcely have maintained itself without agriculture, and the surrounding plain must have been extensively cultivated, though few agricultural tools have been discovered. Numerous grinding stones have been found, however, and chemists have been able to identify carbonized grains of barley and wheat, and seeds of melons and dates, taken from kitchen jars, some of which also contained bones of animals and fish. That the people knew how to spin and weave is obvious from countless spindles of pottery and glazed ware. A stone bust of a man wears over his left shoulder a shawl decorated in a three-leaved pattern. One of the most remarkable finds is an actual bit of cotton cloth, the oldest piece of cotton cloth known to the world, preserved in the corroded surface of a silver jar of jewelry dug up from its original hiding place under a floor in one of the houses. It has helped to establish the claim that Indians were the earliest users of cotton cloth. The rest of the ancient world, apart from the Chinese after their discovery of silk, used linen, wool, skins or bark, before they became acquainted with cotton.

From the amount of jewelry unearthed it is clear that the people of Mohenjo-daro dearly loved to adorn themselves, and various small statuettes of stone, clay and bronze show their exact mode of dress. The women wore short skirts, elaborate girdles, rings, bracelets, necklaces, nose studs and hair ornaments. Their necklaces were made of beads of gold, lapis lazuli, turquoise, jadeite or carnelian, sometimes inlaid. The beads were beautifully polished and always perfectly bored, showing a remarkably high standard of the stone-cutter's art. Both men and women took great pains with their hair. They combed it with ivory combs and dressed it with thin gold fillets or ornamental hairpins. The men appear to have followed the fashion of shaving the upper lip but keeping a thick beard. Bronze razors of four different patterns have been found.

Another prominent characteristic of the Indus people was their love of children. Innumerable toys have come to light, such as miniature household articles, clay whistles in the form of birds, marbles and gamesmen, animals with wagging heads, little two-wheeled carts drawn by humped oxen. A remarkable bronze model of such a cart was found at Chanhu-daro, with the driver actually seated in it, holding a whip. Gambling must have been a fairly common amusement of the older people, if large numbers of dice made from ivory or stone are a correct indication. A charming bronze figurine of a dancing girl shows appreciation of the art of dancing, and representations of various kinds of musical instruments carved on the seals express the love of music.

The unique Indus Valley seals, or amulets, are usually made of soft white limestone and are most commonly square, measuring from a half inch to two and a half inches across. A perforated knob at the back suggests that they were intended to be strung on a cord and perhaps worn on the arm or neck. The distinctive and characteristic feature of the Indus seals is the finely carved animal and the line or two of pictographic writing on the front face. This same sort of writing is occasionally traced on metal tools and pottery, but no large stone inscriptions have been found. Up to now, in spite of many valiant efforts, the Indus script has not been successfully deciphered. It is not even known what the Indus language was, and until and unless there is some lucky find, perhaps of a two-language seal, there is little hope that the secret of the mysterious language and script can be solved.

What gives the Indus seals their special import, apart from the distinctive script, is the fact that they are engraved with characteristically Indian animals, though sometimes they are also adorned with fantastic mythological creatures possessing two or three heads, or the fabulous unicorn. The unicorn, in fact, seems to have been a great favourite with the Indus people, since more seals are found with this device than with any other. The humped Indian bull, however, is extremely popular, as are also the elephant, the tiger, the buffalo, the rhinoceros, the fish-eating crocodile, the goat and the antelope. There are no elephants or tigers in Sind today, but on the strength of the seals it appears that formerly they roamed the Indus Valley which must obviously have been wetter then than now. Indeed, the provision for so much drainage in the houses of Mohenjo-daro is proof of the fact.

It is possible that the animals were worshipped as symbols of different deities, after the Egyptian fashion. Not a few of the seals depict a fight between two fantastic animals or between a

SEALS from the INDUS Valley · 5000 yrs. old

man and an animal. One seal portrays what appears to be a three-headed horned deity seated cross-legged on a low stool or throne. Around this figure are grouped various animals, as if in devotion. Another seal shows a tree spirit with a man bowing before it. Most popular of all, however, was the worship of the Mother Goddess, whose clay images have been found at Mohenjo-daro in great numbers. She was universally worshipped in ancient times throughout western Asia, as well as in India.

The sudden end of the well-established Indus culture remains a mystery. None of the ancient cities appears to have been occupied after about 2500 B.C. Mohenjo-daro and Harappa were apparently deserted first, Chanhu-daro a century or two later. Startled excavators at Mohenjo-daro came upon a few skeletons in distorted positions at the bottom of a staircase leading to a well, and again in one of the streets, as if the victims had been suddenly trapped, or had died in some agonizing epidemic. Did some warlike neighbours fall upon the unsuspecting Indus cities, and after destroying them carry most of the inhabitants off into captivity? Or did the floodwaters of the Indus rise one night, without warning, and overwhelm the land? Who can say?

CHAPTER III

Aryan Morning

THE story of the gradual Aryan expansion in India begins with the legend of the Indian Flood, first described in an ancient Sanskrit work of about 1000 or 800 B.C., the *Satapatha Brahmana*. After the subsidence of the waters, Manu, a mythical descendant of the Sun-god, came down from the top of a mountain where he had tied his boat after being guided to safety by a big fish. He then divided the land among his offspring, and all the later royal Aryan dynasties of India are supposedly descended from his nine sons and one daughter. The eldest son, Ikshvaku, became king of Ayodhya and founder of the great line of solar kings. Pururavas, his daughter's son by the grandson of the Moon-god, became king of Prathisthana (Allahabad) and founder of the line of lunar kings.

Ever since Europe discovered Sanskrit less than two centuries ago, European scholars have been busy trying to prove that the Aryan Indians migrated to India from some other place, but actually only one relevant fact and one certain date are known. An archaeological signpost was discovered in Asia Minor, near Ankara, the present Turkish capital. The little village of Bhogaz-Koi marks the site of the onetime capital of the powerful Hittite kingdom, which came into prominence in the twentieth century B.C. Here, two Hittite inscriptions in cuneiform writing record a victory of the Hittites over their southern neighbours the Mitanis, and mention a royal marriage arranged to cement the peace treaty between the two nations. Five Aryan divinities are invoked as witnesses or are invited to give their blessings to the royal pair, Indra, Varuna, Mitra, the Asvins under the name of Nasatya (the familiar Gemini of the western zodiac). Since this Hittite victory is definitely known to have taken place in or about 1400 B.C., it is clear that Aryan gods were being worshipped in Asia Minor at this date. Which way the signpost points, however, cannot be proved.

The early Indo-Aryans, subject of so much controversy in modern times, have left behind a vast literature which has the unique advantage of having been composed by themselves. The *Rig-veda* consists of 1028 hymns addressed to various deities, divided into ten parts. It may without question be called the

2

oldest book in the world. On the basis of its archaic Sanskrit, it is held to be the earliest of the four Vedas. Afterwards, a number of manuals and philosophic works to explain the Vedas were composed. This Vedic literature was, of course, the work of many authors, and its composition must have covered a very long time, possibly two thousand years. It is the source of all our knowledge about the early Indo-Aryans.

The Vedic Aryans, as the scroll begins to unwind, are found actively engaged in taking possession of the land of the Seven Rivers represented by the Indus and its principal tributaries (later to be known as Punjab, or " Five Rivers "). The western-most limit of Aryan wanderings can be traced by the names of rivers unmistakably identified with the present-day rivers of eastern Afghanistan. The Ganga and the Jumna are mentioned in the *Rig-veda*, but the main setting of Aryan activity is northwestern India, and there is no reference to any land of sacred memories other than the Himalayas. The Indus Valley, as already seen, was no mere wilderness. Great cities had grown up there, and trade and agriculture flourished. Writing and the arts were well developed. Of all this, however, the *Rig-veda* is curiously silent. The Vedic Aryans called their enemies simply *dasas*, or *dasyus* — " slaves " — or by various tribal names such as Danava, Daitya, Simyu, Pisacha, Pani, Rakshasa or Naga. At a much later date, when all these tribes had been absorbed by the Aryan conquest, the names lost their tribal significance and several of them came to stand for races of legendary and mythological beings, more or less unfriendly to men, like giants and demons.

The dasyus are described as " black-skinned ", " malignant ", and " non-sacrificing ". At the same time, their tribes are many, and the Aryans are few. Indra, the Aryan War-god, is often called upon in the hymns with a mixture of praise and flattery to come into the battle on the side of his worshippers. He is invited to make good use of his thunderbolt, to collect the heads of the enemy and crush them under his wide foot.

The Aryans are depicted as driving furiously into battle on chariots drawn by horses, the warrior standing on the left side of the charioteer. The dasyus, not familiar with horses, experienced fear and consternation. Swords, battle-axes, javelins and slings were wielded, but chief of all weapons was the bow, first among Aryan warriors, the archer. The bow was large and was drawn to the ear. At the archer's back hung a quiver of reed arrows, feathered and pointed with deerhorn or metal. A leather guard protected his arm from the friction of the cowhide bow-string. Thus the Aryans extended their conquests and gradually established themselves throughout the greater part of northern India.

They advanced as warriors, but their herds and their women-folk accompanied them, and some hymns of the *Rig-veda* give very human glimpses of the tribes struggling on wearily in search of pasture lands. Pushan, the Sun as pathfinder for herdsmen, is implored to lead the travellers to pleasant tracts covered with green grass, or Brihaspati, the Lord of Prayer, and Indra are jointly solicited for guidance when they have lost their way.

The pastoral Aryans loved their freedom and had a poetic appreciation of nature. They were not at first inclined to build cities and showed an aristocratic contempt for trade, preferring to live in fortified camps or the villages they cleared for themselves in the great forest then extending over vast areas of India. They chose as an auspicious site a place where good water was available. Then the village was laid out as a rectangle divided

Symbolic figure called Nandyavarta, meaning " The Abode of Bliss " or Happiness

into four equal quarters, with gates, or watchtowers, facing the four directions. At the intersection of the main streets an open platform was constructed, shaded by a thatched roof or a tree, where the village council of elders, which came to be known as the *panchayat*, met. As villages grew into larger centres, a council house replaced the simple village platform, and an assembly, or *sangha*, took the place of the council of five. A common grazing ground was set aside, and the village fields radiated from the village centre.

The general picture of the pastoral and agricultural life of the early Indo-Aryan community has an appealing charm. For everyone there was a special duty to perform. The small boys took the cattle out to graze on the edge of the forest land and brought them back in the evening to the shelter of the village. The Vedic maiden's duty can be guessed from her name of *duhitri*, which has the same root as daughter, derived from *dugdha,* " milk ". She was obviously the little milkmaid of the family. She also plaited mats and wove cloth from sheep's wool.

She danced and she collected the sacred *kusa* grass to spread on the ground for sacrifices. She helped to make the sacred *soma* juice. As water was added to the crushed plants, she stirred the juice with her fingers, pressing it through a woollen strainer into a sacred vessel.

The men, when they were not fighting, tended the fields, with the help of their horses and oxen. They sowed barley and wheat, and cut the grain at harvest time with sickles and transported it on carts. They were tenderly considerate of their animals, and ever grateful to the gods of field and sky through whose bounty they prospered. The Vedic field songs, of which there are many, ring with a lusty joy of living.

The Aryans always considered themselves as free men, and originally they were all of equal status. They could be soldiers, herdsmen or farmers, as occasion required, and every Aryan father in his own household daily performed rites of worship and hymn chanting. It was these rites which mainly distinguished the Aryans from the " non-sacrificing " aboriginals, whose strange religious practices were looked upon as outlandish.

Gradually the original five tribes of the Indo-Aryans spread out and multiplied. For purposes of mutual protection, tribal villages combined into larger units under the rule of a chosen *raja*, or king, their protector and leader in battle. Sometimes in their wars, rival Aryan kings made alliances with powerful non-Aryan kings. An account of the great battle on the Ravi, in which Sudas, king of the Bharatas, defeated an alliance of Ten Kings, five Aryan and five non-Aryan, comes down from the dim period of the *Rig-veda*. Both sides had their family priests. On the side of Sudas and the Bharatas was Vasishta, on the side of the Ten Kings, Visvamitra.

Bigger and bigger wars necessitated the maintenance of large forces of trained fighting men. Since the welfare of the whole community depended on good crops, however, those who showed themselves to be the best farmers, in due course, were permanently excused from fighting. The king, who had to spend much time in camp, was prevented from attending in strict detail to religious ritual, and so a royal chaplain, or priest, was appointed to perform religious observances on behalf of the king, and especially to conduct the big sacrifices which now began to be celebrated on an ever-increasing scale.

Thus a special class of Brahmins, or " prayer men ", emerged in Aryan society. They were the specialists in all religious affairs, particularly in matters of ritual. They chanted the appropriate hymns. Famous Brahmin families, or lines of priests, came into existence. Seven books of the *Rig-veda* represent collections of hymns mainly associated with such priestly families. The Kshatriyas, or warriors, from among whom the king himself was chosen, also acquired a separate professional standing in the expanding Aryan community. Below them, came the commoners, Vaisyas — herdsmen, farmers, traders and superior craftsmen, such as goldsmiths, armourers, metal-workers and carpenters. They still remained free and relinquished none of their old privileges as self-respecting Aryans, entitled to a full say in all the affairs of the community. These three groups called themselves ' twice-born,' because their boys underwent a special initiation ceremony, marked by the putting on of a sacred belt or cord, as they began a study of the sacred scriptures, knowledge of which was deemed to bestow a second, or spiritual, birth.

During the period of Aryan expansion in the north, the earlier inhabitants of the land were by no means exterminated, in spite of Indra's mighty thunderbolt. Beyond the Vindhyas, in the Deccan and southern India, the non-Aryans continued to follow their own pursuits. Some of the more primitive inhabitants fled away to remote hills and forests. Those who were conquered by the Aryans were pressed into service to perform the less inviting tasks of life as labourers, menials or petty craftsmen. With the passage of time, these people adopted the customs and beliefs of their Aryan overlords, and though they were excluded from the rite of Vedic initiation, they acquired a respectable place in the economic and social life of the Aryan community.

Slowly, too, some of the primitive folk who had fled away came back. They hung on the outskirts of the mixed Aryan and non-Aryan villages and timidly offered for barter their humble wicker baskets, their clay pottery or their jungle produce. To them was eventually assigned the most menial of the village services, and they remained entirely beyond the pale of Aryan society. From this ostracized fifth group have descended most of the so-called " depressed " and " untouchable " sections of Hindu society today. The Aryan acceptance of a society divided on a basis of colour and labour, flexible at first, tended to become more and more rigid as time went on, until it produced the Hindu caste system. Traditionally, a person is born, marries and dies in a particular community, without ever having the opportunity to leave it. But in the present-day India, caste distinctions are less strict, and " untouchability " has been legally abolished.

To begin with, trade was apparently distasteful to the freedom-loving and poetic Aryan temperament, and business was probably left largely in the hands of capable non-Aryans. Yet barter, or some form of selling and buying, was inescapable, and the *Rig-veda* makes it clear that values were measured in terms of cows or gold. Highways linked the larger towns, and along these merchants travelled in caravans. They also made journeys by sea. The *Rig-veda* has several references to ships. Varuna, the Sky-Ocean-god, is said to know the paths of the sea over which ships go, just as he knows the paths of the birds in the sky.

In periods of leisure, between war and work, the Vedic Aryans amused themselves in various ways. They loved singing, poetry and music. They played on drums, stringed instruments and flutes. Chariot races and archery contests were a source of keen delight. They hunted with the bow and arrow, captured lions and birds in snares, antelopes in pits, and boars with the aid of hunting dogs. They were passionately addicted to the use of intoxicating liquor, of which they had two kinds. The sacred *soma,* offered in sacrifices, was made from a mysterious plant which cannot now be identified, and *sura* was made from fermented barley. Gambling, too, exercised a dangerous fascination over the Indo-Aryans. A vivid description of the plight of a ruined gambler appears in a Rig-vedic hymn to Savitar, the Sun-god.

In the domestic realm, the picture of Aryan life usually seems a happy one. The joint bliss of the married couple is often sung. The father, or oldest male member, was head of the family, and this patriarchal system characteristic of Aryan society markedly differed from the matriarchal system observed among the Dravidians and many of the tribes among whom descent is traced from the mother's or sister's side. Monogamy appears to have been the general rule in Aryan society, and the Aryan mother certainly held a high and honourable position. Sons, indeed, were welcomed as future warriors, but daughters, who would become the mothers of warriors, were affectionately cherished in the Vedic home. Considerable freedom of choice in marriage was allowed to young people and there was no practice of child marriage, nor acceptance of a bride price. On the contrary, the Aryan maiden was given away with an ample dowry of gold, cows, chariots and horses.

As wife and mother, the woman of Rig-vedic days was looked upon as a distributor of blessings. Her responsibilities were the care of the house, the preparation of the food, the upbringing of the children, the provision of clothing for her family, the kindly management of the household servants and concern for the welfare of domestic animals. Although she did not undergo any special ceremony of religious initiation, she received instruction from the family priest, and her presence was required in all the religious sacrifices and rites observed in the household. If her husband died before she did, and she had no children, she could, if she wished, marry again. A widow did not burn herself on her husband's funeral pyre. The bereaved wife is addressed thus in a Rig-vedic funeral hymn : " Rise up, woman, thou art lying by one whose life is gone ; come to the world of the living, away from thy husband."

But hymns were not sung merely to tell unborn generations how the Indo-Aryans lived as human beings in northern India four or five thousand years ago. They were composed with awe and love for the mysterious forces which the minds and hearts of the ancient poets and seers informed them lay behind every aspect of the visible world of earth, sky and sea, as well as behind other invisible worlds whose presence they dimly felt. These forces seemed to them like gods and goddesses, friendly to worshippers and ever ready to give help, if only they were approached with prayers and proper rites. The steadfast mountains, the rushing rivers, the blue-black storm clouds, wind and rain and flashing lightning, the life-giving sun, the rhythmic moon, the bright fire, dawn and twilight, the fertile earth, the invigorating soma drink — all inspired homage and devotion.

The objectives of the rituals, through which the deities were invoked, were quite practical and material. Success in battle, the safe outcome of a journey, long life, wealth in progeny and cows — such were the ends for which the Vedic Aryans generally prayed or made sacrifices. But sometimes, too, the request was for spiritual knowledge. The best-known of the Rig-vedic hymns is a very short one, the " Gayatri," addressed to Savitar, the sun. It has been translated as follows : " We meditate on that effulgent light of Savitar. May he enlighten our understanding."

The Vedic religion deified the powers of nature, but the Indo-Aryans had no temples and no images, other than one of Indra carried in battle. Each god in turn is hymned as all-powerful, all-knowing, omnipresent, creator and sustainer of the universe ; the idea of an all-embracing unity is also manifest. " They call It Indra, Mitra, Varuna : That which exists is One, though the wise call It by many names." This verse appears in the first book of the *Rig-veda*.

The ancient seers could not accept the idea that " something " could ever be created out of " nothing." So the visible universe was conceived as unfolding from a finer invisible form, to which it returns again, coming out and going back in an endless procession of revolving cycles. Evolution is merely the unfolding process of a particular cycle ; dissolution, its end. Countless universes have preceded the present one, countless are yet to come.

Among Vedic deities, Agni, god of Fire, is the chief presiding deity of earth, who acts as messenger between men and gods. Two hundred hymns in the *Rig-veda* are dedicated to him alone. Earth, Prithivi, is a goddess and the rivers are goddesses. Prajapati, lord of creatures, Yama, who rules over the realm of the blessed dead, and Soma, whose cup ceaselessly fills and empties with the waxing and waning moon, are important deities of the Vedic period. To Soma the whole ninth book of the *Rig-veda* has been dedicated. The Sun is, of course, the all-powerful lord of the luminous region, and his one-wheeled chariot is described as rolling across the sky, drawn by seven horses. But the sun has many aspects and is variously known as Savitar, Vivasrat, Surya, Mitra and Vishnu. Vishnu, lord of morning, noon and evening, occupies a minor place in the Vedic pantheon, but becomes one of the chief gods of later Hinduism. Associated with the Sun is Ushas, the Dawn. The Asvins represent the two half-lights between day and night, and act as physicians to the rest of the gods. The wide Sky, in its endless moods, particularly appealed to the Vedic Aryans, who found many sky deities to worship.

One of the most important is Varuna, god of the wide expanse of both Sky and Ocean. The Vedic Aryans are a little afraid of him, and when they pray to him they remember their sins and ask his forgiveness. Varuna is said to see all, to know the innermost thought, to perceive what two men plot in secret. He sends his thousand spies from heaven to survey the world. As a player wields dice, so Varuna wields the universe.

Most popular of all, however, is Indra, the Rain-god, lord of the firmament and king of all gods. Two hundred and fifty hymns of the *Rig-veda* sing his glory. Indra became the national War-god of the Vedic Aryans, and is credited with many exploits, including the slaying of Vritra, a dragon who long withheld the waters of earth in a cave. Indra is perhaps the most human of all the Vedic gods. He has a body, wears golden armour, wields the thunderbolt as a weapon and presides over the court of the gods.

The tenth book of the *Rig-veda* contains many hymns which are abstract and philosophic. These hymns express the solemn searchings of the soul and seek answers to profound questions about the origin and nature of the universe, the mysteries of life and death, the relation of human beings to the Eternal. They clearly foreshadow the religious thought of the next period of Indian history.

CHAPTER IV

A Priceless Heritage

TANGIBLE remains of Indo-Aryan culture between 2000 and
500 B.C. consist of only a few stone *yupa*-posts, once used
in sacrificial Vedic rites, and perhaps a characteristic painted grey
ware, unearthed from many sites in northern India, including
Rupar, Hastinapur and Delhi, and also found in Greece and
Iran. No contemporary Aryan monuments, no historical records
like the early chronicles of China, however, have survived. In
spite of this, a vast archaic literature has been handed down,
which faithfully preserves the ideas and ideals of those far-off
times. It establishes the wonderful continuity and depth of civilization in north India. The only limiting aspect is that the authors
of the Vedic literature were almost invariably Brahmins or high-
caste Aryans to whom it did not occur to present any view of
life but their own. No comparable voice echoes down the corridors of time to speak for non-Aryan India, in the same ancient
period.

With the end of the creative period of hymn making, a new
geographical background and a more advanced social and intellectual life are reflected in the literary materials. The Indus land
so majestically praised in the early hymns seems to have lost
interest for the Indo-Aryans. Sometimes it is contemptuously
classed with Anga and Vanga (eastern Bihar and Bengal) as
outlying territory, where proper Aryan rites are not performed.
The Indo-Aryans are now seen to have settled down permanently
in the Gangetic Valley. Aryavarta, as they call the region of
the upper Jumna and Ganga, is politically divided into the two
great kingdoms of the Kurus and Panchalas, heirs of the old-time
Bharatas. Farther east, in the " middle country " — Madhya-
desa — is the powerful kingdom of Kosala. Its capital is
Ayodhya, identical with the well-known city in Uttar Pradesh still
bearing the old name. Kasi, or Banaras (Varanasi), and Videha
and Magadha, corresponding to northern and southern Bihar, are
other important Aryan kingdoms. The Yadava kingdom with its
capital at Mathura is another. The great *rishi* Agastya has
already passed south of the Vindhyas, the first missionary to bear
the torch of Aryan culture and religion to the non-Aryan, independent peoples of southern India.

With the rise of the new Aryan kingdoms, the power of the king has greatly increased, but it is by no means autocratic. It rests on the approval of the people, expressed through an assembly of respectable citizens and state officials. The king, who must be a Kshatriya by birth, is surrounded with councillors representing all classes of the citizens, and he is expected to follow their advice on matters of state policy. In return for the protection he gives his subjects, his administration is maintained by a tax on the produce of the land, ordinarily not exceeding one-sixth of the crop. If the crop is poor, the king gets less. He also administers justice, but he must follow the law, not his own whims. If the king does not perform his kingly duties properly, he can be deposed and driven into exile. There is no idea of " divine right of kings."

Like the royal power, the power of the priestly class has also become greatly augmented. The Brahmin is now not only the sole priest of Aryan society, but also its teacher and law-maker. But he does not attempt to share worldly power with the king or wealth with the trading classes. He vows himself to poverty, and sets himself the ideal of being content with his religious and intellectual superiority. His poverty, voluntarily self-imposed, wins him the profound respect of society as a whole. He lives on the gifts he receives. However, the religious sacrifices and ceremonies over which he presides, both in private and in public, tend to become more and more extravagant. The great Coronation Ceremony (Rajasuya) is exceeded in splendour only by the Horse Sacrifice (Asvamedha) prescribed for a king who succeeds in making himself king over kings, in other words, a universal monarch. Such State sacrifices may take a full year to complete. When they are finished, the royal treasury is all but empty.

The Brahmins and rishis, or great seers, have asserted a jealous custodianship of the sacred Vedas, described as " eternal, without beginning or end," and looked upon as the expression of those eternal truths and principles directly perceived by enlightened souls. They depend on no one personality for their sacred character. Tradition ascribes to the sage Vyasa the orderly re-arrangement in the remote past of the original Veda into four parts, for greater convenience. The Four Vedas are considered so sacred that no further change is tolerated. Volumes of commentaries and explanations can be written, but not a word can be added or taken away from the Vedas themselves. On this account the Vedas have undoubtedly suffered less corruption than the ancient scriptures of any other people.

The Four Vedas are the Rig, the Sama, the Yajur and the Atharva. The *Rig-veda* is the repository of the archaic hymns recited at Vedic sacrifices. The *Sama-veda* is a collection of verses from many of the same hymns, with some later ones also included, intended to be sung. The *Yajur-veda* is a book of prayers and *mantras* or mystical formulae. The *Atharva-veda* is really a very ancient book of magic, enshrining much of the most primitive lore of the Indo-Aryan people.

Around the Vedas there soon grew up various supplementary works. Each Veda had various *Brahmanas,* or explanatory prose manuals, attached to it, for the guidance of officiating priests of different schools. The *Brahmanas,* in turn, gave rise to the *Aranyakas,* or forest books, which interpreted the Vedic rituals symbolically instead of literally, for the benefit of those who had renounced worldly life and retired to the forest hermitages to practise austerities. As a last chapter to the forest books came the imperishable *Upanishads,* also called the *Vedanta,* or end portion of the Vedas. There are eleven early *Upanishads,* going back to about 800 B.C. These works have nothing to do with rites. They consider, chiefly in the form of philosophic dialogues between pupil and teacher interspersed with illustrative stories, the most profound questions the mind can ask about the purpose of life, the nature of experience, the meaning of death, the relation of man to nature and of soul to God, the ultimate spiritual Oneness of all that exists. The Vedic gods are not altogether discarded, but they are growing dim. The idea of one all-comprehensive unity is emphasized, an eternal, impersonal principle, neither male nor female, but neuter, which is called *Brahman* or *Atman,* and which is to be identified with the innermost being of the awakened self.

How is the impersonal *Brahman* to be known? "As oil in seeds, as butter in cream, as water in river-beds, as fire in wood, so is the Self to be seized within the self." There is no image of him. No one perceives him with the eye. But *Brahman* may be known through steadfastness of purpose, through self-control, goodness, truthfulness and meditation.

As Indian sages pondered on the problem of good and evil, they were confronted with the apparent injustices and cruelties of the world around them, and this state of affairs was finally reconciled with the idea of *Brahman* by the conception of a universal ethical law applying to all life. This law was proclaimed as the law of *karma.* In the words of the *Upanishads,* " As is a man's desire so is his will, and as is his will so is his deed, and whatever deed he does that he will reap." What we have thought and done in the past has made us what we are today, and what we think or do today will make us what we shall become in the future. The idea took root that to experience the full effects of past actions, good or bad, we must be born again and again. What the West calls inheritance, tendencies, or merely tempera-ment, India calls the accumulated effects of our own past *karma* trailing along with us. Rebirth and *karma* are not just an inevitable law of punishment and reward, but the great trial-and-error process by which all living things are given equal opportu-nity, through an infinite period of time, to learn to choose the better way. Eventually all will reach the same high destiny.

Obviously this kind of teaching was not for ordinary persons. Both teacher and pupil had to have very special qualities, and above all the teacher had to have actual experience and realization of the knowledge he taught. Although the Upanishadic wisdom was most generally taught by rishis in the forest schools, the names of great legendary kings, like Janaka of the Videhas and Jaivali of the Panchalas, are honoured to this day. Janaka and Jaivali, having learned the lesson of non-attachment to fleeting objects of sense enjoyment, continued to administer their kingdoms dispas-sionately and, at the same time, by example and precept, taught the supreme truth of the spiritual unity of life. They were knowers of *Brahman.*

The many stories scattered through the *Upanishads* all stress the same theme, this great truth of *Brahman,* which has first to be heard, then to be meditated upon and finally to be realized within one's own self. But this truth can become known by different ways to different persons, by intuition, by reasoning, by direct teaching, and there are stories to illustrate all methods. Among the best known and loved are those of Satyakama Jabala and Svetaketu in the *Chhandogya Upanishad,* and of Nachiketas in the *Katha Upanishad.*

Towards the end of the Vedic period, a new idea began to grow up, that life, at least for a Brahmin, should be divided into four stages. The first is *Brahmacharya,* or student discipleship, followed by the *Grihastha* stage, in which, as a householder, a man is expected to fulfil all his duties towards gods, ancestors, Brahmins, society and his own family. When a man sees his children's children, the time has then arrived for him to renounce worldly affairs and become a *Vanaprastha,* or forest dweller. Accompanied by his wife, should she wish to join him, he retires to some quiet hermitage far removed from the distractions of town or city, there to live a life of austerity and meditation. Finally, severing the ties even of the hermitage, he should give up all attachments, become a wandering *Sannyasin,* or renouncer, and strive for the ultimate knowledge of God alone. The various stages were known as the four *Ashramas.*

The school-going ceremony of the *Upanayana,* normally performed for a Brahmin boy at eight, for a Kshatriya, at eleven, and for a Vaisya, at twelve, meant admission into the sacred Aryan inheritance. This ceremony of putting on the sacred thread is still performed among orthodox high-caste Hindu families. Simple dignity attended the symbolic rite of initiation. After a ceremonial bath, the boy was given new garments, a deerskin to sit on, and a triple-plaited grass girdle. He was then formally presented to Agni, the Fire-god, who was requested to endow the young scholar with his own brilliance and vigour. Standing on a stone, the boy was enjoined to be firm as a rock in the diligent pursuit of knowledge. Finally, he was given a staff, as a symbol that he was about to start on a long journey, which, if untiringly pursued, would lead him to the wonderful realm of knowledge. He then left home and took up his residence in the Brahmin teacher's house on the edge of the forest, where he was henceforth treated like a son, both by the teacher and his wife. Normally he spent twelve years at his teacher's house, the minimum deemed necessary for mastering a single Veda. If he wanted to learn all the Four Vedas, he might spend a lifetime. There were no fixed school fees, but at the end of the course he presented a " teacher's fee," in accordance with the means and position of his family.

During his school life, a student was expected to wait on his teacher and beg food for his master's family and himself. He had to rise regularly at half past four in the morning, say his prayers, gather wood in the forest to keep alight the sacred Vedic fire, fetch water, prepare toothsticks cut from some medicinal tree, and tend the cattle. Rich and poor students alike went out on the daily begging round for food, which had to be accepted from all who offered it, without distinction of caste. Thus the young students were taught humility and a spirit of equality. Even a king's son followed the same routine. The students became aware of their dependence on society for help in getting their education, and society was made to assume a direct responsibility for seeing that the younger generation got its education. Since character building was considered an essential part of education, a student was taught to shun anger, laziness, jealousy, pride, untruthfulness and cruelty. He was not expected to indulge in luxuries, such as perfume, flower garlands, meat and spiced food. Except for long journeys, he did not put on shoes or carry an umbrella. He was disciplined to observe a life of strict chastity, and to pay reverence, respect and implicit obedience to his teacher.

The method of teaching was oral, and boys had first to learn their alphabet and elementary arithmetic. *Ganita,* calculation, was sometimes called " dust-work," because the figures were written with the forefinger in the dust or on a board spread with sand, and were rubbed out as the calculation proceeded. The earliest form of writing used by the Indo-Aryans was Brahmi, from which all the alphabets of all the purely Indian languages, including the Dravidian, were believed to be derived. Brahmi was presumably invented in India by the Brahmins, around 1000 B.C. Within six centuries, it came into use all over India, and thus became the earliest national Indian script.

Having mastered his preliminary subjects, the student was ready for his serious preoccupation with his Vedic studies. Everything had to be learned by heart, and sitting decorously on his deerskin, he would first begin to repeat after the teacher, syllable by syllable, word for word, the hymns of the *Rig-veda,* naming the rishi associated with each hymn and explaining the meaning of every abstruse word. Already the spoken language of the Aryan people, Prakrit, though allied to the archaic Sanskrit of the early Vedic period, had developed on its own lines. Extreme care had to be taken to learn the correct pronunciation of each sacred syllable. Every syllable had long ago been carefully counted, every line of the hymns tabulated. There were exactly 153,826 words, made up of 432,000 syllables, in the 1,028 hymns of the *Rig-veda.* It was believed that any mistake, even the accidental mispronunciation of a single word, might bring disaster to the unwittingly guilty person and to the whole community as well. To prevent their falling into wrong hands, they were not written down, even after writing came into vogue. In fact, it was not until the eighth or ninth century A.D. that a bold Kashmiri Brahmin, Vasukra, had the courage to defy tradition and reduce the Vedas to writing.

The Vedic student had also, of course, to wrestle with grammar, etymology and poetic metres. The science of grammar was so highly regarded that it was called " Veda of the Vedas." One name stands out above all others among the world's early grammarians, that of Panini, but Panini, born in Gandhara in northwest India probably around 500 B.C., gives the names of more than sixty grammarians who had already preceded him. Panini's grammatical treatise on Vedic Sanskrit is presented in eight lectures of four thousand aphorisms. In order to compress the subject into the shortest possible space, he used a kind of shorthand, with arbitrary symbols or letters, like those of algebra, to denote specific rules and combinations of letters. Before the rules themselves can be understood, Panini's code has to be thoroughly mastered. It was on the foundation of Panini's grammatical analysis that, after the decay of Vedic Sanskrit, a polished literary Sanskrit (the word itself means " constructed " or " perfected ") was artificially reconstructed in the classical period of Indian history, about the beginning of the fourth century A.D., and it was the discovery of Panini's grammar by Europeans in the eighteenth century that opened up the new science of language study, or comparative philology.

Another important branch of Vedic study was geometry, which also included astronomy. The laying out of the sacrificial ground for religious ceremonies and the building of the Vedic altars were considered matters of supreme importance. The size and shape of altar for each kind of sacrifice was minutely prescribed. Bricks had to be laid according to a precise plan. Altar-building posed many intricate geometrical problems, whose solution was a great achievement in those early times, such as the squaring of a circle or the opposite, finding the square of a diagonal, constructing equivalent squares and rectangles or constructing triangles equivalent to squares and rectangles.

Some knowledge of astronomy was likewise necessary for the proper performance of Vedic ceremonies. Sacrifices had to be begun at fixed times of the day or year and also to end at fixed times. The movements of the heavenly bodies, observed without the aid of any modern instruments, were checked over long periods of time and gradually made to yield the secrets of orderly progression. In the later Vedic period, astronomy became a distinct science, and an astronomer was called a star observer, or calculator. In spite of the allegorical language often employed, many astronomical facts were clearly and correctly noted. The star observer reached the conclusion that the earth was a sphere, that it was suspended in air and was held in place by the mysterious power of the sun. The year was divided according to both solar and lunar months. The ancient names of the lunar months are still in everyday use. To adjust the difference between the two calendars, a thirteenth month was inserted every five years to bring them together. The day was divided into thirty hours of forty-eight minutes. The moon's path in the course of a month through twenty-seven or twenty-eight stellar stations was carefully recorded. Summer and winter solstices and equinoxes were known, and six seasons were recognized : winter, spring, summer, rainy season, autumn and dewy season. The four directions were accurately measured by ascertaining the sun's position at noon. At least five planets had been distinguished.

In the field of mathematics, the Vedic Indians, from the very beginning, were using the decimal system of numbers, a discovery probably their own, which the whole world has since adopted. They also made use of extremely large numbers. In the fourth century B.C. the highest number used by the Greeks was the myriad (10^4), and the Romans never advanced beyond the mille (10^3), but the Vedic Indians centuries before had already proceeded to the use of 10 to the fourteenth power. Time they conceived on a vast scale of *yugas*, or ages, eternally repeating themselves. They are named Krita, Treta, Dvapara and Kali, representing the numbers on dice — 4, 3, 2 and 1. Each age diminishes in length and loses one-fourth of its virtue, in comparison with the previous age. At present, the world is in the Kali Yuga, and has only one-fourth of its ancient virtue left.

Other sciences can also be traced back to the Vedic period. Medicine seems to have made remarkable progress at an early date. Two famous names are Charaka and Susruta, whose actual dates are unknown. Seven birch-bark manuscripts, written in Sanskrit characters of the fourth century A.D., came to light in central Asia about half a century ago. Three of the manuscripts gave extensive quotations from both Charaka and Susruta, and the latter was quoted as an ancient authority. According to a Chinese source, Charaka was an Indian physician in attendance at the court of Kanishka, the Kushan king who ruled in northwest India about the beginning of the Christian Era, but Charaka's famous medical treatise was based on the much earlier teachings of Atreya, whose date has been assigned to the sixth century B.C.

The most remarkable part of Charaka's work is his classification of remedies drawn from vegetable, mineral and animal sources. Over two thousand vegetable preparations derived from the roots, bark, leaves, flowers, fruits, seeds or sap of plants and trees are described, and Charaka also gives the correct time of the year for gathering these materials and the method of preparing and administering them. Charaka sounds surprisingly modern. He devotes a good deal of attention to children's diseases, discusses proper feeding and hours of sleep and stresses the care of the teeth. Diagnosis in Charaka's time was primarily based on a careful study of the pulse. That he had a good idea of blood circulation is apparent from this passage in his treatise : "From that great centre (the heart) emanate the vessels carrying blood into all parts of the body — the element which nourishes the life of all animals and without which it would be extinct." High ethical standards to be maintained by the medical profession are also stressed by Charaka. He says : " Not for money nor for any earthly objects should one treat his patients. In this the physician's work excels all vocations."

Susruta, whose date is sometimes placed as early as 700 B.C., was a surgeon. He calls surgery " the first and best of medical sciences." He insists that those who intend to practise it must have actual experimental knowledge of the subject. One who possesses only verbal knowledge of texts he likens to a donkey, conscious of the weight, but not of the quality, of the load he carries. Much later, the higher Hindu castes were forbidden to touch a dead body. Susruta had no such compunctions. He says : " No accurate account of any part of the body, including even its skin, can be rendered without a knowledge of anatomy ; hence anyone who wishes to acquire a thorough knowledge of anatomy must prepare a dead body, and carefully examine all its parts." For preliminary training, students were taught how to handle their instruments by operating on pumpkins or cucumbers, and they were made to practise on pieces of cloth or skin to learn how to sew up wounds. Major operations, as described by Susruta, included amputations, grafting, setting of fractures, removal of a foetus and operation on the bladder for removal of gallstones. The operating room, he declares, should be clean, and both before and after an operation it should be disinfected with cleansing vapors. He describes 127 different instruments used for such purposes as cutting, inoculation, puncturing, probing and sounding. Cutting instruments, he declares, should be of " bright handsome polished metal, and sharp enough to divide a hair lengthwise."

Medicine and surgery, like military science and music, were subjects of specialized study, not directly related to the Vedas, yet somehow were brought under their all-embracing wing. The six orthodox systems of philosophy, all taking their starting point in the authority of the Vedas, later formed a regular part of the advanced curriculum of study. Each system had its own distinctive text or texts, surviving in the form of *sutras*, or " threads ", short abbreviated aphorisms as memory aids to the student, after the subject had been thoroughly expounded by the teacher. The six philosophic systems are the Purva Mimamsa, stressing the significance of rituals ; Vedanta, the ultimate search for the *Brahman* of the *Upanishads* ; Yoga, meditation and rules for bodily and mental self-discipline as a means to supreme knowledge ; Samkhya, numbers, or numerical categories of relationship between nature and soul ; Vaiseshika, an atomic theory of the universe ; and Nyaya, logic and reason.

The intellectual standards of the Aryan aristocracy of ancient India were obviously of a high order, but what was the position for ordinary people ? Even Vaisyas, eligible for the higher Vedic studies, could scarcely have afforded to carry on those studies up to the age of twenty-four. For simple folk, an excellent technical education was provided through the caste and guild systems. The knowledge and the skill of the father were automatically passed on, free of cost, to the son, who began his apprenticeship at his father's knee.

For the edification and entertainment of all, there were the popular *itihasas* and *puranas*, with their mingled accounts of gods, kings and sages. The eighteen puranas, though of post-Vedic date, certainly preserve much historical material handed down from the most ancient bards and ballad makers, and they represent the Kshatriya, as well as the Brahmin, tradition. Thirteen puranas give more or less similar royal genealogies, purporting to cover the earliest Aryan kingdoms. Genealogies of the famous sages, reckoned by discipleship, are also included.

Even more important, however, from the general cultural point of view, are the two great Sanskrit epics, the *Ramayana* and the *Mahabharata*. These, too, in their present textual forms, are held to be only about fifteen centuries old, but the core of both goes back to a far earlier period. Rama must have been a real king, before he was transformed into an incarnation of Vishnu by Valmiki, and the great fratricidal war between the descendants of Bharata must have been an actual war, which probably took place about 900 B.C. In any event, as epics, what the *Iliad* and the *Odyssey* were to ancient Greece, the *Ramayana* and *Mahabharata* were, and still are, to India. The *Mahabharata* has the further questionable distinction of being the longest poem in the world. It is seven times as long as the *Iliad* and the *Odyssey* together, and even the *Ramayana* is three times their combined length. Century after century, at the courts of kings, on occasions of religious ceremony, at places of sacred pilgrimage, within the forest hermitages, these stories have been told and retold, and in countless humble villages of mud and thatch the glories of Epic India live on undimmed, in the hearts of men.

One may follow the epics like children, for their dramatic value, and be thrilled by the exciting wars between gods and demons, by the pageantry of royal courts, by the miraculous feats and brave deeds of Hanuman, the monkey devotee of Rama.

One may take them as a noble expression of the social ideals of loyalty, chastity, love, self-control, obedience, truthfulness and unselfishness. One may study them for the light they throw on the mythological or historical background of India itself and on the evolution of important religious ideas. One may read them as source books, tracing back to their inexhaustible inspiration the mighty streams of sculpture, painting, poetry and drama of later Hinduism. Or one may read them for the profound spiritual teachings shining through their pages. It is because they continue to have something vital to say to all, irrespective of age or sex or social position or education, that they are so treasured and loved in India.

The events and episodes portrayed in the *Mahabharata* are popularly supposed to belong to a later period than the *Ramayana*, mainly because Krishna, the real hero of the *Mahabharata*, is believed to be a later incarnation of Vishnu than Rama. But unlike the *Ramayana*, the *Mahabharata*, often called the " Fifth Veda " because of its attribution to Vyasa, compiler of the Vedas, is not a unified piece of work, either in authorship or in time of composition. The story of the great war between the Kauravas and Pandavas, the two branches of the Bharatas, which forms the main theme of the epic, is the glorified memory of some national event of great historic significance, but this story constitutes only about a fifth of the entire poem. Woven into its fabric is a stupendous miscellany of mythology, legends, fables, stories and philosophic discourses, many of them complete works in themselves. The whole epic is a veritable encyclopedia of human psychological types, and well has it been said that what is not in the *Mahabharata* is not in India.

A tiny fragment embedded in its vast mosaic is the *Bhagavad-Gita*, the Lord's Song, in the form of the discourse held on the battlefield between Krishna and the Pandava hero Arjuna, just before the great battle begins. It gives in a wonderfully dramatic and living way the essence of the highest philosophy of the *Upanishads*, and at the same time unites with it a new doctrine of salvation through love and devotion to the personal God.

CHAPTER V

The Yellow Robe

THE political and religious centre of Indian interest next shifts to the rising eastern kingdom of Magadha, on the fringe of ancient Kosala. For the first time, fairly correct historical dates for actual events associated with real persons can be cited. In the sixth century B.C., two great religious leaders emerge in Magadha. Vardhamana, better known as Mahavira, the "Great Hero", is identified with the religious system of Jaina, or Jainism, and Siddhartha Gotama (Gautama) — more simply the Buddha, or "Enlightened One" — becomes the founder of Buddhism. Bodily relics of the Buddha, found within an inscribed receptacle taken from a Buddhist *stupa*, or relic mound, have proved beyond doubt that he really lived. These bits of bone and ash are now carefully preserved at Sarnath, near Banaras.

It is scarcely by accident that two important religious movements, in many ways remarkably alike, should spring up at the same time and in almost the same locality. The spirit of the new age initiated by the *Upanishads* was one of free inquiry, opposed to rituals and sacrifices. It expressed itself in an intellectual rebellion against the Brahmins and their claim to act as sole interpreters and intermediaries between gods and men. It was also in part a reaction against the cruelty of animal slaughter in the name of religious sacrifice. Another important factor explaining the rapid growth of the new reform movements was that both Mahavira and Gotama taught in Prakrit, the ordinary spoken language of the people in their area, abandoning Sanskrit to the Brahmins and scholars.

This same spirit of independence began to show itself in popular forms of government, a little appreciated chapter of Indian history. The typical government in ancient India was monarchical in form, but no Aryan king ever held completely autocratic powers. He could never say "I am the State", and it was his duties, rather than his privileges, that ancient texts of statecraft always impressed upon him. Even during the epic period, when royal power was at its apex, village councils, general assemblies, and caste and guild organizations fostered a healthy tradition of self-government among different sections of the people. There now arose a number of small independent states, in the Punjab and Sind, in Rajputana, and in eastern India, with a genuinely republican and democratic form of government. The grammarian Panini refers to this type of government as *gana* government, or government by " numbers ". Greek writers of the fourth century B.C. also describe some contemporary Indian republics and federations. Altogether, the names of eighty-one of them have been preserved.

In the sixth century B.C., this democratic atmosphere particularly prevailed in the areas where both Mahavira and Gotama were born and grew up. Videha, or northern Bihar, was part of a republican federation with the neighbouring territory of the Lichavis, and it was at Vaisali, the Lichavi capital, that Mahavira was born. The Sakyas of Kapilavastu, a small state to the north, near the border of Nepal, also had a republican type of government. The ruler was called a raja, but he was regularly elected from among the members of the Sakya clan. It was to this clan, or family, that Gotama, afterwards known as Sakyamuni, the Sage of the Sakyas, belonged, and at the time of his birth, his father was raja. It is significant that both Mahavira and Gotama modelled their religious *sanghas*, or orders, on the political *sanghas*, or free assemblies, familiar to them in their own territories.

In spite of the reform spirit that animated both men, making them reject the final authority of the Vedas and of the priestly Brahmins, neither made any claim to have discovered the principles of a new religion. Both Jainism and Buddhism are typically Indian, with roots buried deep in the past. The ideal their founders preached was not fundamentally different from that of the *Upanishads*. Both rejected any idea of an original Creator, and hence offered no god to worship. Both accepted the current concepts of rebirth and karma, and the ascetic ideal of renunciation of the world and its pleasures. Buddhism taught that the world is impermanent and fleeting, that every compound must ultimately resolve back into its component parts, that there is no soul or permanent entity of being, and that attachment to what is impermanent inevitably brings pain. Jainism taught that while both matter and soul are permanent, the temporary association of soul with matter through karma inevitably brings pain. Both insisted that salvation is attainable through strenuous effort in this very life, and is not something to be won after death as a reward of ritual sacrifice. Salvation — *moksha*, or *nirvana* — is the state of freedom attained with spiritual enlightenment and understanding of truth, with or without blissful consciousness, achieved by a pure life and concentrated awareness. It is an extinction not necessarily of being, but of ignorance and craving, and it alone can free an individual from the monotonous rounds of birth and death.

According to Jain belief, Mahavira was not really the founder of Jainism, but only the twenty-fourth and last, in this world cycle, of the great *Tirthankaras,* or " ford makers ", also called *jinas,* " conquerors." Although all are said to have preached exactly the same message, only the last two, Mahavira and his predecessor Parsva, are historical figures. Two centuries or more before Mahavira, Parsva lived in Banaras, where he founded the ascetic order of the Nirgranthas, those " without ties." This order still survived in Mahavira's time, and his parents are said to have been strongly attracted to it.

Mahavira was an older contemporary of Gotama. His father was a Vaisali nobleman and his mother was the sister of one of the Lichavi chiefs. He was also connected by family ties with Bimbisara, at that time king of Magadha. He was therefore a Kshatriya by birth, like all the twenty-three *Tirthankaras* who preceded him. Mahavira married, but at the age of thirty he renounced the world and devoted the next twelve years of his life to severe austerities, undergoing almost unendurable hardships. It was during this period that he discarded all his clothes, as a symbol of bodily consciousness, and for the rest of his life he went about entirely naked. When he was forty-two, a mystic experience of deep significance came to him, after which he preached his religious ideas until his death at the age of seventy-two at the little town of Pawa, near Rajagriha, the Magadha capital. The date of his death is usually given as 527 B.C., but the *Cambridge History of India* puts it sixty years later. He left behind him 14,000 followers, firmly united in a religious order made up of monks, nuns and householder disciples.

For the attainment of salvation, the Jains laid down that right faith, right knowledge and right conduct must all be present together. One alone was insufficient. Right conduct meant the fulfilment of five vows, or abstinences, enjoined on both monks and laymen, though monks were expected to observe them with greater rigidity and strictness. The vows were not to injure, not to lie, not to steal, not to be unchaste and not to strive after luxury and possessions. Superfluous wealth was to be given away in charity, particularly in providing medicines, building of asylums for decrepit animals, copying sacred books and supporting religious teachers. Non-injury was the vital heart of Jain ethics. The smallest creature alive was credited with a soul. Therefore causing death to any living thing, whether by accident, by the nature of one's occupation, in self-protection, or for the mere wanton pleasure of killing or gratifying one's appetite, was considered the greatest of sins. Water must be strained, lest invisible insects be swallowed. A monk must not walk at night, lest he tread upon an unseen worm.

In spite of its extreme asceticism, Jainism spread rapidly to different parts of India, and the royal patronage it received did much to help its growth. About 300 B.C., as a result of a severe famine, Bhadrabahu, the eighth great sage after Mahavira, departed with a group of *sravanas*, or monks, for the south. Broadcasting their teachings throughout the Deccan, they founded a Jain colony at Sravana Belgola, in what is now Mysore State.

In time, a split arose between the southern and northern monks, and two sects came into existence. Although there were no differences in regard to Jain doctrine, the two groups disagreed on minor matters of discipline. The southern group, which took the stricter view, became known as the Digambaras, or "sky-clad" — that is, naked — because its members adhered to the practice of going without clothes. The northern Jains were called Svetambaras, or "white-clothed". The Digambaras still maintain their chief hold in the south, but are also strong in eastern Rajputana. The present centre of the Svetambara sect is in western Rajputana and Gujarat.

In succeeding centuries, the Jain contribution to art and literature in India was considerable. The peculiar style of Jain painting, with heavy outlines and bold brilliant colours, is preserved in the illustrations of medieval Jain manuscripts. The sculpture is associated with Jain temples and cave retreats. The twenty-four *Tirthankaras* are represented with crossed legs and folded hands or standing stiffly straight, all exactly alike, except for a tiny differentiating symbol engraved on the bare breast of each figure. The Jains also carved colossal freestanding statues and giant bas-reliefs of their saints. The most famous of these is a huge tenth-century stone image of Gomata, son of the first *Tirthankara*, Rṣabhanatha, at Sravana Belgola. This image, fifty-six and a half feet high, is completely nude, like all Jain statues, and termite nests carved at the saint's feet and vines gracefully entwining his lower limbs and arms suggest the timeless concentration of the questing soul for ultimate illumination. On the whole, however, the ascetic ideals of Jainism discouraged a virile expression in art form. Jain sculpture lacks the variety and charm, both in subject matter and technique, of Buddhist art, and equally misses the dramatic intensity of later Hindu art.

JAIN Colossus 57 ft. high · Rock of GWALIOR·
A Sky-clad JINA or Spiritual Conqueror

The medieval Jain temples are nevertheless amazingly beautiful. On out-of-the-way mountain tops, remote and secluded, the Jains built remarkable temple cities. White and shining against the blue sky, Girnar and Palitana, both in Gujarat, have an ethereal unreality. Palitana has 863 temples closely packed along the crest, enclosed within a massive battlemented wall. The exquisite white marble temples at Mount Abu, in Rajputana, dating from the eleventh and thirteenth centuries A.D., are unrivalled in the whole of India for their delicate carvings and lavish traceries.

In the realm of literature, the Jains produced an immense amount of notable work, both religious and secular. Their earliest scriptures, or *Agamas*, were written in the Ardha-Magadhi, or " half-Magadhi " vernacular current in northern India. Other early works were composed in a Jain Prakrit which seems to have been a parent of modern Mahratti. They also made good literary use of whatever language was spoken wherever they established themselves. Jain influence in early Tamil literature is clearly discernible, and from about the tenth century, they began to make Sanskrit translations of their sacred scriptures. Nor did the Jain authors limit themselves to religious commentaries and expositions. They made original contributions in the field of poetry, drama, moral tales, grammar, philosophy and logic. The best known Jain author is Hemachandra, who lived in Gujarat at the end of the eleventh and beginning of the twelfth century.

It was Buddhism, however, that was to stir most deeply the heart of Asia and to awaken a whole continent to new, intense spiritual life. We know that the historical Buddha was almost certainly born in 563 B.C. and died at the age of eighty in 483 B.C. But legend says that he was preceded, like Mahavira, by a long line of great beings. Twenty-four previous Buddhas had each made a great resolve to become perfectly enlightened, and then, as a *Bodhisattva* — one destined to become a Buddha — had striven through countless lives to do good and to acquire the Buddha qualities. In exactly the same way, Siddhartha Gotama is said to have been born again and again, before his historical appearance on earth. He had been born as a monkey, a lion, a tiger, an elephant, a deer, a jackal. He had been a rat, a fish, a lizard, a frog and a snake. He had been crow, peacock and woodpecker. He had been potter and smith, gambler and thief, king and king's son, ascetic and Brahmin. But in each of his previous lives he had performed some noble act of self-sacrifice, and had journeyed a little farther along the path to Buddhahood.

Then, it is said, as a result of accumulated good deeds, he
reached the Tusita Heaven of those destined to become Buddhas.
Considering carefully the conditions for his birth, he chose
Kapilavastu as the country, Suddhodana of the Gotama family
of the Sakyas as his father and Maya as his mother. Then he
descended from the Abode of Bliss, in the shape of a six-tusked
white elephant, bearing a white lotus in his silvery trunk, and
entered the womb of Queen Maya as she lay asleep on her
couch on a day of full moon, during the midsummer festival.
When Brahmins were summoned to explain the queen's strange
dream, they prophesied that a son would be born, who, if he
lived the household life, would become a universal monarch, but
if he retired from the world, would become a Buddha and roll
back the clouds of sin and folly of this world.

In due time, in the pleasant grove of Lumbini, not far from
Kapilavastu, Queen Maya gave birth to her child, and in the
selfsame moment were born Yasodhara, afterwards to become

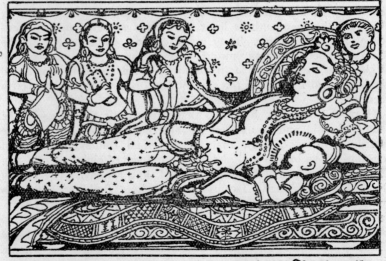

Queen Maya with the baby Prince Siddhartha

the mother of Rahula, his son, his faithful groom Channa, his
horse Kanthaka, his playmate Kaludayin, his favourite disciple
Ananda, and the sacred Bodhi tree, under which he was to receive
illumination. When he was five days old, the child was named
Siddhartha, " he who has achieved his aim." On the seventh
day, Queen Maya died and he was given into the charge of his
kindly aunt Queen Maha Prajapati.

King Suddhodana did not like the idea that his son would renounce the world. He inquired what would induce him to do so, and was told that when Siddhartha saw the four omens — an Old Man, a Sick Man, a Corpse and an Ascetic — he would make the great renunciation. Thinking to himself, " From this time forth, let no such things come near my son," Suddhodana had three mansions for the three seasons built for Prince Siddhartha, and enclosed them within a great walled garden. Then he placed guards without, to insure that the sights of ill omen should never meet the eyes of the prince, and he sought to beguile him with amusements and to chain his mind to worldly things.

The time came when the prince had reached manhood, and a wife was to be chosen for him. She was his cousin Yasodhara. Her father, the chief minister, thinking the young prince too softly nurtured, demanded that Siddhartha first be put to the twelvefold test of skill in mental and physical accomplishments with other youths of his age, but he triumphed over them all. So the marriage was richly celebrated, and still within his guarded palace Siddhartha knew not the meaning of sorrow.

Did the king really think to hold back Siddhartha from his destiny ? One day the prince ordered Channa, his charioteer, to bring his chariot, with its four white horses, and drive him to the royal park. Near one of the city gates of Kapilavastu there suddenly appeared before him an Old Man, wasted with age, gray-haired, bent double and leaning on a staff. " What kind of man is this ? " he asked. At the other gates he saw in turn a Sick Man, a Dead Man and a Hermit. From the serene expression on the face of the ascetic, he alone, it seemed, was free from suffering and beyond the reach of life's ills. Thus, Siddhartha came to know that all men born must indeed suffer sickness, grow old and die, and can in no wise escape. He was plunged in grief for the fate of men, and his face was wet with his first tears.

At this very moment, a messenger arrived from King Suddhodana, announcing that a son had been born to Yasodhara. On hearing of the birth of his son, the prince cried out, " An impediment has come into being, a bond has come into being ! " When this saying was reported to the king, he named the child Rahula, or " Fetter."

That night Siddhartha lay down as usual on his couch. The women of the palace, seeing his indifference, dropped their instruments and fell asleep. They lay in uncomely attitudes, their clothes in disarray, and the prince was filled with loathing. " Roused

into activity like a man who is told that his house is on fire,"
in the words of a Buddhist text, he rose swiftly. The great renunciation, from which there would be no turning back, was already
made. He would seek, and would not rest until he found, a
way out of sorrow and suffering, despair and death, not for
himself alone, but for all mankind. Calling his charioteer, he
ordered him to saddle the horse Kanthaka, and rode away into
the night. At last he dismounted on the farther side of a river,
where he took off his ornaments and bade Channa carry them
back to the king. Next he exchanged his rich dress for the
tattered ochre-coloured garments of a hunter. Then he continued
on foot to Rajagriha, the capital of the Magadha kingdom, where
Bimbisara was then king. He went through the streets begging
his food, accepting whatever was placed in his alms bowl.
Having conquered disgust, he partook for the first time in his
life of the beggar's dole. Refusing the king's offer of honour
and wealth, but promising that after he had become a Buddha
he would again return to Magadha, the future Buddha then under-
went prolonged fasts and endured the uttermost penance and
mortification of the body for six long years. Realizing at last
that his penances were no more than an attempt to tie the air
into knots, he went again to beg ordinary food in the village of
Uruvela, receiving from the hands of Sujata, a village maiden,
a bowl of sweetened rice and milk.

When evening came, he walked towards the Tree of Enlightenment. On the path he met a grasscutter. Accepting from him a
gift of grass, he spread it beneath the tree and sat down. There
he made this resolve : " Let my skin, my nerves, and my bones
dry up, and likewise my flesh and blood ; let this body dissolve
back into primal nothingness, if need be : but until I attain
Supreme Enlightenment, I will not leave this seat ! "

He remained motionless, his mind fully concentrated, steady
as a flame in a windless place. In the first watch of the night,
it is said, the endless procession of his past lives in all their
details was revealed to him. In the middle watch, his Buddha-
eye opened, and all worlds, past and to come, lay stretched out
before him. In the last watch, the secret of universal suffering
and the way out were made known to him. Ignorance was dispelled, and knowledge arose in him. Darkness was dispelled,
and light arose. He had attained the goal. He had become a
Buddha.

He then proceeded to the Deer Park near Banaras, where he
preached his first sermon after his Enlightenment. It was called
the setting in motion of the Wheel of the Law, the symbolic

Wheel appearing on the Indian national flag today. He exhorted men to avoid the two extremes, pursuit of worldly pleasures, on the one hand, and performance of useless austerities, on the other, and to follow instead the Middle Path. He expounded the Four Noble Truths regarding suffering, namely, its nature, its origin in desire, its extinction by ending desire, and the eightfold means of doing so by the practice of right views, aspirations, speech, conduct, living, effort, thought and meditation. Having converted his listeners, he then founded the first Order of Buddhist Monks, and sent out sixty disciples to preach in the ordinary language of the people. " Go forth and journey from place to place," he said, " for the welfare of many, for the happiness of many, out of compassion for the world. Preach the Law. Proclaim the Holy Life."

He himself, in fulfilment of his promise, proceeded to Rajagriha, where Bimbisara came to meet him with a large retinue of Brahmins and householders, and the Buddha addressed them. He prescribed no rites or sacrifices, but spoke of alms-giving, morality and the blessedness of renunciation. When their minds had become softened, " like a clean cloth ready to take the dye," he told them how to find peace, through the knowledge that gives peace, by living a holy life. King Bimbisara on the following day presented to the Buddha the garden known as the Bamboo Grove, as a residence for the monks, and this became the first Buddhist monastery. It was also at Rajagriha that Sariputra and Moggallana, his foremost disciples, were converted and accepted into the Order.

King Suddhodana, hearing that his son was now staying at Rajagriha, sent a messenger requesting him to return to Kapilavastu. There many of the Sakyas gave up the world and followed him, as also Upali, the barber. At that time, Yasodhara sent Rahula to his father one day with instructions to say to him : " Father, I am the prince. Give me the treasure ; for a son is heir to his father's property." The boy came and stood near the Blessed One. " Happy, O monk, is thy shadow ! " he said. Then he repeated his mother's message. The Buddha, looking down at him, reflected with grave tenderness, " I will give him today the wealth obtained under the Bodhi tree and make him heir to a spiritual kingdom." Rahula was taken into the Order. His aunt, the venerable Maha Prajapati, earnestly besought permission to become a nun, and Ananda, the favourite disciple, pleaded for the admission of women into the Order, so that they too might become fully established in the path of renunciation and holiness. The Blessed One acquiesced, and the mother of

Rahula also joined the Order and became one of the first Buddhist nuns.

Throughout Magadha and the neighbouring kingdom of Kosala, and in the villages bordering the Ganga, the Buddha and many thousands of disciples tirelessly preached the new religion. Innumerable converts put on the yellow robe and followed him. Gravely the monks walked from village to village, from city to city, spreading the message, but during the four months of the rainy season, they went into retreat, according to the rules laid down by the Blessed One.

At Jetavana, lying just outside the Kosala capital of Sravasti, the Buddha is said to have spent no less than twenty-five rain-retreats during his lifetime.

Forty-five years after his enlightenment under the Bodhi tree, when he was eighty years of age, looking back for the last time at Vaisali, departing from Rajagriha where Ajatasatru was then king, he passed northward through the villages of the Malla clan, knowing that the end of his long ministry was approaching. At Kusinagara, not far from the borders of the Sakya country of his birth, he asked Ananda to prepare a bed between two *sal* trees in a grove outside the town, and he lay down with his head to the north, resting on his right side. Ananda leaned against a doorpost of the monastery and wept. The Blessed One sent for him and reminded him that all things are transitory in this world. " Enough, Ananda, do not weep. Have I not already told you, Ananda, that it is in the very nature of all things near and dear to us that we must divide ourselves from them ? How is it possible, Ananda, that whatever has been born, has come into being, is organized and perishable, should not perish ? "

When the third watch of the night came, he addressed the monks for the last time, saying, " And now, O monks, I take my leave of you. Decay is inherent in all component things. Work out your salvation with diligence."

His body was cremated, and the relics were divided into eight portions and stupas built over them. Two hundred and fifty years later, King Asoka redivided the relics and distributed them among thousands of stupas all over India. A few of the ruined Asoka stupas still remain.

The earliest existing form of the Buddhist scriptures is contained in the Pali Canon, written down in Ceylon about the first century B.C. Pali itself means " text ", but the word has come to signify both the canonical language and the script itself. The Pali language is a literary form of Prakrit, allied to Sanskrit, and obviously derived either from the actual speech used by the

The Life of Gotama Buddha

Buddha in the fifth and sixth centuries before the present era
or the Magadha court language of the third century B.C.

The Pali scriptures consist of twenty-seven books. Out of
84,000 sections, 82,000 are made up of the words attributed to
the Buddha, the small remainder being ascribed to his disciples.
The Canon is divided into three *Pitakas,* or "baskets." The
first is the *Vinaya,* which contains the monastic rules laid down
by the Buddha. The second is the *Sutta* portion (the Pali equivalent of Sanskrit *Sutra*), which gives the Buddhist doctrine, or
law, preached by the Buddha in the form of sermons, discourses
and sayings, in both prose and verse, as also a few discourses
by disciples. Included in this portion are the fascinating Jatakas,
in each of which the Buddha tells a story related to one of 550
previous births. The third section of the Pali Canon is the *Abhi-
dhamma,* an analysis of the psychology and metaphysics on
which the Buddhist doctrine is based.

The material embodied in the Pali scriptures clearly represents
the memorized teachings of the Buddha, as first handed down
orally among the Buddhist monks in India and passed on to
those in Ceylon. There is every reason to believe in their accu-
racy and faithful transcription. The First Buddhist Council was
called at Rajagriha almost immediately after the death of the
Buddha. His direct disciples then came together under the leadership of the venerable Kassapa and recited the precepts in
unison, so that nothing should be forgotten. Just over a hundred
years later, in 377 B.C., a Second Buddhist Council was held
at Vaisali, to settle a dispute which had arisen among the monks
in regard to some of the rules of discipline. Still a Third Buddhist Council was held at the instance of Asoka in the Mauryan
capital of Pataliputra in about 240 B.C. It was at this Third
Council that the Pali Canon was revised, completed and finally
closed. A year later Asoka sent his son and daughter, who had
joined the Order, to carry Buddhism to Ceylon. With them must
have gone the Canon, very much in the form in which it survives
today.

For a thousand years after the death of the Buddha, Buddhism
continued to grow in popularity and to expand in all directions.
It developed numerous sects. Yet the great majority of the people
in India always remained loyal to the older forms of religious faith. Buddhism attacked the authority of the Brahmins.
It ignored the old rituals. It refused to recognise most of the
Vedic gods. It undermined the family by encouraging monasticism. Presently a Hindu revival movement began to gain head-
way, and Buddhism began to languish. Yet because Siddhartha

Gotama was a true son of India, uncompromisingly committed to the Aryan search for truth and knowledge, Hinduism found little difficulty in eventually claiming him for itself. He was accepted, like Rama and Krishna, as another Descent of Vishnu.

And what, exactly, was the message of the Buddha? Whenever his own disciples or their rivals approached him and tried to draw him into a theoretical discussion about the burning questions of the day — is the world eternal or not eternal, is it infinite or finite, are soul and body identical or separate, is there life after death for one who has become fully enlightened? — he merely replied : " The religious life does not depend on the dogma that the world is eternal ; nor does the religious life depend on the dogma that the world is not eternal. There still remain birth, old age, death, sorrow, lamentation, misery, grief and despair, for the extinction of which in the present life I am prescribing."

On another occasion he picked up a handful of leaves and asked the assembled monks which were greater in number, the leaves in his hand or those in the grove. " The leaves in the grove," answered the monks. " Just so," he replied, " those things that I know, but have not revealed, are greater by far in number than those things that I have revealed. And why, brethren, have I not revealed them ? Because they are not concerned with the holy life, they do not lead to Nirvana."

It was the living of the holy life that was the centre of his teachings, because it was right, because it was good, because it alone could lead to the spiritual knowledge which would extinguish suffering and ignorance.

So he taught men to understand the three hindrances to enlightenment — lust, greed and delusion. He taught them to recognize the nine fetters of the mind — covetousness, ill will, anger, deceitfulness, jealousy, obstinacy, arrogance, vainglory, heedlessness. He taught them to strive after the ten perfections — generosity, goodness, renunciation, wisdom, firmness, patience, truthfulness, resolution, kindness and equanimity. By his own life and by stories and parables, he showed them how all beings, even animals, are capable of noble self-sacrifice. He taught them to be gentle and courteous to all. Even after two thousand five hundred years, his words still ring with noble truth.

" O ye monks, like as the great ocean has but one savour, the savour of salt, so has this religion and order but one, the savour of renunciation."

" All men tremble at punishment, all men fear death ; remember that you are like unto them, and do not kill nor cause slaughter."

4

" The fault of others is easily perceived, but that of oneself is difficult to perceive. A man winnows his neighbour's faults like chaff, but his own faults he hides."

" Better than matted hair and ashes are truth and discipline."

" Let one overcome anger by love, let him overcome evil by good, let him overcome greed by liberality, let him overcome deceit by truth."

" Not by hatred is hatred quenched ; by love is it quenched. This is an eternal law."

CHAPTER VI

The First Indian Empire

WHILE SIDDHARTHA GOTAMA was still a young man, certain events, unknown to him, were taking place in the north-western corner of India and beyond. Cyrus the Great, founder of the Achaemenian Dynasty in Persia, was laying the foundations of the mightiest empire the world had yet seen. After absorbing Media, Lydia, the Ionian Greek settlements of Asia Minor, Babylonia and Bactria, Cyrus led his Iranians in the direction of the Indian border. After Cyrus came Darius I, who succeeded to the throne in 522 B.C. Darius promptly annexed the territory of the Punjab and Sind, and in two of his famous rock-cut inscriptions the Indus country is clearly called a part of the great Persian Empire. It constituted the twentieth satrapy, and contributed one third of the total revenues of the Persian Empire in the form of an annual tribute of ten tons of gold dust.

Darius is said to have sent a naval expedition to explore the Indus and find a new sea route to the west. The expedition was put under the command of a Greek captain named Skylax. The fleet was assembled on the upper Indus in the Gandhara region. It sailed down to the sea, then westward around Arabia and up the Red Sea to Arsinoë (modern Suez), which was reached two and a half years after Skylax had first embarked on his bold enterprise. His own lost account of the expedition, surviving in fragmentary quotations, appears to have been the first book by a Greek author dealing with India.

The organizing genius of Darius made itself felt throughout the whole of his vast territory. He divided his empire for purposes of administration into satrapies, with a satrap, or viceroy, at the head of each province. The headquarters of the Indian satrapy was Takshasila, called Taxila by the Greeks. The extensive ruins of this city lie ten miles from Rawalpindi, in Pakistan. In early Buddhist literature, it was famous for its great university to which princely youths were sent even from far away Banaras, to be trained especially in military science and medicine.

To facilitate administration and trade, Darius introduced a new script into northwestern India. This was the Kharoshthi script derived from the Aramaic script then in wide use throughout the Persian Empire. Like all Semitic scripts — but unlike the Indian Brahmi — it was written from right to left. The Kharoshthi form of writing gradually spread from northwest India to central Asia, where it was still used as late as the fifth century A.D. Persia's gold and silver coinage also appeared in northwest India at the same time.

Each province of the Persian Empire was expected to raise levies for the imperial army in time of war, and the Indian province was no exception. Indian mercenaries marched with the expedition of Darius against Greece. They also took part in the second Persian campaign against Greece under Xerxes, successor to Darius. They were again present on the battlefield at Arbela, near Nineveh, when Darius III, last of the Achaeme-

nians, was routed by Alexander the Great. According to the Greek historian Herodotus, the Indian soldiers were dressed in cotton and carried bows of cane and arrows tipped with iron. Their contingents consisted mainly of light infantry, but there were also divisions of cavalry, elephants and chariots, and the chariots were drawn by asses as well as horses. Fierce Indian hunting dogs also accompanied the armies. India and Greece thus first came into touch with each other through Persia.

A direct connection was established when Alexander of Macedonia successfully challenged the might of Persia towards the end of the fourth century B.C., and overthrew the Achaemenian Empire.

Alexander's raid into India, when he was just thirty years old, was, from all military standards, a truly extraordinary feat. He had set out from Greece with an army of 30,000 to 40,000 men. Within four years, he had conquered all the important cities and strongholds of Asia Minor, Syria, Palestine and Egypt, and had advanced deep into the heart of the mighty Persian Empire. At last, trailing down over the Hindu Kush, Alexander crossed the Indus above Attock and entered the Punjab early in the spring of 326 B.C.

Ambhi, the raja of Taxila, greeted him with presents and flattery, welcoming him to Taxila as an honoured guest. He even offered to supply Alexander with 5,000 Indian soldiers, to add to his polyglot army of Balkans, Thracians, Ionian Greeks, Cypriots, Cretans, Phoenicians, Egyptians, and Parthians from central Asia — but mainly, of course, Macedonian veterans trained in a hundred battles. To India, all were foreigners known simply as Yavanas or Yonas — Ionians.

Ambhi's pliability was not inspired by love of Alexander, but by fear of his powerful neighbour to the east, whom the Greeks called Poros. When Alexander imperiously summoned all the Indian princes to meet him at Taxila, Poros replied that he would indeed meet him — but armed, and on the borders of his own territory. Alexander had boats transported overland in sections from the Indus and put together again on the Jhelum, in full sight of Poros and his army, encamped on the opposite bank. The rainy season had begun, and the river was in high flood. One stormy night, Alexander and a small picked force of 11,000 men and their cavalry horses managed to cross the Indus before the alarm could be sounded. Poros had superiority in war chariots and elephants, but the Parthians, shooting with deadly aim as they galloped, bore down in a surprise attack, followed by the famous Macedonian cavalry, with Alexander himself at their head. The unwieldy chariots were soon bogged down in the mud, and the elephants stampeded backwards instead of forwards. Poros, mounted on a great elephant, was severely wounded. Brought into the presence of Alexander, he was asked how he should be treated. " Like a king," he replied haughtily. Alexander was impressed. He reinstated Poros in possession of his former territory.

Alexander then continued his march eastward until he reached the Beas (Hyphasis), last but one of the five rivers of the Indus system. Eighty miles ahead lay the Sutlej, and beyond that, with only a narrow strip of desert between, stretched another great Indian river system, that of the Ganga, and the rich eastern kingdom of Magadha, with its capital at Pataliputra (Patna).

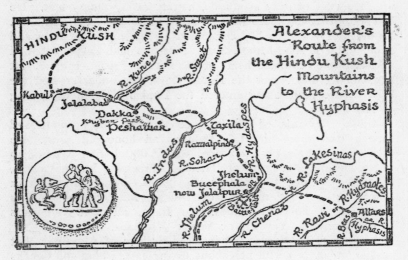

Self-confident as ever, Alexander dreamed of advancing all the way to the Eastern Ocean — wherever that was — and making the whole of India his prize.

On the march through Afghanistan, Bactria and Sogdiana, as well as at points along the Indian rivers, Alexander had already laid out a string of new cities. In these he had planted Thracian and Macedonian garrisons to protect the little colonies of Europeans left behind. The soldiers did not like being left behind, and murmurings of discontent were steadily growing. At last, the war-weary Macedonians, 3,000 miles from home, flatly refused to go one step farther, and Alexander reluctantly gave in. After building twelve great altars to mark his farthest advance — they must have been constructed along the Beas not far from Amritsar — he ordered a retreat — back to the Ravi, to the Chenab, to the Jhelum. There, prompted no doubt by Skylax's feat two centuries earlier, Alexander suddenly made up his mind to sail down the Indus to the Indian Ocean. His armada, consisting of about a thousand boats collected or built in India, was entrusted to the Cretan Nearchus. Some eight thousand of the troops, several thousand horses and quantities of supplies were embarked. The remainder of the army marched in two detachments along either bank. Alexander stood up in the prow of his vessel, piloted by Onesikritus, a former pupil of

the Greek philosopher Diogenes, and solemnly poured libations
to the Indian rivers and to the Greek and Egyptian gods, while
crowds of Indians on shore danced and sang with wild joy,
speeding the Yavana departure. Having spent just nineteen

Alexander the Great

months in India, Alexander and one section of the army then
set out overland for Persia by way of the terrible Makran Desert,
while Nearchus and the fleet continued their more leisurely way
up the Persian Gulf. Two years later, Alexander died in
Babylon.

Among the companions who had accompanied Alexander to
India were surveyors, city planners, geographers, historians and
philosophers, as well as able Macedonian soldiers like Ptolemy,
afterwards king of Egypt, and Seleukus, who inherited the Asiatic
conquests. At least four of these men — Ptolemy, Nearchus,
Onesikritus and Aristobulus — wrote books about their Indian
experiences, which were drawn upon freely by all the later
classical Greek and Roman authors.

Climate, the vastness of the rivers, the tides, the strange
animals and plants, the manners and customs of the people, the
political institutions, the peculiar religious and philosophic ideas,
all were commented upon with naive interest by the foreigners.
They admired the " vegetable wool " of India (cotton), the
" honey-bearing reeds " (sugar cane) and the trees that sent
down branches to root as new trunks (the banyan). Like all
tourists, they were fascinated by pythons, monkeys and elephants.
Elephants, they reported, were so intelligent and teachable that
they could be taught to sew, and there were ants as big as foxes,
trained for gold digging! Nearchus recorded that for letter
writing Indians made use of closely woven cloth. Aristobulus

took note that anybody who discovered a new poison and
revealed it without first making known the antidote, was put to
death in India.

One of the famous Greek anecdotes describes a meeting
between Onesikritus and fifteen naked ascetics — probably Jains
— at Taxila. Alexander saw some of these men in the street
and sent Onesikritus to say that he would like to inquire of them
about their wisdom. The fifteen ascetics were located ten miles
from Taxila, sitting naked on the burning rocks under the blis-
tering sun. Onesikritus duly delivered Alexander's message,
through a series of three interpreters. With scant courtesy, he
was told that no one wearing European clothes could possibly
learn this wisdom! Moreover, any attempt to learn this wisdom
through three interpreters was as futile as trying to get clear
water through mud. Yet they themselves inquired about the
conclusions of Greek philosophy, and were told about Pytha-
goras, Socrates and Diogenes. One of the Indian ascetics,
Kalyana, was later persuaded by Ambhi, the raja of Taxila, to
accompany Alexander when he left India. An account of his
strange end at Babylon has survived. Suddenly he announced
that he intended to commit suicide, and nothing could dissuade
him. While the Greek trumpets sounded and the Greek soldiers
stood watching with mingled horror and disgust, Kalyana calmly
climbed upon a huge pyre, sat down cross-legged in the prescribed
posture of the *yogi,* and in motionless serenity allowed the flames
to consume him.

Alexander's meteoric flash across the Indian sky, so impressive
to the Greeks, was scarcely noted by India. His name is not
even mentioned in the whole of contemporary Indian literature.

But if India as a whole was singularly indifferent to the Greek
adventure, there was one ambitious young man, an exile at Taxila
from the Magadha court of Pataliputra, who must have watched
the Yavana advance with shrewd interest, and on whom the
lessons of the superior Greek tactics and military strategy were
certainly not lost. He was soon to become known as Chandragupta Maurya, founder of the first real Indian Empire.

Chandragupta's ancestry and early history are obscure. He
has been called both an upstart and a scion of the Nanda family
of Magadha. He probably held a post in the Magadha army
to begin with. The Saisunaga Dynasty, which had replaced the
line of Bimbisara and Ajatasatru of the Buddha's time, gave
way in 413 B.C. to the dynasty of the Nandas, and Magadha
began to expand at the expense of its neighbours. It absorbed
Anga (western Bengal), the Lichavi territory and the powerful

kingdom of Kosala, which had itself just absorbed Kapilavastu
and perhaps Kasi as well. Under the Saisunaga kings, the rival
power of Avanti to the southwest, with its capital at Ujjain, was
also destroyed. When the Nandas supplanted the Saisunagas,
they became heirs to the wealthiest and the most important
kingdom of northern India.

It was against the contemporary Nanda king that Chandragupta fomented a rebellion. When it failed, he was compelled
to flee to Taxila, where he fell in with a certain astute Brahmin
named Kautilya, also known as Chanakya, who himself had some
sort of grievance against the Nanda court. It is just possible
that Chandragupta met Alexander in Taxila, and even urged him
to invade Magadha and put an end to Nanda. When news
reached India of Alexander's death in Babylon, Chandragupta
lost no time in making an alliance with Kautilya. He placed
himself at the head of the Indian revolt in the Punjab and after
exterminating what remained of the Greek garrisons there, set
off with a good-sized army for Pataliputra. The unpopular
Nanda was overthrown and murdered, and in 321 B.C. Chandragupta became the first king of the new Mauryan Dynasty. It is
said that he raised his forces in Magadha to huge proportions,
maintaining a standing army of 30,000 horses, 8,000 chariots,
9,000 elephants and 600,000 infantry. No power in India was
capable of contending with such a force, and Pataliputra became,
in effect, the national capital.

Chandragupta presently had an opportunity to show just how
strong he was. In 305 B.C., Seleukus, who had obtained the
lion's share of Alexander's Asiatic conquests, foolishly imagined
that he could repeat Alexander's exploits and regain for himself
the lost Indian provinces. He was promptly disillusioned.
Chandragupta's victory was so complete that Seleukus not only
hastily withdrew all the way to Syria (where he founded the
city of Antioch), but in token of his defeat gave his daughter
in marriage to Chandragupta and handed over, by way of dowry,
Baluchistan and a good part of Afghanistan. In exchange,
Chandragupta gave only five hundred elephants. The Hindu
Kush now became the boundary between the Indian empire of
Chandragupta and the Asiatic empire of Seleukus.

Most of what is known about the Mauryan Empire during the
reign of Chandragupta comes from Megasthenes, Greek ambassador from Seleukus, who arrived in Pataliputra in 302 B.C., and
from Kautilya's manual of statecraft, the *Artha Shastra*. Though
frequently referred to in early Sanskrit works dealing with
government, it was only in the present century that a complete

manuscript copy of the *Artha Shastra* was unexpectedly discovered, along with twelve other old manuscripts, in the library of the Maharaja of Travancore.

As described by these authors, the Mauryan capital, originally a fortress camp built by Ajatasatru at the meeting place of two rivers, the Sone and the Ganga, was nine miles long and a mile and a half wide. It was surrounded by a heavy wooden palisade guarded by more than five hundred watchtowers and pierced by sixty-four gates. A moat two hundred yards wide and sixty feet deep provided security and drainage. Outside the city, a hundred bow-lengths away, were sacred groves for ascetics and resthouses for travellers, and beyond these were the public burial and cremation grounds. Parts of the ancient teakwood rampart of Pataliputra and sunken platforms to give strength for buildings have been excavated in modern times.

Chandragupta's wooden palace, set in a spacious garden with fountains and ponds filled with fish, once occupied the centre of the city. It had many pillared halls, and Megasthenes, who had certainly visited Persia, thought it more magnificent than the famous royal palaces of Susa and Ekbatana. The pillars were encased with flowering vines worked out in gold and silver, after the fashion of the silver-plated cypress pillars of the Persian palaces. Chandragupta might well have heard of the skill of the Persian craftsmen, and encouraged his own workmen to rival their accomplishments. The quantities of royal vessels of gold, silver and copper, many richly studded with precious stones, filled the Greek envoy with amazement.

The city was divided by two wide cross streets into quarters, on the traditional Indo-Aryan plan, and houses were two and three storeys high. Each quarter had a temple dedicated to its guardian deity. Guildhalls were erected at the corners of the city, and in the northwestern section were located the bazaars and hospitals. Megasthenes notes the general fondness of the people for delicate flowered materials, bright colours, jewels and gold ornaments. When the better class of citizens went abroad, they were accompanied by attendants carrying sunshades.

The danger of fire in a city of wood, like Pataliputra, must always have been great, and very elaborate provisions were made for fire fighting. There was a well for every ten houses. No thatched roofs were permitted within the city limits. Vessels filled with water had to be kept in readiness along the main streets and in front of the palace. Every householder was required to have ladders, leather water-bags and other fire-fighting equipment on hand. Fines were imposed for carelessness in starting a fire, or for failure to run to the assistance of any neighbour in whose house a fire had broken out. It was recommended that a person found guilty of arson should be thrown into the fire of his making.

Chandragupta, in his later life, seems to have lived a secluded life within the palace. During the day he heard reports and petitions, passed sentences, attended to matters of finance and defence, and listened to the confidential reports of his secret agents and spies. But he seldom appeared in public, except to review the army, to go hunting in the royal forest preserve or to hold public audience once a year on the occasion of his birthday, when a ceremonial public washing of the royal hair took place. He may also have watched at times the popular court amusements — chariot racing and combats between rhinoceroses, elephants, rams or bulls — to which zest was added by gambling.

Megasthenes describes the strange bodyguard of armed foreign Amazons always in attendance upon the Mauryan king, present even in his sleeping quarters. A few centuries later, an item of " Greek girls " appears on lists of commercial imports into India, and the " Yavana Guard " became a feature common to the court of many an Indian prince. Chandragupta evidently wore his imperial crown none too easily. Constant care was taken lest he be poisoned, and special servants were employed to taste both food and medicine before they were offered to him. It is said that the king changed his sleeping apartment every night.

Ultimately renouncing his throne, according to tradition, Chandragupta joined Bhadrabahu, the Jain sage, and journeyed to South India, where at Belgola he eventually slowly starved himself to death, in the way permissible to a Jain monk after he has completed twelve full years of ascetic discipline.

The Mauryan administration doubtless owed its efficiency to the highly intelligent but coldly calculating Kautilya, Chandragupta's chief minister. The system of justice, however, which permitted torture both for extracting confessions and punishment, was considered harsh by the Greeks. The war office was divided into six departments, each placed in charge of five key men. Four departments were responsible for the four traditional branches of the Indian army — infantry, cavalry, chariots and elephants. The fifth department looked after proper coordination between army and navy, and the sixth handled the transport, commissariat and menial services. There was even a " Red Cross " and " Ambulance Service " for active war duty. Surgeons, with instruments, medicines and dressings, were in attendance in the rear of the battlefields, and women provided food and beverages for the wounded at first-aid stations.

The finances of the empire were drawn from varied sources. Agriculture paid the usual one-sixth of the produce, and fishermen handed over one-sixth of their catch. The Crown Lands, reserved as the king's property, yielded a substantial income. Salt was a monopoly of the government. Other income was derived from the working and leasing of mines and pearl fisheries, taxes on gambling and drink, a sales tax, fines, ferry dues, rental of government ships plying the rivers and coastal waters and making regular journeys to Persia, Arabia, Burma, Ceylon and possibly even to China. For general revenue purposes, villages under the Mauryan Empire were divided into three classes. To the first belonged the important religious and educational centres, which were tax-free. In the second class were villages contributing soldiers to the army and exempt from further taxation. Other villages paid taxes in gold, grain, cattle, dairy produce, manufactured goods or free labour for public works. Registers were kept of all citizens, showing occupation, caste, income, livestock owned, number of servants employed, and tax payable.

Supreme administration of the empire was vested in the king and his council of ministers, normally eight in number. High officials were nominated to the control of departments such as army, justice, finance, religion, foreign affairs, irrigation, public roads, prisons, the mint, parks and agriculture. The empire itself was divided into provinces under viceroys. Kautilya candidly analyzes the problem of royal princes, who may easily be tempted to try to usurp the throne for themselves. He recommends that they should be kept at a safe distance from the capital, and suggests that the best way to dispose of them is to make them provincial viceroys.

Roads and irrigation received constant attention and support from the Mauryan empire-builders. The Royal Road, modelled after the Persian Royal Road, extended 1,200 miles from beyond Taxila all the way to Pataliputra. Megasthenes says it was sixty-four feet wide and was marked with a pillar at every *stadia,* that is, every mile and one eighth. It was planted with trees and at regular intervals were wells, post and police stations and hostels for travellers. Imperial officers were charged with looking after it, and the towns and villages through which it passed had to maintain it in good condition. Fines were imposed on anyone damaging the road or causing obstruction to traffic.

Public irrigation works were also well organized in the Mauryan Emipre. Water rates were in force and the matter of fair distribution of water from canals was strictly controlled. An ancient inscription at Girnar, in Kathiawar, pays tribute to one of Chandragupta's provincial governors who dammed up a lake in that region. This irrigation project was later enlarged and was kept in repair for eight hundred years.

The affairs of Pataliputra itself were subject to minute supervision, and probably the same general rules were enforced in all the provincial capitals and large towns. There was a municipal board of thirty members, and there were six city departments. The first dealt with handicrafts, wages and fraud. The second supervised strangers, passports and lodging arrangements, and also provided medical assistance for foreigners and in the event of their death arranged to bury them and send their effects back to their relatives. The third department was responsible for keeping a register of births and deaths. The fourth controlled retail trade and issued licences. The fifth handled manufactures. The sixth department collected the municipal tax of 10 per cent on bazaar sales.

Regulations in connection with drink and gambling were very strict. Taverns must be decent, and were required to have suitable furnishings, including such amenities as scents and flowers. A special officer was to be on hand to note how much the patrons habitually drank. The value of the jewelry of intoxicated persons was to be carefully noted down, and the tavern keeper himself had to make good any loss by theft. Gambling was licensed on the basis of 5 per cent of the profits to the State. Dice were supplied by a regular official, who watched the games to see that fair play was observed.

Megasthenes, a cultured Greek gentleman, was naturally interested in some of the intellectual and philosophic aspects of life at the Mauryan capital, at the close of the fourth century B.C. Like other Greeks, he was not very clear about the gods worshipped in India. He confused them with Greek gods, identifying Shiva with Dionysos and Krishna with Herakles. Nor did he know the difference between Buddhists and Jains and other forest recluses. Yet he has given a revealing glimpse of a religious grove outside Pataliputra, where ascetics and monks were to be found " living sparely, practising celibacy and abstinence from flesh-food, and listening to grave discourse." Perhaps Megasthenes saw things a little too idealistically when he wrote, " No Indian has ever been convicted of lying," but he has left as his testimony that witnesses and seals were unnecessary, and that there was almost no litigation among Indians.

Kautilya, on the other hand, cannot be accused of a too rosy vision. He describes at length forty different methods of embezzlement, and complains that it is as hard to find out guilty officials as to discover whether fishes in a stream are drinking or not. The sinister Mauryan spy system was considered next to the army in importance ; it was based on the assumption that everybody, ministers as well as the general public, was to be regarded with suspicion and kept constantly under watch. Battalions of spies were employed. Information was to be obtained from public women, bazaars, taverns, the " four corners " of streets. News writers were employed to make regular reports, often by secret code, to a central bureau of information. Carrier pigeons brought urgent messages from distant parts of the empire. For the disposal of proved or suspected enemies, Kautilya gives a long list of poisons, which it was the duty of the official poison-mixers to administer. There were lingering poisons, instantaneous poisons, poisons which would take effect in just the requisite number of days or weeks. The *Artha Shastra* considers the subject so important that it devotes a whole chapter to poisons, and Kautilya has no qualms in freely recommending their use.

Chandragupta's son and successor, Bindusara, probably ascended the throne in about 296 B.C. Like his father, he engaged in successful military campaigns, and he also kept up relations with some of the Greek rulers in Asia and Africa. A new Greek ambassador arrived at Pataliputra from the Syrian court, and Ptolemy Philadelphus, son of Alexander's old general, sent a special envoy from Egypt. There is a Greek reference to an amusing correspondence carried on between Bindusara and Antiochus, who by this time had succeeded Seleukus. The Mauryan ruler asked for a sample of Greek wine, some figs ,and a philosopher, and promised to pay a good price for the latter. Antiochus replied that he took pleasure in sending the wine and the figs, but that among the Greeks it was not considered good form to trade in philosophers. Little more is known about Bindusara except that he married a lady from Champa, in other words, a Bengali, who became the mother of his son, the great Asoka, the Sorrowless One.

The third Mauryan emperor was not only one of the greatest rulers the world has ever known, but one of its greatest men. His own words tell us much about him. For with noble purpose and transparent sincerity, Asoka composed and had engraved on boulders, rocks and monolithic pillars in various parts of his empire a series of royal edicts and messages, embodying his laws, detailing many of his deeds and expressing his hopes and prayers for both the material and spiritual well-being of his subjects. Ten such pillars are still standing in a good state of preservation, and fragments of another twenty or more have been found and about the same number of inscribed rocks, in different parts of India.

The Asokan inscriptions give us authentic information about Asoka and the India of his day, but the Ceylonese Chronicles and Buddhist legends in Pali, Sanskrit and Chinese also speak of him. There is a legend of how the Bodhisattva, before his enlightenment, passing one day on his accustomed begging round, met a child playing in the road. The child looked up at the benign countenance and felt a quivering of love. Having nothing else to offer, he scooped up a handful of dust and innocently dropped it into the begging bowl of the Blessed One, who smiled and passed on. That child, so the story goes, was reborn as Asoka Priyadasi, Beloved-of-the-gods. Another tale narrates how Asoka, after the death of his principal queen, married Tishyarakshita, a young and vain woman, vengeful by nature. Jealous of Asoka's great love and reverence for the sacred Bodhi tree, by an evil spell she caused it to sicken and droop. When word of this was brought to Asoka, he hastened to Bodh-Gaya, filled with grief and anxiety, and miraculously revived the holy tree by pouring perfumed water over its roots. This scene has been charmingly depicted on one of the magnificent gateways of the Sanchi Stupa in Bhopal, which dates from the first century B.C.

Other legends tell how Tishyarakshita fell in love with the beautiful eyes of Prince Kunala, Asoka's eldest son. When he repelled her, she plotted a horrible revenge. She addressed a letter to the commander of the army at Taxila, where Kunala was posted as viceroy, and sealed it with the royal seal obtained by stealth. Kunala was accused of conspiring against Asoka's life, and the commander was ordered immediately to seize and blind him. A large ruined stupa is still to be seen crowning a hill near Taxila. It is popularly known as the Kunala Stupa, and is supposed to have been built by Asoka over the spot where Kunala was blinded at the instigation of his wicked stepmother.

Bindusara, Asoka's father, had died in 274 B.C. At that time, Asoka was serving as viceroy at Ujjain. Previously he had served his apprenticeship as viceroy at Taxila also. His coronation ceremony, for reasons unknown, did not take place until four years after he had actually begun to reign. In the twelfth year of his reign, Asoka fought his one and only war of aggression. This was the war against Kalinga, the country extending southward along the Bay of Bengal, comprising what is now

Orissa. It was then inhabited by a large number of forest tribes. Against them Asoka launched his mighty Mauryan army, and, in his own words, 100,000 Kalingas were slain, 150,000 others were borne away as captives, and countless more perished from famine and disease. The conquest of Kalinga brought no joy to Asoka. Instead, he was filled with remorse. He became a lay member of the Buddhist Sangha, and from this time forth publicly renounced war and all conquest by force.

Other notable events of his long reign of forty years, recorded in the inscriptions, were a grand tour of the Buddhist holy places, including a visit to Lumbini, the birthplace of the Blessed One, the calling of the Third Buddhist Council at Pataliputra (245 B.C.), and his dispatch of missionaries to the kingdoms of South India, Ceylon, Kashmir, Gandhara, and countries of the far West, beyond the borders of India. Five Greek kings are named to whom his emissaries were dispatched — Antiochus of Syria (the half-Persian son of Seleukus), Ptolemy Philadelphus of Egypt, Antigonas of Macedonia, Magas of Cyrene and Alexander of Corinth. Asoka is also credited with having founded two important cities, Srinagar in Kashmir and Lalita Patan in Nepal.

His later years seem to have been devoted almost entirely to pious works. He is said to have opened seven of the eight stupas in which the relics of the Buddha were originally enshrined and ordered their redistribution in thousands of new stupas he had built in all parts of his empire. He raised a temple round the Bodhi tree at Gaya and built so many *viharas*, or monasteries, in Magadha that it became known as the vihara country — Bihar. He was tolerant and generous in his attitude to all religions, but he made Buddhism the state religion of India. Though he continued to administer his empire until his death about 232 B.C., it is probable that toward the end of his life he was actually ordained as a Buddhist monk.

The Mauryan dynasty did not long survive its greatest ruler. Asoka's grandson Dasaratha succeeded him, and then came several weak kings. The last of them was murdered in 184 B.C. by a Brahmin commander of the army, Pushyamitra. Chandragupta, founder of the Mauryan line in 321 B.C., had risen to power by murdering the last Nanda king. By a curious twist of fate, his own dynasty was destroyed by a similar act of violence, within a century and a half.

The famous Asokan inscriptions fall into two principal series, those on natural rocks and those on sandstone pillars. Among detached inscriptions found elsewhere is a dedication of the

Barabar caves near Gaya, excavated for the use of hermits of the Ajivika sect, founded by a rival of Mahavira. Like the Buddha, Asoka deliberately chose Prakrit as the language of the inscriptions. Two rocks in the extreme northwest make use of the Kharoshthi script. All others are in the Brahmi alphabet, which was first successfully deciphered a century ago by James Prinsep, assay master of the Calcutta Mint.

The great emperor's simple personal confessions are a human document of rare charm and high moral significance. In the remarkable edict on the Kalinga conquest, Asoka humbly records that " If a hundredth, nay, a thousandth part of the persons who were then slain, carried away captive or done to death were now to suffer the same fate, it would be a matter of remorse to His Majesty." Renouncing war, he declares " The conquest of the Law alone is a conquest of delight." After his conversion, Asoka tried by progressive steps to discourage and ultimately to stop the slaughter of animals throughout the empire. He abandoned the royal hunt and recommended, as a better form of amusement, pilgrimages, religious processions and edifying spectacles. He cut down the supply of meat and game for the royal kitchens to two peacocks and one deer a day, and finally even these were given up. Animal sacrifices in the capital were strictly forbidden. A closed season was declared, and fish were not to be caught or sold on a fixed number of days in the week. Branding and castration of animals were also forbidden. Along the public highways he planted shade trees and established watering places " for the comfort of cattle and men ".

In spite of his tender regard for the life and happiness of all creatures, Asoka did not abolish capital punishment, though he tried to mitigate the harsh punishments of Chandragupta's time. He allowed a condemned man three days of grace to make an appeal and to prepare himself for death. He appointed officers to examine cases of prisoners to see that they had not been falsely condemned, and to supply money to their families if they were in need. On the anniversary of his coronation, an amnesty was granted to certain classes of prisoners.

In administration, Asoka was no doubt a benevolent autocrat. He considered all men as his own children, and the happiness of his subjects, " in this world and the next ", was what he strove for. His governors were to think of themselves as " good nurses ". They were to be careful in their conduct, and were to avoid violence, harshness, envy, impatience and idleness. He himself was a model of devotion to duty. " At all times and in all places, whether I am dining or am in the ladies' apartments,

5

in my bedroom or in my closet, in my carriage or in the palace gardens, the official reporters should keep me constantly informed of the people's business, which business of the people I am ready to dispose of at any place."

Commissioners were to tour their respective areas every five years, inquiring into the grievances and needs of the people, and looking after their spiritual education. Viceroys, including his sons, were to follow the same procedure. "Everywhere in my dominions, the commissioners and the district officers every five years must proceed on tour, not only to execute the ordinary duties but to give instruction in the Law" — the *dharma*, or code of moral duties laid down for oneself, one's family and society. The secret-service department of Chandragupta was transformed into a new service in which "overseers of the Law" were to report on the religious progress of the people. These men were also charged with seeing that all state charities and even private donations from members of the royal family were distributed impartially.

Asoka's tolerance was one of his most outstanding traits. In spite of his own loyalty to Buddhism, he enjoined upon the people respect for Brahmins, for the followers of all religious sects, for teachers and for elders. Above all, "father and mother must be hearkened to". He advocated freedom of religion for the varied population of his vast empire, representing different levels of cultural development, but insisted that the people must be united in observing moral principles and good manners. Thus did Asoka earnestly strive to fulfil the ancient Indian ideal of kingship and the Buddhist ideal of humility and love for all living creatures.

Asoka was also responsible for introducing a new development in Indian architecture. It was during his reign that, for the first time, stone came into wide use in India, both for sculpture and building purposes. The only surviving stone sculptures from pre-Mauryan or even pre-Asokan times are a few crude life-size figures of those supernatural beings called Yakshas and Yakshis, found near Patna and Mathura. This does not mean that Indian sculpture was non-existent until the third century B.C., but rather that materials easier to handle and work, like wood, ivory and baked clay, were generally preferred. Then, quite suddenly, from Asoka's time, royal artisans began to produce works of high merit in stone, such as Asoka's "Pillars of Piety". Stone also made its appearance in architectural monuments.

Whether Asoka copied or adapted his pillars from Persian or Greco-Persian models and imported Persian workmen for their execution, as is sometimes asserted, is pointlesss. Greek, Persian and Indian were all descended from Aryan stock, and if at one period or another of their separate histories they interchanged ideas or cultural influences, this was natural enough. Tall poles with a fluttering pennant at the top — a sort of flagstaff — were erected in Vedic India at the site of the sacrificial altar. Asoka simply erected columns of stone, and used them as a commanding means of publishing his messages to his people. The Pali inscriptions are always found near the base of the shaft, in a position easily seen.

The Asokan pillars are of fine-grained sandstone, varying from forty to fifty feet in height and weighing about fifty tons. All

LION CAPITAL OF ASOKA PILLAR

came out of the Chunar quarries, not far from Banaras. They rise abruptly from the ground, without any sort of pedestal. The rounded tapering shaft is perfectly plain but highly polished, and this glasslike lustre is, indeed, the chief characteristic of all Asokan stonework, without exception. The single piece of stone forming the shaft is crowned by a bell-shaped capital (more properly, an inverted lotus-petalled capital) and a round slab, which usually supports a large finely carved animal — elephant, horse, bull or lion — or sometimes the forepart of a group of lions seated back to back. A finely executed Lion Pillar found at Sarnath also supported a great metal wheel, symbolic of the Buddhist Doctrine, or Law.

The feat of moving these great stone pillars long distances and setting them in place certainly required technical and engineering skill of a high order. They have been found in eastern and central India, as far north as Lumbini in Nepal, as far west as Rajputana. No doubt they once adorned the main routes of pilgrimages or were placed near important cities, in association with stupas or other sacred structures. Sometimes they were pushed up to the top of considerable hills, like the pillar which once stood at Sanchi. The ingenuity of the Indian labourers who accomplished such work without any modern devices to make it easy commands our highest admiration.

Asoka's dome-shaped stupas seem to have been made originally of brick, but with stonework embellishments. The processional path around the base was marked off by a massive stone railing, and a similar smaller railing of stone was built round the relic box, usually at the top of the dome. Above the relic chamber, an umbrella of carved and polished stone, symbol of royalty and sovereignty, was another characteristic feature. In later centuries, many old stupas were enlarged and provided with a stone facing and tall carved gateways at the four sides.

Acres of crumbled brick and dust are all that are left today of the great Mauryan cities, but the noble ideals and principles of the great Asoka, committed to writing on imperishable stone, have fortunately been saved for posterity.

CHAPTER VII

Foreign North

PUSHYAMITRA SUNGA, commander-in-chief in Magadha, must have had the army behind him when he assassinated the last of the Mauryas as he was reviewing the imperial forces. But the new Sunga house did not last much more than a century. About 70 B.C., it was replaced by the short-lived Brahmin dynasty of the Kanvas, and following them came the Satavahanas, also of Brahmin origin, who first arose in the western Deccan and then swept eastward across Andhra, homeland of the Telugu-speaking Indians. For the next two and a quarter centuries, kings of the Satavahana line dominated both the Deccan and Magadha.

Brahmin dynasties in India were doubtless a sign of unsettled conditions following the collapse of the Mauryan Empire. Brahmin ministers, by encouraging a return from Buddhist democracy to Hindu orthodoxy, sought to climb the dizzy height to kingship with the help of the non-Buddhists.

Pushyamitra Sunga burned monasteries and even placed a price in gold on the heads of monks. Buddhism had almost put a stop to animal sacrifice. Pushyamitra revived the great " horse sacrifice " in pretentious claim to world rulership. He and his successors were devout Krishna worshippers. Yet persecutions of Buddhists under the Sungas could not really have lasted very long, for some of the most beautiful of all Buddhist monuments were erected in Sunga territory, during Sunga times.

Pushyamitra also gave practical encouragement to Brahmin scholarship. The *Purana*, or *Puranas*, and both the great Sanskrit epics were probably revised and greatly enlarged under his patronage. To the Sunga period, also, belongs Patanjali, the author of an important explanatory work on Panini's Sanskrit grammar, which stimulated a reversion to the use of Sanskrit from the Prakrit or Pali of Asoka's day.

Still another interesting and important work of Sunga times is the *Manava Dharma Shastra*, the Code of Manu. It is no law-book in the modern sense of the term, but a mixed collection in Sanskrit verse, based on an earlier prose treatise, of religious, ethical, ceremonial, civil and criminal rules and precepts taught by a particular school of northwestern Brahmins, called Manavas.

Manu is a mythical author only, whose name was written into the work to give age-old sanctity. In the middle of the eighteenth century, Warren Hastings, the first British governor-general of India, chose this work out of forty-seven different Indian law-books submitted to him, and had it translated for use by East India Company officials as a legal guide in their dealings with Hindus.

The Code contains many fine statements of principles but they are sometimes contradictory, and many of the rules are inappropriate to modern conditions. Women are placed by Manu under the permanent authority of fathers, husbands or sons. Brahmins are given a position of superiority. Child marriages are enjoined as a guarantee of chastity, and widow remarriage is forbidden to the higher castes. Yet who can say that the stiff and arbitrary rules of old " Manu ", unpalatable though they be, may not have done much to hold Hindu society together, in the face of impending foreign invasions ? Ideals of self-sacrifice and self-control were inculcated. Self-sacrifice still ranks ahead of self-expression in India, and the Hindu social structure, whatever its faults from a modern, democratic point of view, has shown high survival value.

While Pushyamitra was consolidating his power in Magadha, the old colonies of Asiatic Greeks in Bactria on the far side of the Hindu Kush, decided to try to advance their fortunes in India. Having previously thrown off allegiance to the Seleucid rule in western Asia, they declared themselves independent from the middle of the third century B.C., when the Parthians, a virile mountain tribe of northeastern Iran, known to the Indians as Parthavas or Pahlavas, also established their independence. The first king of independent Bactria was Euthydemus, and his son Demetrius, leading a Greek army down into India, called himself *Basileus Indikon*, " King of the Indians ". While Demetrius was adventuring in India, however, a usurper, Eukratides, established himself in Bactria. He, too, presently appeared over the mountains and vigorously disputed with Demetrius the rulership of the newly won Indian territory. In the end, princelings of the two rival Greek houses of Euthydemus and Eukratides set themselves up in northwestern India, the former in the eastern Punjab, the latter in Gandhara and western Punjab. A century and a half of Indo-Bactrian supremacy followed, during which at least thirty kings and two queens of Greek descent were ruling over Indian subjects in northwestern India.

Most of these kings are known only from their coins, which are fine examples of the Greek coin art, with very lifelike royal portraits. Though the later Indo-Bactrian coinage degenerated, the types established by the early Bactrians were repeated in India again and again, long after the disappearance of their last descendants.

Regular coinage issued from a royal mint and bearing the head of the ruling king was one of the important contributions of Greece, but metal money itself was not new. Coins were already circulating freely in India as early as 600 B.C., certainly long before the arrival of the Greeks. The Greek historians themselves state that Alexander received as part of the tribute paid to him by Ambhi at Taxila eighty talents of " stamped silver ". The ancient Indian money consisted of silver punch-marked coins and die-struck and cast coins of copper. In the Mauryan period, punch-marked coins came into general use, and huge quantities of them have been found all over India. They were both square and circular, and the symbols or devices punched on them were trees, plants, mountains, animals, birds, human beings, Buddhist symbols, weapons and solar and plane-tary signs. These may have been the trade-marks of well-known guilds or moneylenders.

Archaeology and literature have added a few meagre details of Indo-Bactrian history. The Bactrians first occupied Taxila in the early part of the second century B.C., and then built a new city for themselves at Sirkap, close by. Other known centres of Indo-Bactrian occupation were Kapisi, north of Kabul, Push-kalavati (Charsadda) on the Swat River in eastern Gandhara, and Sakala (Sialkot) in the Punjab. Sakala was chosen as his capital by Menander, best remembered of Indo-Greek kings and known to the Indians as Milinda. A Pali Buddhist work of about the beginning of the Christian era, the *Milinda Panha*, or " Ques-tions of Milinda ", gives a flattering description of the busy and prosperous life of the royal city, as it is supposed to have been in Menander's lifetime. The massive fortifications, the wide streets and pleasant parks, the wealth of products displayed in the bazaars, the cosmopolitan character of the population, are pictured in great detail, and it is inspiring to learn that the streets of hospitable Sakala constantly resounded " with cries of welcome to teachers of every creed ".

Menander was a great soldier and he overran many small neighbouring Indian kingdoms. Contemporary Indian works refer to Greek attacks on Mathura, Ayodhya, Pataliputra and some place in Rajputana. Menander is not remembered for military exploits, however, but rather because he became a Buddhist. When he died, about 150 B.C., his loyal subjects are reported

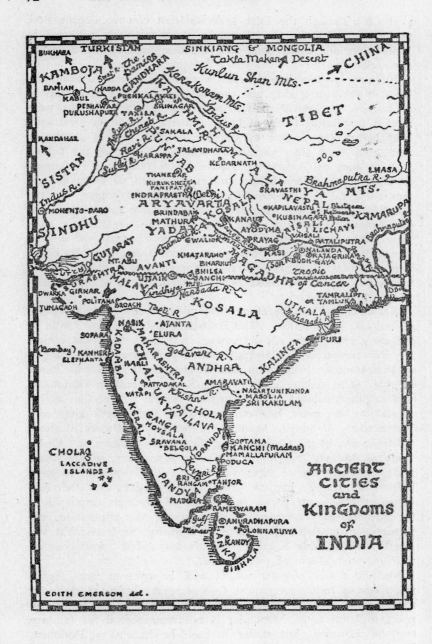

to have fought amongst themselves for possession of his earthly remains.

A trace of the influence of Indian religious thought on the Greek mind of the time is also reflected by a Brahmi inscription on a stone pillar at Besnagar, in the Gwalior region, a few miles from the site of ancient Vidisa, the Sunga capital in eastern Malwa. The Greek ambassador Heliodoros, sent by Antialkidas of Taxila to pay his respects to the Sunga king, commemorated his visit to central India by erecting a pillar bearing an image of Garuda, Vishnu's sacred bird. What lends special interest to the Besnagar pillar and its inscription is that Heliodoros describes himself as a Bhagavata, or worshipper of Vishnu. The Hindu faith, as well as Buddhism, had already begun to attract converts from among high-placed foreigners visiting India in Sunga times.

About 135 B.C., cultured Bactria was suddenly overwhelmed by nomad Scythian tribes from central Asia. The Scythians, or Sakas, were then pushed out of their central Asiatic grazing lands by the Yueh-chi, advancing from the Chinese borderland. The Sakas spread southward into Afghanistan and Baluchistan, permanently bequeathing their name to the region, afterwards known as Sakastan, Seistan, or Sistan. Toward the beginning of the first century B.C., they pressed forward into India, rapidly reducing the Indo-Bactrian states there to weak units.

The first Saka king to march into India was Maues. He installed himself at Taxila, taking the high-sounding Persian title of " king of kings ", which he put in Greek letters on his coins, copied from those of his Bactrian predecessors. After Maues came Azes I. He subjugated the Punjab and extinguished the line of Euthydemus. Saka dominion in India was then extended to Mathura, Malwa and western India. Azes I was probably the founder of the puzzling Vikrama, or " victory ", era, also known as Samvat era, which begins with the year 58 B.C.

Under Saka rule, the Persian system of governing provinces through satraps and military rulers was applied to India. Taxila remained the administrative headquarters, but Saka satraps in western India presently became so powerful that they were able to found independent dynasties of their own. By this time, however, the Sakas were becoming thoroughly Indianized. They had taken Indian names, intermarried with Indian ruling families and become Hindu or Buddhist in religion. The great satrap of Ujjain, last to bear the title, was finally defeated and killed by Chandragupta Vikramaditya, in A.D. 388. Thus Saka rule in India came to an end.

Meanwhile, an independent Pahlava kingdom had arisen in Sistan, and its leader, Vonones, had also begun to call himself " king of kings ". Sakas and Pahlavas naturally came into conflict, but their rivalries were settled when the two kingdoms were united under the Pahlava ruler Vindapharna — called Gondapharnes by the Greeks and Gaspar by the Syrians — in the first quarter of the first century A.D.

Tradition says that Gondapharnes, or Gaspar, king of Taxila, was the second of the Three Wise Men who came out of the East, following the Star, to pay homage to the Christ Child in his manger at Bethlehem. According to another legend, however, Gondapharnes was converted at a later date by the Apostle Thomas. The earliest account of this story is found in the *Acts of Judas Thomas*, a work belonging to the third century A.D. and preserved in Syriac, Greek and Latin. Immediately after the Crucifixion, the Apostles are said to have cast lots to see to which country each should go to preach Christianity. To the reluctant Thomas fell India. " I have not strength enough for this, because I am weak. And I am a Hebrew ! How can I teach the Indians ? " he lamented. The Lord then appeared to the rebellious Thomas in a vision, but still obdurate, he cried, " Withersoever Thou wilt, our Lord, send me ; only to India I will not go." His protests were vain. An Indian merchant opportunely arrived on the scene, sent by Gondapharnes of Taxila to fetch a skilful carpenter to build him a palace at Taxila, and the Lord sold Thomas to the Indian merchant for twenty pieces of silver. At the court of Gondapharnes, Thomas proceeded to spend in charity all the money given to him by the king for building the palace. He was consequently thrown into prison, but after his release, he was able to convert Gondapharnes to Christianity.

The story of St. Thomas in relation to India does not end here. His name is far better known in connection with an apostolic mission to south India, where he is said to have landed at a port in Malabar in the year 51. Chronologically, it is quite possible that he could have gone to southern India after the death of Gondapharnes, which probably occurred in A.D. 45. After residing for some years in Malabar, he is supposed to have carried his missionary labours to the east coast of India, where he suffered martyrdom while in the act of saying his prayers. The traditional site of his martyrdom is at St. Thomas Mount, a few miles south of Madras, and he was buried at Mylapore, in the suburbs of Madras, where the Portuguese built the Cathedral of San Thomé in the sixteenth century. In any case, the Syrian Christian Church was established in south India early in the first century A.D.

The Pahlavas, though probably followers of the popular Zoroastrian religion of Iran, were ardent admirers of Greek culture, and the ruins around Taxila have yielded ample proof of how they were charmed by Hellenism. Outside the north gate of Sirkap are the foundations of a large temple built on a plan closely resembling that of the Parthenon at Athens. Its Ionic columns and pilasters might have been taken straight from classical Greece. Numerous small objects of pure Greek workmanship have come to light — a silver plaque of Dionysos, a small bronze statuette of the popular Egyptian-Greek child-god Harpocrates, a gold figure of a winged Aphrodite, a Cupid medallion. On the other hand, the majority of their Indian subjects were loyal Buddhists. Many small stupas have been found in front of the remains of private houses at Sirkap and the foundation walls of a large Buddhist temple, with porch, nave, circular apse and processional path. Dating from not later than the middle of the first century A.D., this is actually the earliest freestanding Buddhist temple yet known.

Harpocrates god of Silence The Greek Horus

Image of 300 B.C. found at Taxila

Most of the jewelry and the ten thousand coins dug up at Sirkap came from under the floors of the houses. Possibly they were hidden away in haste when Taxila once again faced foreign invasion. Already it had suffered three foreign invasions by Bactrians, Sakas and Pahlavas. Now came the Kushans. Sirkap was sacked, and Kushan Taxila sprang up a few miles away. The exact date of the Kushan conquest is not known, but a

Kharoshthi inscription from a stupa of Taxila bears a date corresponding to A.D. 78, and it clearly states that in that year the ruler of Taxila was the " Great King, Supreme King of Kings, Son of Heaven, the Kushana."

Who was this illustrious personage, bold enough to appropriate to himself the Greek title of " great king," the Persian title of " supreme king of kings " and the Chinese title of " son of heaven " ? His name is not given. But on small silver coins recovered from Taxila are found the portrait and name of one Vima Kadphises bearing similar titles, and these titles invariably appear on the coins of his successor, the famous Kanishka, under whom the Kushan capital was shifted from Taxila to Purusha-pura (Peshawar).

The Chinese Annals of the Han Dynasty (202 B.C.–A.D. 220) fortunately provide a good deal of information about the background of the Kushans, who might otherwise seem to have descended into India from empty space. They were nomads, probably of eastern Turkish stock. When the Chinese first came into contact with them, they were occupying the borderlands of northwestern China, and the Chinese called them Yueh-chi. Other nomads, the Hiung-nu, or Huns, fierce Tatars from the north, later drove the Yueh-chi westward. Slowly the whole tribe moved on across central Asia, with their women and children, their carts and horses, their sheep and oxen, until they arrived in the region of Farghana (Bukhara), along the upper reaches of the Amu Daria, or Oxus. Here they found the Sakas encamped, and since there was no room for both, the Yueh-chi drove the Sakas southward into Bactria. Pleased with their new home, the Yueh-chi were just settling down comfortably, when their old enemies the Hiung-nu caught up with them. Once more they had to flee. Following the path of the Sakas, they moved first into Sogdiana, then into Bactria, where they remained for about a century. Here they gave up their nomadic habits and showed a surprising capacity to absorb the higher culture of both Bactrians and Parthians. Under Kujula Kadphises, a contemporary of Gondapharnes, their five clans were welded into one, and they became known as Kushans. There was still restlessness in their blood, however, and about the beginning of the Christian era they poured down into the Kabul Valley and Gandhara. Ultimately the new empire they created stretched from central Asia to the edge of Bengal.

While the Kushans, or Yueh-chi, were still in Bactria, they received a visit from the Chinese general Chang Kien. This was an important event, because it led indirectly to the opening up of relations between China and India. Chang Kien had set forth from China in 138 B.C., sent by the Han emperor Wu-ti, to obtain help in fighting their old common enemy the Hiung-nu. The Yueh-chi saw no reason to help a Chinese emperor who had never done anything in particular to help them. Chang Kien went back empty-handed — but not quite. He collected seeds of alfalfa and grapes, as he passed through Farghana, and he also learned the secret of how to make grape wine. Emperor Wu-ti listened spellbound to Chang Kien's recital of the marvels seen on his long journey, but the emperor's heart quickened when he heard of the beautiful big horses of Farghana, horses with powerful breasts and croups and slender feet, very different from the shaggy little Mongolian ponies which were the only horses the Chinese knew. Wu-ti made up his mind to have some of these splendid horses, and in due course dispatched a second mission to Farghana, with suitable presents to exchange. The Chinese emissaries received no horses, and were killed in the act of trying to steal some. The insult was unbearable. The mighty emperor of the Han country equipped an army and sent it westward. Farghana was chastised and made to pay a heavy fine, principally in horses. Seeing the fate of Farghana, other little states of central Asia hastened to pay tribute of their own accord and acknowledge themselves vassals of China. The shadow of Han now began to lengthen across Asia.

The Kushan king, either Vima Kadphises or Kanishka, decided upon a trial of strength. He demanded the hand of a Chinese princess. When the Kushan envoy was arrested, a large Kushan force boldly crossed a 14,000-foot pass in the Pamirs and attacked the Chinese army encamped in the plains of Yarkand, in central Asia. It was a foolhardy venture. The Chinese fell on the exhausted Kushans and annihilated the whole force. The Kushan ruler now had to pay the usual penalty of defeat by rendering an annual tribute to China.

A time came, however, when Kanishka wiped out the humiliation. First he conquered the whole of northern India, Bactria and Afghanistan. A Kushan satrap ruled at Banaras. The wealth of India enabled him to send a much larger and better-equipped army over the Pamirs, and Kashgar, Yarkand and Khotan, on the famous Silk Road to China, became part of the Kushan Empire. The tribute previously paid to China was stopped, and the Kushans carried back with them a number of Chinese hostages. The Han Annals say these hostages were well treated in India. They were given residences suitable to the different seasons, at Kapisi, in Gandhara and in the Punjab. It

is they who are thought to have introduced the peach and the
pear into India.

Kanishka dreamed of a still greater empire, to embrace the
four quarters of the world. At last the people grew weary of
endless compaigning far from home. "This king does not know
when to stop," they murmured to one another. The story is
told that, when he fell ill one day, they simply smothered him
by holding a quilt over his head. Two sons succeeded him,
Vasishka and Huvishka and inscriptions of the former have
been found at Mathura and Sanchi. Huvishka reigned thirty
years, and like his father, was a patron of Buddhism. He
endowed a large Buddhist monastery at Mathura and another at
Huvishkapura, a town he founded and named for himself in
Kashmir.

The last great Kushan ruler was Vasudeva, who lived in the
second century A.D. His coins have turned up in the Punjab
and Uttar Pradesh. Perhaps he no longer exercised authority
over the territories farther north. The first king of the new
Sassanid Dynasty of Iran raided India about this time. The
coinage of both the later Kushan princes and the Saka satraps
of western India suddenly begin to reflect Persian influence.
Even the inscriptions on them are sometimes written in Persian,
and a Zoroastrian fire altar appears on some types. Coins of
Vasudeva depict the Kushan king in Persian dress. Soon after
his time, the great Kushan Empire, which had lasted two centuries, disintegrated. The branch known as the Kidara Kushans,
however, managed to hang on to power in the Kabul Valley for
a few centuries longer.

It was during the period of Kushan rule that relations actively
developed between India and Rome in the West, and China in
the East. When Augustus proclaimed himself Roman emperor,
some of the Indian kings thought it expedient to send missions
of congratulation. The Greek historian Strabo mentions one
such Indian mission from a "lord of six hundred kings." He
is sometimes called Poros and sometimes Pandion. The head
of this mission carried a letter, written in Greek, inviting Augustus to form an alliance with him and offering Roman citizens
free passage throughout his dominions. The party set out from
Barygaza, or Broach, at the mouth of the Narbada River, in
25 B.C. It sailed over the Persian Gulf, travelled up the Euphra-
tes and struck out overland to Damascus and then on to Antioch.
A Buddhist or Jain monk accompanied the expedition, and this
man, like Kalyana of old, greatly startled the Athenians by later
burning himself on a pyre at Athens. It took the mission four

years to reach Augustus, on the island of Samos. Here they delivered their Greek letter and the gifts they had brought — tigers, a python, some gigantic tortoises, a Himalayan pheasant and an armless boy who shot arrows with his toes ! The tigers were publicly shown in 13 B.C. at the opening of the Theatre of Marcellus in Rome, the first tigers ever to be seen in Europe. Subsequently, a Kushan embassy was received by Emperor Trajan in Rome in A.D. 99. The Indians were honoured by being given senators' seats.

The Kushans greatly admired the Romans, and were quick to perceive that the splendid Roman gold coins possessed international value. They struck the first gold coins in India, in imitation of those of Rome, with almost identical weight and fineness. On one side were portraits of themselves, with pointed beards, peaked caps, long belted coats with flaring skirts, and huge knee-length boots with turned-up toes. On the other side were the images of various deities, both foreign and Indian, including Shiva with Nandi his bull, Shiva's son Skanda, god of war, and Buddha.

India was immensely rich in all those articles of luxury for which Rome now had an avid taste — jewels and fine muslins, ivory and tortoise shell, indigo, drugs, cosmetics, perfumes, condiments and spices. Tiberius, the emperor who followed Augustus, complained that such vast amounts of Roman gold were flowing to India to buy pearls and diamonds for the Roman ladies, as well as Chinese silks imported by way of India, that there was actually a serious lack of precious metals to carry on the military administration and defend the frontiers of the Roman Empire. Under the first five Roman emperors, the imports into Italy from India and the East mounted higher and higher until they reached a climax during the extravagant reign of Nero (A.D. 54-68). India, in exchange, imported from the West only limited quantities of linen, coral, glass, antimony, copper, tin, lead and wine. The balance of trade was thus always heavily in India's favour, and Rome had to settle her bills in gold.

At first the bulk of the western trade passed along the overland routes crisscrossing Asia. Persian, Greek, Arab and Indian ships had, of course, long been cautiously plying along the coast between India and the Persian Gulf, Aden, Mocha and Solomon's ancient port and iron foundry town of Ezion-Geber, at the head of the Gulf of Akaba on the Red Sea. But pirates of many nationalities lay in wait to snatch the rich cargoes and the danger of shipwreck or becalming was all to real. Therefore over-

land routes, though longer, were considered safer. It was not·
until a Greek captain named Hippalus in the first century A.D.
suddenly observed — what must already. have been common
knowledge to Indian and Arab sailors — that during the summer
months a regular wind blew steadily from the southwest across
the Indian Ocean, that sea-trade took precedence over land-
trade. It was then discovered that by setting out from Africa
in July, and cleverly utilizing the newly discovered " trade wind,"
ships could steer right across the middle of the Indian Ocean
to any ports on the west coast of India. This reduced the time
necessary for the journey between India and Alexandria, the
principal entrepôt for the Indian trade with Rome, to a bare
two months, and as many as 120 ships began to sail from the
Red Sea for India each season. On their return voyage to
Africa, three months later, they unloaded cargoes and passengers
on the Egyptian side of the Red Sea from where the caravans
passed overland to the Nile, and thence ·the goods were again
sent by boat down to Alexandria, on the Mediterranean.

The great city of Alexandria had by now replaced Athens as
the chief centre of Greek culture, and was second only to Rome
in splendour. In the early centuries of the Christian era, it was
a meeting place for the traders and adventurers, the philosophers
and scholars, the saints and mystics, of three continents and
India must have made its own distinctive contributions to
Alexandrian culture.

The first Indian known to have visited Alexandria was a
humble shipwrecked sailor, picked up at the entrance to the
Red Sea and taken to Alexandria in the second century B.C.
Indirectly he was responsible for opening up new geographical
vistas. The Egyptian government generously provided a ship
for him to pilot himself home, and along with him went an
interesting Greek explorer, Eudoxus. Eudoxus became convinced
that India might also be reached by sailing in the opposite
direction, around Africa. Eventually he succeeded in fitting out
an expedition and set sail from Cadiz, in Spain, but never
reached his destination. Sixteen hundred years later, Vasco da
Gama accomplished what Eudoxus had vainly tried to do.

By the third century A.D. some Alexandrians had certainly
gathered a fair knowledge of India, from one source or another.
Clement of Alexandria, an early Church Father of Greek birth,
had learned a good deal about India from his tutor, who had
been to India as a missionary. Clement's writings refer to the
Brahmin abstention from meat and wine, and clearly differen-
tiate between Brahmins and Buddhists. " There are some

Indians," he wrote, " who follow the precepts of *Boutta* (Buddha), whom by an excessive reverence they have exalted into a God." When St. Anthony emerged from the solitude of the Egyptian desert in the third century A.D. to found the first order of Christian monks, some of his monastic ideas — the ringing of bells, the use of the rosary, the strict discipline imposed on the brotherhood — may well have been borrowed from familiar accounts in Alexandria of Buddhist monasticism, already eight hundred years old.

Indian numerals, commonly miscalled Arabic, were introduced by Indian merchants into Alexandria probably as early as the second century A.D. Asoka had used written numerals in his Brahmi inscriptions, but it was not until about a century before the beginning of the Christian era that an unknown Indian mathematician made the greatest of all contributions to arithmetic. He invented the place-value system and zero. Numerals now had a value depending on their place, or position, in a series of numbers, built up on the decimal plan. The same numerals, 12 or 21, for example, express a different value, depending on their order. The whole world today takes for granted this ingenious Indian numerical system, by which all arithmetical calculations can be worked out by the use of only nine numerals and zero. The earliest references to the new system in India appear in Sanskrit literary works of slightly before and just after the beginning of the Christian era. From the end of the fifth century, all Indian mathematicians were already using the new system. It soon made its way eastward to Sumatra, Cambodia and Annam, and was adopted by the Arabs in the West. The Arabs, to begin with, possessed no numerals of their own, but used Greek or Coptic signs and did their calculations on the abacus. They were not slow to perceive the superiority of the Indian system and gave full credit to India. Subsequently they introduced it into the countries they conquered, and from Spain it passed into Europe. Europe first tentatively began to use Indian numerals and the Indian numerical system in the tenth or eleventh century, but it was not until the seventeenth century that they came into general use in the Western world.

The majority of Kanishka's Indian subjects in the north were probably already Buddhists when the Kushan Empire took shape but Kanishka was himself converted to Buddhism by Asvaghosha, a gifted Brahmin, himself a recent convert to Buddhism. The Kushan ruler, according to tradition, forcibly carried away Asvaghosha from Ayodhya to his capital of Peshawar. Originally of a haughty temperament, Asvaghosha now turned into a sort of strolling minstrel. He went about singing and reciting poetry and staging edifying Buddhist plays. Fragments of a palm-leaf manuscript of one of his plays, about the conversion of the two Buddhist elders, Sariputta and Moggallana, were unexpectedly recovered in distant Turfan, in central Asia, in the present century. Asvaghosha is best known, however, as the author of a famous poetical work in Sanskrit, the *Buddha-charita*, or Life of Buddha. This popular work translated into Chinese and from Chinese into English, inspired the well-known poem of Sir Edwin Arnold, *The Light of Asia*.

Kanishka, like Asoka, was fired with missionary zeal. Stupas and monasteries and temples and chapels sprang up all over the northern land. In Bactria, in the Kabul Valley, in Gandhara, in Swat, in Kashmir, in the Punjab, the white walls of Buddhist monasteries and the gilded and painted stupa domes soon dominated every rocky crest. They stood out against the green slopes of the lesser hills, and towered impressively from the plains in the vicinity of important cities. Traders saw them, pilgrims visited them. The contagion spread outward to the oases of central Asia and along the Silk Road to distant China. The Great Illuminator offered peace and joy to all who accepted him, without distinction of race or caste. Chinese Buddhists came to revere Kanishka among kings of India next only to Asoka, for it was he who did more than anyone else to make Buddhism a living creed for the people beyond India.

At least eighteen Buddhist sects had arisen by the first century A.D., and each claimed to represent the only true teaching of the Blessed One. Kanishka, puzzled and troubled by the conflicting views, decided to summon a council to settle the disputes. This was the Fourth Buddhist Council. Five hundred eminent monks and scholars from all parts of India assembled, and the deliberations lasted six months. The council produced new commentaries in Sanskrit on the three *Pitakas* of the Pali Canon, and also other works. Kanishka afterwards had the commentaries engraved on sheets of copper and a stupa erected over them, but neither stupa nor copper plates have ever been found, and it is only through early Chinese translations that the commentaries have been preserved. By the king's order, the Pali Canon was also officially translated into Sanskrit for Buddhists in northwest India who did not know Pali.

To the first three centuries A.D., including Kanishka's period, belong four basic Sanskrit texts of Mahayana Buddhism, all by unknown authors. They are the *Lalita-vistara,* a miraculous life of the Buddha, the *Saddharma-pundarika Sutra,* "Lotus of the

True Law ", the *Mahaprajna-paramita Sutra,* on " Transcendental Wisdom ", and the *Lankavatara Sutra,* on " Self-realization of Noble Wisdom ". These important works were quickly translated into Chinese, and a little later into Tibetan, and when the Sanskrit originals were subsequently lost in India itself, it was through the medium of these foreign translations that the texts were restored to the Buddhist world.

The new Buddhism differed greatly from earlier Buddhism. Its followers called it Mahayana, or the Greater Vehicle, and referred a trifle condescendingly to the teachings of the earlier Buddhist school as Hinayana, the Lesser Vehicle. Both types of Buddhism, however, shared a belief in rebirth and in the reward and punishment of good and bad deeds in future lives. Both believed in the possibility of the individual's attainment of Nirvana, or release from rebirth, through spiritual knowledge gained by right living and right thinking. Both accepted with the utmost loyalty the Three Jewels — Buddha, his Doctrine, and the Brotherhood, or Church. But Hinayana Buddhism looked upon the Buddha as a human sage and a Great Teacher, who by his own life showed men the path he wanted them to follow. Mahayana Buddhism called the historical Buddha the earthly shadow of an Eternal Buddha, a Divine Being to be worshipped as God and Saviour. The goal of the Hinayanist was his personal Nirvana. The goal of the Mahayanist came to be best expressed in the teaching of the heavenly Bodhisattvas, who gave up individual emancipation for the salvation of others.

Hinayana Buddhism flourishes today in Ceylon, Burma, Siam and Cambodia, while Mahayana Buddhism is the form found in Nepal, Tibet, China, Mongolia, Korea and Japan. In the land of its birth, Buddhism eventually all but disappeared, but quite recently there have been signs of a Buddhist revival movement.

It is not difficult to understand why the Kushans, themselves of foreign origin, looked to the Eurasian craftsmen of Bactria, Gandhara and Kashmir, trained in Greco-Roman art conventions, for suitable forms to express the new ideas of Mahayana Buddhism, instead of to the school of early Buddhist art already well established in the Deccan. To the Kushans, this truly Indian art may well have seemed more alien than Greco-Roman art. They had come into India by way of Bactria, which at the time of their occupation had sixty large Hellenic towns. They had remained there long enough to become thoroughly acclimatized and to feel on the friendliest of terms with the Greek gods whose statues in the temples resembled glorified men. Greek realism was much more comprehensible to them than the restrained and delicate symbolism of the early Indian Buddhist art convention, which considered it unseemly to drag back to earth, as it were, by any form of direct representation, one who had attained the high state of spiritual and bodily emancipation identified with Nirvana. So in this art, the Buddha was indicated only by holy symbols — a lotus for the Birth, an empty throne under the Bodhi tree and a footstool in front of it with the sacred imprints of his feet, for the Enlightenment, the Wheel of the Law for the First Sermon, an umbrella, to mark his presence in other scenes, the stupa for the Nirvana. When Mahayana Buddhism made the Buddha into a god, to be worshipped and prayed to with flowers, perfume and incense, with litany and music, the old restraint lost its meaning. Now, for the first time, Buddha images were set up for ceremonial worship.

The earliest known Buddha image is carved on a gold relic casket originally found inside a soapstone vase, bearing a Kharoshthi inscription, recovered from a stupa at Bimaran in eastern Afghanistan — part of old Gandhara. The vase contained votive coins of the Saka king Azes I, who reigned in the half century immediately preceding the Christian era. The oldest datable image, however, adorns a Buddha relic box of bronze from Peshawar, dedicated in the year I of Kanishka. This casket, which contained a crystal reliquary with a tiny piece of bone, was discovered two feet under the floor at the exact centre of what was once Kanishka's great relic tower at Peshawar. On the lid of the precious casket a small Buddha sits on a pedestal, with a lotus-petalled halo behind his head, flanked by two worshipping Bodhisattvas. Another Buddha, a portrait of Kanishka himself and a frieze of geese chasing one another with outstretched necks adorn the sides of the casket. An inscription states that it is the work of Agisala, overseer of Kanishka's monastery. Agisala seems to be an Indian transcription of a Greek name, and evidently Kanishka's master of works was a Buddhist of Greek or Indo-Greek descent. A standing Buddha, with the word " Boddo " inscribed in Greek at one side also appeared on one of Kanishka's gold coins.

From the Kushan period onward, Buddhist images, dated and undated, began to be executed in great numbers in India and other parts of Asia. Mathura, the southern capital of the Kushan kings, which already had a vigorous Indian art tradition behind it, became a new centre of activity, and from its workshops in the first years of Kanishka's reign appeared dedicated statues of Buddhas and Bodhisattvas, intended for niches and shrines. Some of these were carried as far as Sarnath, near Banaras, where they influenced the development of Gupta art in succeeding centuries. The Mathura sculptors also began to try their hands at portrait sculpture. An inscribed headless statue of Kanishka (now in the archaeological museum, Mathura) is one of the most interesting examples.

In the secluded valley of Bamian, northwest of Kabul, first-or second-century sculptors were also busy hewing from the living rock-face two enormous images of the Buddha, 170 feet and 115 feet high respectively. A man stands just on a level with the big toe of the greater image. Both are still in their original niches, though damaged by nineteen hundred years of exposure and ignorant attempts at mutilation. Bamian was on the main highway from central Asia to India, and for centuries travellers passing this way must have stopped to wonder and marvel at these gigantic images, the chief adornment of a seven-mile cliff into which thousands of caves were cut — the onetime retreat of a great community of Buddhist monks. The art of Bamian presents a strange hybrid of India and the Hellenistic East, overlaid with a strong Iranian influence. It did much to fix the distinctive Buddhist art forms which spread through central Asia to China and on to Japan.

Although Kushan or Gandharan art made use of Greco-Roman ideals in the modelling of the Buddha's head, more like an Apollo than an Indian mystic, and in certain technical details, such as the handling of the folds of the monk's robe, it must not be forgotten that the original conception of the Buddha figure was basically Indian, not Greek, and was evolved in strict accordance with the ideal description of the thirty-two auspicious signs on the Buddha's person, as given in the earliest Buddhist literature. The mark of wisdom between the eyebrows, the protuberance on the top of the head, the long ears, the long arms, the closed or half closed eyes, indicating an inner contemplation, the solemn dignity of the standing figure, the immobility of the seated figure with legs crossed and upward turned soles, the beautiful hand gestures, or *mudras*, denoting spiritual acts such as teaching, blessing, bestowing, calling the earth to witness to the truth of his words — all these are in the Indian tradition and bear no resemblance to anything foreign. Likewise the crowned Bodhisattvas, loaded with jewelry, are typical young Indian princes of noble lineage, and could never remotely be mistaken for the athlete of magnificent body and objective mind, so greatly admired by the Greeks. Gandharan Buddhist art represented something less subtle, more direct and concrete, than the older Hinayana symbolism, but it was nevertheless imbued with Indian ideals. For illiterate worshippers, stone pictures illustrating the Jatakas and the incidents of the life story of the Buddha were also a fine means of spreading the message of Buddhism along the outer rim of India.

Under the Kushans, a new type of Buddhist monastic architecture also emerged. Monastic buildings had hitherto been grouped somewhat at random around open-air stupas, the earliest Buddhist centres of worship. In the north, where political conditions were never very stable and turbulent invasions were always a possibility, monasteries began to assume the form of fortified cities. The monks' cells were ranged in double-storied rows, facing inwards round three sides of an open courtyard. Only blank walls greeted the beholder from without. The fourth side of the courtyard was provided with a massive gate. Since the stupa placed at one end of the open court was now reduced in size, it was given appropriate height by means of a high platform, and the dome was embellished with stucco garlands and festoons, gilded or painted in bright colours. About the base were niches with Buddha images.

Minor stupas and chapels clustered around the main stupa, and from many of these, present-day archaeological researches have recovered fascinating articles. Near the back wall of a chapel associated with the great stupa of Taxila, probably dating from Asoka's time but rebuilt and enlarged under the Kushans, a silver vase was found with a gold casket containing minute bone relics and an inscribed silver scroll. The Kharoshthi inscription, with a date corresponding to A.D. 78, states that the accompanying relics were those of the Holy One, enshrined by the Bactrian Urasaka for the bestowal of health, blessings and honour on the Kushan king, his parents and his friends.

The whole of the northern territory was transformed by Kushan zeal into a second Buddhist Holy Land. The Buddha was popularly believed to have transported himself thither through the air to work various miracles, and incidents connected with his mythical life as a Bodhisattva, or with the lives of previous Buddhas, were also transferred to northern sites. Numerous stupas arose to commemorate these legends and to enshrine the supposed relics, such as the stupa of his staff, the stupa of the begging-bowl, the stupa of the top bone of his skull, the stupa to commemorate the spot where as Bodhisattva he gave his eyes to a hungry tigress.

Hill monasteries in the neighbourhood of Taxila have preserved the evidence of how the flame of Buddhism was suddenly extinguished in northern India, about the middle of the fifth century. Among charred ruins and tumbled heads of clay and stone images, excavators found several skeletons in tortured attitudes, presumably of monks who once inhabited the monastic cells. With barbaric shouts and the loud trampling of horses' hoofs, the White Huns, like a gusty storm, shattered the peace of the great monasteries, spreading death and ruin behind them.

CHAPTER VIII

Indian South

HISTORIES OF INDIA, unfortunately, nearly always show a peculiar northern bias. South India and the great Deccan plateau are neglected, and the distinctive contributions of the Dravidian South to Indian civilization as a whole are overlooked or given scant attention. This neglect of the historian is really due to no fault of his own, but rather to a series of odd circumstances.

No ancient archaeological site as important as Mohenjo-daro, for example, has yet been discovered in southern India. The early Aryans of the north were prolific thinkers and writers, and the background of their vast literature was invariably north India. Tamil, the oldest Dravidian language, has remained a formidable stumbling block for those not having it as their mother tongue, and work of translation has progressed all too slowly, with a resulting lack of balance in our sources of information. Then, for centuries, the easiest route to reach India from Western Asia was by way of the north, as it was also the earliest route of cultural exchange between India and Eastern Asia. Greeks and Chinese, who have filled in many a blank in the written history of India, concerned themselves almost exclusively with north India. Buddha was a Northerner. He did not travel to the South, and it was the northern land of his birth and ministry which became a Holy Land to the millions of Buddhists. The earliest and greatest Indian empires arose in the north. When they disintegrated or succumbed to outside aggressors, foreigners, coming from the north, established their seats of government there. Muslim conquerors in medieval times ruled India from Delhi or Agra for more than six centuries. Their British successors ruled from Calcutta and Delhi for two and a half centuries. Their historians naturally devoted most of their attention to northern India.

Thus, far more historical material is available for northern India than for southern India. Dravidian-speaking people had probably spread over most of India, however, in prehistoric times, and it was only when the Aryans appeared on the scene, that the Dravidians were pressed back into the southern part of the peninsula. And Aryan penetration into South India had already taken place when South Indian history, as such, really begins. Of two great basic types of civilization, Aryan and Dravidian, which mingled and fused in succeeding centuries, each contributed vital elements to make Indian civilization today one of the world's five living distinctive civilizations. If the tall fair-skinned Aryan of the north was the father of this civilization, the slender dark Dravidian of the south was certainly its fertile mother.

The mode and time of the actual penetration is largely guess-work. Tradition says that the Vedic rishi Agastya — the great Aryan pioneer and pathfinder — crossed the Vindhyas and plant-ed Brahmin colonies in the Deccan and the far South, perhaps as early as 800 B.C. Statues of Agastya, with long beard, tower-ing topknot and sacred thread falling across his mighty paunch, are revered in South India even today. They are the affectionate and loyal tribute of later ages to some dim memory out of the past.

Whatever its circumstance, Aryan advance southward seems to have been entirely peaceful. The Dravidian kings welcomed and honoured the Brahmins. The people of the Deccan and the South, however, were materially well advanced. They had pros-perous cities, far-reaching trade connections, skilled craftsmen, a highly developed system of music, fine poetry. The Brahmin merely served to stimulate the Dravidian genius, which soon blossomed out in its highest expression in literature and art, enterprise and industry, an imaginative and deeply emotional religious fervour, a remarkable capacity for mathematical abs-traction, a well-developed village organization, and ultimately in the creation of magnificent, breath-taking temple cities, vast irri-gation works and splendid sculpture in bronze, copper and stone. The principal Dravidian kingdoms of the historical period — Pandya, Chola, Kerala, Pallava in the far South, Andhra and Chalukya in the Deccan — have added many brilliant pages to the annals of India.

The history of the great kingdom of the Telugu-speaking people of Andhra, in the Deccan, begins later and ends earlier than the history of the three older Tamil-speaking kingdoms of southern India, Pandya, Chola and Kerala, but it forms a strik-ing bridge between North and South. With the breakup of the Mauryan Empire shortly after the death of Asoka, the part which did not come under the yoke of foreign invaders was divided among three rival claimants. The central region passed into the hands of the Sungas, who were afterwards succeeded by the Kanvas. In the east, Kalinga (the conquest of which had caused so much heartburning to Asoka) reasserted its independence and kept it until the time of the Guptas. The Deccan plateau became identified with an Andhra kingdom which before long extended from the Bay of Bengal to the Arabian Sea. Andhra rule lasted in the Deccan for about four and a half centuries, from 225 B.C. up to A.D. 225.

The Andhra people were known to and were so called by the Greek ambassador Megasthenes in the time of Chandragupta Maurya, and Asoka was also familiar with them. They seem to have originated in the Telugu country between the deltas of the Godavari and Krishna rivers, and their earliest known capital was Srikakulam, near the mouth of the Krishna. At a later date, Amaravati became their chief southern capital, and Paithan their capital in the west.

In the first or second century B.C., a man named Simuka suddenly acquired power in the western Deccan, where he founded the Satavahana dynasty. Satavahana rulers extended their sway eastward, put an end to the remnants of Sunga power, exterminated the Kanvas, and in due course merged their line with the ancient Dravidian line of Andhra kings. Counting from the time of Simuka, the Puranic royal lists, which make no distinction between Satavahanas and Andhras, give the names of thirty Andhra kings. Dates are very uncertain, however, because the title of Satakarni is commonly used in Andhra inscriptions without any personal name attached, and the puzzling Dravidian system of chronology records events not by any fixed era, but by the sequence number of the fortnight in the particular season — hot, rainy or cold — of the regnal year of the individual king concerned.

One of the earliest inscriptions in which the name, or title, of Satakarni appears is found near Bhubaneswar, in Orissa. It is the celebrated cave inscription at Udaigiri, singing in one hundred and seventeen lines the praises of one King Kharavela of Kalinga, who probably belonged to the second century B.C. The inscription states that Kharavela (otherwise unknown to Indian history) ascended the Kalinga throne at the age of twenty-four, after completing his princely education in writing, mathematics, law and finance. He then carried out important works of public utility such as renovating and extending certain old irrigation canals and fought a number of successful campaigns. In the second year of his reign he fought a war with Satakarni. Kharavela also invaded Magadha twice, overawing an unnamed Yavana general. He compelled the Sunga king at

Rajagriha to sue for peace and return a famous Jain image which had been carried away from Kalinga by an earlier Magadha ruler. In the thirteenth year of his reign, Kharavela made war against the Tamil country of Pandya, in the South, obtaining as fruit of victory a great booty in horses, elephants, rubies and pearls. With this bit of information, the royal chronicle comes to an abrupt end.

From the opposite side of India, in Maharashtra, come Satavahana inscriptions of about the same early period. One of them asserts that Satakarni, son of Simuka, made extensive conquests and performed Vedic sacrifices. A somewhat later inscription from Nasik, in the name of the queen mother Balasri, proudly boasts that her son Gotamiputra Satakarni, " the unique Brahmin ", crushed the conceit of the Kshatriyas, properly expended the taxes levied in accordance with sacred law, restored the observance of caste rules, overthrew Sakas, Yavanas and Pahlavas, and re-established the glory of the Satavahana race. Gotamiputra inflicted a crushing defeat on Nahapana, the Saka satrap of Nasik, and thus arrested the further advance of alien influence into the Deccan. Under his son, about A.D. 130, Satavahana sway was extended to the Andhra country.

Defeat of the foreigners from the north was ultimately accomplished in another way. Gotamiputra's son married the daughter of Rudradaman, Saka satrap of Ujjain, and Nahapana's daughter and her husband Ushavadata both adopted the Hindu faith. A Nasik inscription records that Ushavadata granted sixteen villages to Brahmins, himself married into Brahmin families eight times, and fed one hundred thousand Brahmins every year. From the time of Rudradaman onward, all Saka satraps of Ujjain bear Indian names. On the famous Girnar Rock in Kathiawar carved with a set of Asoka's Fourteen Edicts, an inscription in Sanskrit prose by Rudradaman also appears. This is the inscription relating to repairs on the dam of the artificial lake originally excavated in the time of Chandragupta Maurya. It shows that in the Saka-Andhra lands of western India, a typically Indian culture had supplanted foreign influences by the middle of the second century A.D.

The rule of the last great Andhra king, Yajna Sri Satakarni, continued up to the end of the second century A.D. Under him, the Andhra kingdom stretched from sea to sea. The western capital, Paithan (now a ruined site on the upper Godavari), rivalled Amaravati in the southeast. Paithan was connected by a good road with Kalyan, the principal western port of the Deccan, and Andhra commanded an important share of the rich trade then being carried on with Alexandria. One of Yajna Sri Satakarni's coins bears the device of a two-masted ship, and Andhra possessed a considerable fleet of merchant vessels for maintaining its sea-borne trade.

Early in the third century A.D., there came an abrupt collapse of Andhra rule. No destructive invasion or large-scale war is known to have occurred, but suddenly Abhira and Naga tribes-men are found roaming unchecked over the western Deccan. The Vakataka dynasty then asserts itself, and finally in the sixth century the Chalukyas gain ascendency. Meanwhile, the illus-trious Pallavas (not to be confused with the Iranian Pahlavas of the North) become heirs to the southern and eastern parts of the Andhra domain. There will be more to say about these later kingdoms of the Deccan in the next chapter.

Early Andhra rulers seem to have been extraordinarily tole-rant. In spite of the honour accorded to Sanskrit, their seven-teenth king, Hala, is credited with the authorship, in the first or second century A.D., of a poetic work in the ancient Maha-rashtri language, consisting of seven hundred verses on love, the " Seven Centuries ". One of Hala's ministers produced a Sanskrit-Prakrit grammar and still another, Gunadhya, was the author of a collection of popular tales, the *Brihat-katha*, in the Paisachi dialect. In matters of religious faith, Hindus, Jains and Bud-dhists were all allowed equal freedom in Andhra.

Andhra is especially honoured for its famous Buddhist monu-ments, which have survived the ravages of centuries, and perhaps tell us more of the high culture existing in the ancient Deccan than we could learn from any other source. Sanchi, Amaravati and Ajanta — what names to conjure with ! If India had produced only Sanchi, she would have established herself before the world as a land of supreme artistic genius. Compared with contemporary clumsy Gandharan art, the grace and beauty and spiritual quality of the artistic creations of Andhra were superb.

The early Buddhist art tradition was centred in the stupa, or relic mound, probably derived from some prehistoric type of burial. As the chief object of early Buddhist worship, the stupa had acquired all its characteristic features by the time of Asoka. In its earliest form it consisted of an uncovered mound in the form of a solid hemisphere, made of large unburnt bricks over-laid with earth or whitewashed plaster. A small railing and a pinnacle in the symbolic form of the royal umbrella crowned the structure. Around the base, a massive circular wooden ground railing, with gateways at the four cardinal points, marked off a

broad path for monks and lay pilgrims to circumambulate the
stupa, and a second narrower terrace and railing often circled
the drum of the stupa some little distance from the ground. A
stone reliquary was invariably placed within the stupa, either
near the top or at floor level, and this usually contained a smaller
receptacle of some precious material like gold or crystal, enshrin-

Umbrella of stone from a Stupa

ing a bit of bone or ash, with offerings of gold flowers, pearls or
other precious stones. The most sacred relics were those of
Gotama Buddha, distributed by Asoka in the third century B.C.,
but in the course of time his great disciples were also given relic
stupas of their own. Stupas were naturally erected to mark traditional sacred Buddhist sites.

In late Mauryan and Sunga times, stone was substituted for
brick and wood. The original brick stupa was then encased with
stone slabs and the wooden railings were replaced by stone.
Stone was an excellent medium for carving, and surfaces now
came to be adorned with reliefs in the shape of small panels or
medallions and floral borders. The Jataka stories, episodes connected with the life of the Buddha, the legendary lives of the
previous Buddhas, and actual incidents of known Buddhist
history, were considered fitting subjects for sculpture. The
earliness or lateness of all Buddhist works of art, however, is
determined by the absence or presence of the Buddha figure.
If the presence is indicated merely symbolically, the work belongs
to the early period.

Two carved railings, one from Bharhut, near Allahabad
(150 B.C.), and the other from Bodh-Gaya (100 B.C.), and a
single Bharhut gateway, represent the earliest existing Buddhist
sculptures in India after Asoka's time. The Bharhut railing and
gateway are now in the Indian Museum at Calcutta. A fragment

of the Bodh-Gaya railing has been re-erected beside the temple at present standing at Bodh-Gaya. This railing and the Bharhut gateway both bear Sunga inscriptions. The sculptured medallions of the Bharhut railing are of particular interest, because they have Brahmi titles identifying several of the Jataka stories and life episodes. The small archaic Sunga reliefs might easily have been the work of ivory or wood carvers not yet perfectly familiar with the technique of handling stone, and they are directly related to Andhra sculptures of Sanchi and Amaravati, in the immediately following period. There is the same crowding into a small space of many figures, the same remarkable capacity to tell a story in stone, the same dramatic device of repeating the central figure to indicate the successive episodes of action within the same composition, the same decorative exuberance, the same charming familiarity with animals, birds and flowers, the same utter sincerity of purpose, the same fervent faith, the same child-sweet emotion and innocence.

Though the Great Stupa of Sanchi, near modern Bhopal — best preserved of all Buddhist monuments in India — is the chief object of interest, the low stone hill which it crowns is strewn with remains of temples and monasteries and smaller stupas, and indeed the whole neighbourhood of Sanchi is incredibly rich from an archaeological point of view. From the time of Asoka, through the Sunga and Andhra periods, and well into the Gupta age, Sanchi was apparently the chief Buddhist site in the Deccan. Its monuments extend over a building period of thirteen centuries. Yet forgotten Sanchi was only rediscovered in 1818 by an English military officer, and it was in the twentieth century that Sir John Marshall, Director General of Archaeology, completed the work of clearing away the accumulated debris, so that the Great Stupa emerged once more in all its splendid and solemn magnificence.

Important as Sanchi was, strangely enough it does not seem to have had any connection with any known incident in the life of the Buddha. The place is barely mentioned, under the name of Chetiyagiri, in early Buddhist literature. Perhaps it was only because Asoka's Queen Devi happened to be born at Vidisa (Bhilsa, or Besnagar), five miles from Sanchi, that Asoka selected the spot for erecting a stupa there. The original brick structure still exists, inside a later stone enlargement of the Sunga period, but the Buddha relics themselves long ago disappeared. An Asokan pillar stands near by. Queen Devi herself dedicated a sumptuous monastery in the neighbourhood. From two of the smaller Sanchi stupas have come relic caskets of unusual interest. One stupa yielded two reliquaries inscribed with the names of Buddha's two chief disciples, Sariputta and Moggallana. In the other were found four boxes on whose lids or sides were the names of ten Buddhist saints and teachers, among whom some are known to have taken part in the Third Buddhist Council, called by Asoka, and some to have been sent by him on missions to the Himalayas and elsewhere.

The fame of Sanchi rests, above all, on the four intricately carved gateways, known in Sanskrit as *torana*, erected on the hilltop around the main stupa in the first century B.C., when Sanchi lay within the Andhra kingdom. A similar gateway stands fifty yards away, in front of the stupa dedicated to the two chief disciples. All these gateways, with only one exception, were still standing in their original positions early in the nineteenth century, exactly as they had stood for two thousand years. How they could have remained intact all this time is a mystery since from the architectural point of view the structures would appear quite unstable. The supporting pillars of gray stone are only two feet thick, rising from the ground with no support of any sort to a height of thirty-five feet. The top-heavy superstructure consists of three massive horizontal crosspieces, twenty feet in breadth. Heavy lion capitals and tree dryads swing gracefully from the carved openwork branches at both ends of the lowest lintel. The top one bears a great Wheel of the Law, flanked by attendants bearing yaktails and the *triratna* device, standing for the Buddha, the Law and the Order.

The upright posts and the three crosspieces of the Sanchi gateways, both on the inner and outer faces, are completely covered with an exquisite series of sculptures in relief. They depict various Jataka stories, the Birth, Enlightenment, First Sermon and Death of Gotama Buddha (always without the figure of the Buddha), and historical events associated with Asoka and some of his pilgrimages. There are royal and relic processions emerging from fortified gates protecting the picturesque moated cities of Rajagriha, Kapilavastu and Kusinagara. Asoka appears in one scene paying homage to the sacred Bodhi tree. There are numerous delightful village scenes. Village women, wearing their hair loose, clad in short skirts and adorned with heavy anklets and armlets, husk and winnow grain or make bread beside their open doorways. Clusters of beehive huts, with conical roofs of thatch — round huts are still to be found in the Deccan — leafy hermit dwellings and elaborate palaces with pillared halls are all faithfully depicted in the Sanchi sculptures. Within the palaces, young bejeweled rajas are seen leaning in graceful

postures, attended by lovely queens, and aristocratic little damsels
peer forth from upper balconies and windows, to watch with
vivid interest what goes on in the street below. There are wonderful forest scenes, too, in which the Bodhisattva as king of a
mighty herd of elephants disports himself with dignity among
his females and young, while a cruel hunter lies in wait to kill
him at the bidding of a jealous queen of Banaras. Or there is
the moving episode of the Bodhisattva as the monkey king, making
a sacrificial bridge of his own body to allow his monkey subjects
to cross over in safety and thus escape the soldiers sent to shoot
them by the king of Banaras.

The whole contemporary Andhra world, of city, village and
wilderness, teeming with human, animal or floral life, lives again
in the gray rain-washed stones of Sanchi, which were perhaps
once tinted red. Inscriptions on gateways and railings, as well
as on many of the paving stones of the processional path, make
it clear that contributions for the work came from rich individuals and various artisans and guilds. A lute player, a banker,
the foreman of the Andhra king Sri Satakarni, the ivoryworkers
of Vidisa, are among those who have left a record of their
donations. Gifts of money and the income of specified villages
for feeding mendicants and maintaining votive lamps are also
recorded. The Great Stupa was a popular shrine to which offerings were gladly made by innumerable persons.

The eastern Andhra country at the delta of the Krishna was
another early Buddhist centre, and numbers of stupas and architectural remains have been found in this region. The most important belong to Amaravati, Jaggayyapetta and Nagarjunakonda.
The stupa at Nagarjunakonda shows a unique plan of construction not found in any northern Indian example. It was built in
the form of a giant wheel, symbolizing the Wheel of the Law,
or Doctrine, with hub, spokes and tire clearly indicated in the
brickwork. An inscription says this stupa was erected by the
Princess Chantisiri and was built for the monks of Ceylon.
Nagarjuna, whose name is associated with this site, who lived
at the end of the second or early part of the third century A.D.,
is said to have passed the greater part of his life at this
place. It was he who is thought to have founded the Mahayana
system of Buddhism which afterwards spread northward from
the Deccan. Today, after careful removal of all possible archaeological remains, Nagarjunakonda has been sacrificed for building
the great Nagarjunasagar project, on the Krishna, which is to
irrigate thousands of acres.

The Great Stupa of Amaravati, originally 192 feet in diameter (the Sanchi stupa is 120 feet), existed at the beginning of the nineteenth century, but subsequently disappeared. Fortunately, numerous carved white marble slabs, which once adorned the lower half of the great dome, have been dug out, and these now repose in the British Museum and the Madras Museum. Replicas of the stupa itself are carved on many of them, and it is

Chaitya Slab from the Amaravati Stupa

possible to have a fairly correct idea of how it looked in the days of its glory. It was much more elaborate in appearance than the Sanchi stupa, due to the jewel-like carving of its glistening white marble base, and the upper dome was decorated with a great necklace, or garland, in stucco relief, probably gilded and painted. The Amaravati stupa possessed one curious feature not known elsewhere. The upper terrace around the dome had four projecting balconies each supporting five pillars twenty feet high. Their exact significance is not known.

The reliefs of the Amaravati school range over a fairly wide interval, from about 200 B.C. to the third century A.D., and cover the transitional period from earlier to later Buddhist art forms. Considerable development in technique is also apparent by the end of this period. There is greater freedom of movement than in the Sanchi carvings, and an almost infinite variety in the

7

treatment of figures, which have an ethereal grace. They run, dance, fly or float through space, with wonderful agility. At the same time, the virile realism and the earnestness of the moral message, characteristic of early Indian art, are still present in the Amaravati school. It would be hard to surpass in charm, for example, the little circular medallion from Amaravati, which has been given the title of " The Taming of the Elephant ". It shows an elephant let loose for the purpose of killing the Buddha by his jealous cousin, Devadatta. In the left half of the circle the elephant is dashing a helpless victim head downwards against the pavement, and at the same time trampling another under-foot, while the frightened inhabitants of the city run for safety or cling to each other, petrified and terror-struck. In the right half of the panel, the elephant bows in humble submission before the calm and majestic figure of the Blessed One, while the monks behind him observe the miracle with folded hands.

About the time when Buddhist stupas were beginning to receive their splendid stone embellishments in the Deccan, an entirely different kind of Indian religious architecture was gaining in popularity. This was the architecture of rock-cut caves. Some of the earliest appear in Orissa, at Khandagiri and Udaigiri, where Jain excavations took the form of oblong halls with or without pillared verandas. Some were double-storied, and one of the more famous of the group, the " Rani Gumpha ", was provided with a courtyard where possibly religious plays were enacted, overlooked by broad stone terraces. The sculptured frieze running around the walls of the upper storey seems to have a dramatic character. One cell is curiously carved out of a jutting rock, in the form of a tiger with open jaws. The chamber inside is eight feet wide, six feet deep and only three and a half feet high. According to an archaic inscription, an anchorite named Sabhuti lived in this tiny retreat, where he apparently passed the whole of his life.

In the Western Ghats, north of Bombay, numerous groups of Buddhist excavations also belong to a very early period — such as those of Bhaja, Kondane, Ajanta, Bedsa, Nasik and Karli. Square *viharas*, or monasteries, have ranges of small individual cells opening out from them, and long, pillared *chaityas*, or worship halls, contain a solid stone stupa as an object of worship or meditation. For about four hundred years, from 200 B.C. to A.D. 200, all these rock-cut dwellings were occupied by communities of Hinayana monks. After Mahayana Buddhism had generally supplanted the earlier form, the same caves were adapted to the requirements of the new form of worship. At the back of the *viharas,* additional chambers were cut out and large Buddhas were sculptured from the solid rock. Until at least the close of the seventh century, Buddhist monks in India continued to construct these monastic establishments, and Jains and Hindus did the same.

Indian ascetics had always retired to natural rock caves in places of solitude, but artificially excavated caves date only from the Mauryan period, so far as is known. In the Barabar Hills, in the vicinity of Gaya, inscriptions of Asoka and his grandson Dasaratha tell us that certain caves were made here, at royal cost, for ascetics belonging to the Ajivika sect of the Jains. These caves show the fine polish which was the distinctive characteristic of all Mauryan stonework. By the second century B.C., a veritable passion to scoop out swallowlike eyries in the vertical faces of lonely cliffs and gorges seems to have taken possession of Buddhist monks all over India. Soon these establishments had become incredible series of magnificent halls of gigantic size, decorated outside and inside with bas-reliefs and elaborately carved pillars and imposing statues of Buddhas and Bodhisattvas, and, as at Ajanta in the western Deccan, with beautiful frescoes covering their walls and ceilings. Then the Brahmins, too, caught the fever. At Elura (Ellora), about seventy miles south of Ajanta, twelve Buddhist, five Jain and sixteen Brahmin excavations, huddle side by side at the base of a tall cliff overlooking a wide level plain. They range in date from the fourth to the thirteenth centuries A.D.

Altogether, there are more than twelve hundred rock-cut temples and monastic halls and cells in different parts of India, but by far the greater number is found in the Western Ghats. The practice went on for about a thousand years, finally dying out only in medieval times. As the religious communities multiplied and required more space, new chambers were excavated at irregular intervals alongside or above or below the earlier ones. Rooms were connected by narrow zigzag ledges or stairs cut in the front face of the rock. One group at Nasik has twenty-three caves. Ajanta has twenty-nine. Kanheri, on Salsette Island near Bombay, has one hundred and nine !

The earliest Indian rock-cut temples and monasteries all faithfully copy the technique of wood-building. Carpenters became stoneworkers and with infinite patience chiseled from the solid rock imitation wooden beams along the barrel-shaped ceilings of the meditation halls. Embrasures of the great sun-windows were carefully given utterly useless stone ribs, as if they added strength. Imitation arcades and decorative balconies and casements and niches were given joinings and railings of the ancient architectural style of wooden buildings which undoubtedly preceded those of stone. Yet the architects and engineers mastered their difficult problems, or their wonderful creations would not have endured these hundreds of years. Some of the Ajanta viharas are ninety feet square. The great chaitya at Karli is 124 feet long, 45½ feet wide and 46 feet high. The largest of the Buddhist cave structures at Elura is three storeys high, with a frontage of 112 feet. It was certainly no small feat for Indian workmen to excavate chambers of such enormous size.

At Ajanta, and elsewhere, a few incomplete chambers reveal just how the workmen set about their task. The outer face of the cliff was first cut back vertically to provide a projecting ledge with space for a columned porch, to give access to the interior. The actual work of excavating commenced on the upper level, above the porch, through the central arched window, designed both to admit light and permit accumulated debris to be thrown outside as work progressed within. The interior cutting, performed with a pick, started at the ceiling. The position and size of pillars for sustaining the immense weight of the stone overhead had to be carefully calculated. The rock was then hewn away, leaving the massive stone columns standing free.

The rough excavation completed, picks were discarded for chisels and brushes. Now began the exquisite carving and painting. Many of the ordinary workmen were capable of transforming themselves into able craftsmen, but the best sculptors and artists of the day must also have been employed. As shown by numbers of inscriptions in the Ajanta caves, rich patrons donated individual viharas and chaityas. Pedestals, capitals, brackets, door-frames, porches, were all elaborately sculptured. Here and there walls and ceilings and the flat sides of pillars were plastered with mud and straw as a base for painting. Traces of very early paintings, darkened almost beyond recognition, still cling in patches to the dark interiors of certain caves, but in the later Gupta period the most magnificent of the Ajanta frescoes were added.

It was to such environments of solitude and strange man-made beauty that Buddhist communities in India, in the centuries immediately before and after the commencement of the Christian era, retired from mundane existence—not to live a life of slothful ease, but of strenuous endeavour. At Ajanta, the abbeys and monasteries stretch in an irregular line for a third of a mile, across the face of a crescent cliff overhanging a charming little stream winding along far below. The earliest excavations are

Bodhisattva with the Blue Lotus. Vihara Cave 1. Ajanta

of the second century B.C. Then, after a long interval, twenty-four more caves were excavated in the fifth and sixth centuries A.D. One can picture the old abbots superintending the work as it progressed without hurry, decade after decade, or even century after century. Students and novices must also have been present from many parts of India, perhaps even from Ceylon and countries far beyond India's borders in the north, for Ajanta was a university as well as a monastery. The atmosphere surely vibrated with a spirit of earnest study and intense devotion.

Imagine the hot glare of the brilliant Indian sunshine without, the monotonous drip of the monsoon rains. Inside the gloom of a great cavern, a carved stupa suddenly becomes illumined by a

Flying Gandharvas from Gupta-period sculpture

shaft of light, striking down through the high sun-window of the façade. The light fades to evening. From the raised music chamber in the chaitya anteroom, sounds the muffled thud of drums, and sonorous trumpets call the monks to their communal worship and meditation. The solemn procession bare-footed, yellow-robed, passes slowly into the prayer hall and along the ambulatory passage, carefully keeping the stupa to the right. The monks sit down cross-legged in long rows and resonantly intone the sacred texts. Oil lamps flicker like a thousand fire-flies, and blue incense trails upward, losing itself in the shadowy vault. Then, gradually the voices cease, the figures fade. Only silence and emptiness remain.... Wild bees are now building their hives among the deserted Buddhas and Bodhisattvas, and bats flicker out and in, weaving intricate patterns in the twilight. Now and then simple cultivators or hunters, overtaken by storm or darkness, seek refuge for a night in the mysterious caves, lighting smoky fires as protection against prowling beasts.... And once more change follows change. Ajanta is accidentally re-discovered within territory ruled by a Muslim prince, the Nizam of Hyderabad. Experts from abroad are invited to repair the frescoes and save them from further disintegration. The caves are thoroughly cleansed, electric lighting is supplied, a fine motor road is built to the foot of the cliff. Nowadays curious visitors, guidebook in hand, swarm to the world-famous Ajanta caves of ancient Andhra, to marvel and admire.

CHAPTER IX

The Dravidian Matrix

IT IS SURPRISING that no very early monuments of either artistic or historic importance, like those of Andhra in the Deccan, have come down from the still more ancient Tamil kingdoms of seagirt south India — Pandya, Chola and Kerala (also known as Chera). By the seventh century A.D., the many Buddhist and Jain monasteries and temples which had once existed there appear to have been deserted and fallen into ruins. The stupendous masterpieces of Dravidian temple architecture seen today at Madurai, Thanjavur (Tanjore), Rameswaram, Srirangam, Chidambaram and Cape Comorin, all belong to later centuries. Yet there must certainly have been an unbroken continuity of Tamil tradition, uniting past and present. Climate, wars and neglect are perhaps the explanation for an absence of the earliest type of architectural remains in southern India.

The first mention of Tamil kingdoms is a reference to Chola and Pandya in the Sanskrit grammatical work of Katyayana, who lived in the fourth century B.C. Next in point of time, the *Artha Shastra* makes casual mention of the famous pearls of Pandya. Megasthenes, the Greek envoy to the Mauryan court, relates a foolish fable about Pandaia, whom he calls a daughter of the Greek god Herakles, who is supposed to have given her name to the southern country where she was born, and over which her amiable father gave her sovereignty. According to Megasthenes, in this remarkable land females at the age of six were quite capable of bearing children. Jain literary tradition mentions the Jain migration to the South about 300 B.C., and a copy of Asoka's Fourteen Rock Edicts, found near Madras, shows that Mauryan influence had certainly penetrated to the far South by the third century B.C. Asoka specifically names Chola, Pandya and Keralaputra (Kerala), along with a fourth region called Satiyaputra, as friendly neighbouring countries to which he sent missionaries to preach the Buddhist gospel. So it is quite clear that by the time the inscriptional history of South India begins, in the middle of the third century B.C., both Jainism and Buddhism had gained a footing in the region, and the Aryanizing process must have been well under way.

Dravidian source material fitfully illuminating the most ancient past is of very uncertain date. Dravidian languages are spoken by approximately one fourth of the Indian population today. Tamil, Malayalam, Kannada and Telugu are the princinpal Dravidian languages. Telugu, spoken over a large part of the Deccan, is the most widely used. Malayalam, confined to the southwestern corner of India, was evolved only in the ninth century, as a mixture of Tamil and Sanskrit. Kannada, the language of the present Mysore State, is considerably earlier, and Tamil, the common language of the three most ancient Dravidian kingdoms of the South, and the pre-eminent language of present-day Madras State, is the oldest and purest of the Dravidian tongues. It has the fewest Sanskrit words in its vocabulary and possesses the earliest regional literature of India apart from Pali.

The dating of Tamil literature, however, is a hazardous affair. Even with regard to the evolution of the Tamil alphabet there are different views. Some would maintain that the Tamils developed their own script even before *Tolkappiyam* was written. Others would say that Tamil, like the present alphabets of all languages in India not of direct foreign importation, derives its script from Brahmi. There are yet others who think that Tamil script owes its origin to no other language but would concede that Brahmi had its own influence in the final evolution of the Tamil script. Tamil poetry, recited by bards at the courts of the Tamil kings, could easily have been handed down orally for centuries, as was the material of the Sanskrit epics in the North. Nor is antiquity, it should be stated, determined solely by survival. The Tamil tradition says that once a large part of the Pandya country sank suddenly into the sea, carrying down with it beneath the waves all the accumulated riches of ancient Tamil civilization.

The oldest known work in Tamil is a grammar. This is the *Tolkappiyam*, roughly assigned to a period about the beginning of the present era, on the basis of language and syntax. Popular sentiment makes the author a disciple of the ancient Vedic rishi Agastya, who lived many centuries earlier. Like its Sanskrit predecessors, this Tamil grammar is a veritable encyclopaedia of information. It discusses not only letters, words and sentence structure, but such diverse subjects as religion, love, the art of warfare, social and civil ideals and the four primary divisions of the people according to occupations determined by geographical features of hill, forest, coast or plain. Chieftains at first governed each class, but hereditary kings eventually arose from among the wealthy agriculturists who owned land but did not cultivate it with their own hands. Each main group had numerous subdivisions. The category of the coastal people of the Tamil land, for example, was divided into fishermen, pearl fishers, boatmen, makers of boats, salt makers, workers in shell and merchants engaged in foreign trade. Fractional organization on basis of occupation had distinct parallels with the caste or colour divisions of Aryan society, but at least to begin with there does not seem to have been the rigid binding by birth to an inherited work in Dravidian society. In South India today, only three main social divisions are significant — Brahmins, non-Brahmins and Adi Dravidas (untouchables — now called Harijans). Brahmins, who constitute about 4 per cent of the population, are traditionally the intellectual class. Non-Brahmins, who make up the vast majority, have a highly respectable status. The Depressed Classes, on the other hand, were pushed down to their lowest level, especially in the southwestern corner of India.

Madurai became the Pandyan capital in succession to the two ancient coastal towns of Korkai and Kayal, which gradually dwindled in importance, owing to the silting up of the river on which they were situated. Three great *Sangams*, or literary academies, are supposed to have flourished in Madurai, during early centuries. The last Sangam disappeared in the second century A.D., after setting its seal of approval on a number of Tamil works now commonly referred to as the Sangam Classics. These include eight Tamil anthologies containing more than two thousand poems, by four hundred and forty-nine different poets, a collection of ten long idylls and eighteen lesser works.

It is scarcely possible to give even a bare summary of the contents of early Tamil literature. Hero worship, love, devotion to duty, ethical teachings, honour and friendship form favourite themes. Three of the eight classical anthologies consist of four hundred love poems each, and one contains four hundred heroic poems in praise of Madurai, together with fifty lyrics. A fifth anthology has twenty-two poems in praise of Madurai and other cities and places. Eighty-eight poems about eight Kerala kings, and a collection of five hundred short miscellaneous verses, make up the seventh and eighth anthologies. The ten idylls range over an equally wide field.

Like Sanskrit, Tamil also has its twin epics, the *Silappadikaram* and its sequel the *Manimekalai*. The first was composed by a monk-brother of a Chera king some two thousand years ago. It has for its theme the love of a wealthy young merchant for a beautiful dancer, and the sorrows and ultimate self-sacrifice of the faithful wife. The second epic continues the story of the dancer's daughter, Manimekalai, and relates how, after hearing religious truths expounded by teachers of various schools, she finally embraced Buddhism. It is in the wealth of their exact descriptive details that these epics provide a wonderful mirror of early Tamil times. On the basis of an account contained in the *Silappadikaram*, it has even been possible for scholars in modern times to reconstruct the entire ancient system of South Indian music, which was thoroughly disrupted after the twelfth century.

Among all the Tamil classics, the most popular is one of the eighteen shorter works included in the early collections. This is the *Kural*, by Tiruvalluvar, a poet of great genius, who probably lived in the first century A.D. In terse couplets in which the rhyme, as in all Tamil poetry, is found at the beginning instead of at the end of a line, the philosopher-author brings his shrewd experience and pointed wisdom to bear on ethical values and problems of his day. The *Kural* is the most beloved and most widely read book in South India. Tamil children begin their education by memorizing its verses.

Tamil kings, like their contemporaries in the North, were constantly at war with one another, and also with rulers of the neighbouring island of Ceylon. The fortunes of war swayed this way or that, but through all vicissitudes, trade went on, and the people of South India clearly enjoyed a high degree of prosperity. Pandya held the monopoly of such valued articles as pearls and beryls, and Pandya and Kerala shared between them the rich trade in spices — above all, in pepper. There was always a great demand for pearls and pepper, and while the Tamil armies fought among themselves, or with their Sinhalese neighbours, Tamil merchants quietly continued to trade with one another and with distant countries of West and East, including the innumerable islands of the Indian Ocean, and even of the vast Pacific. When Alaric the Goth besieged Rome in 410 A.D., part of the ransom he demanded for sparing the city from total destruction was 3,000 pounds of Indian pepper !

After the possibilities of monsoon navigation became known to the Alexandrian Greeks in the first century A.D., and the straight run to the South Indian ports proved the easiest and quickest way to India, a great increase in trade with the West followed. Rome's insatiable demand for precious stones and pepper soon brought a fortune to southern India. Besides pearls from the pearl beds of the Mannar Gulf between the mainland and Ceylon, Pandya supplied beryls from the rich mines near

Madurai. These multicoloured stones, which included the lovely
transparent sea-green aquamarines, were immensely popular in
Europe for seals and cameos. But in the early days the Tamil
South had little taste for anything Europe could offer in exchange,
except gold. Roman gold coins have turned up in astonishing
quantities along the Malabar coast, around Madurai and also
on the east coast. One such treasure trove consisted of " five
coolie loads ". Most of the coins belong to the reigns of the
first five Roman emperors. A unique example among them is
a coin of the Emperor Claudius (A.D. 41-54), struck to commemorate the Roman conquest of Britain. Unlike the Kushans,
who used to melt down the Roman gold and recast it under
their own names, the Tamils did not bother to mint any cur-
rency of their own, but freely used Roman coins for their ordinary trading purposes.

Tamil poetry has preserved several interesting references to
the " beautiful large Yavana ships " which used to come riding
into the Kerala port of Muziris or the Pandyan ports of Nyl-
kynda and Barake, bringing Greek wine and gold and taking
away pepper and spices and precious stones. These Alexandrian
ships had to carry an escort of armed soldiers as a protection
against pirates, and some of the adventurous foreigners elected
to remain behind and hire themselves out as palace mercenaries
to Tamil kings. Roman colonies were actually established at
Muziris and Madurai, and in the former a temple to Augustus
existed at one time. Foreign colonists also found their way
around to the Coromandel coast of the Chola country. The
principal Chola port was Puhar, situated at the mouth of the
Cauveri. It was divided into two parts. One adjoined the
seacoast, and the other, consisting of the palace and residential
quarters, lay westward of the central market place. A vivid
passage in Tamil describes the beach town of docks and ware-
houses, with the settlements of foreign traders from beyond the
seas, all speaking their " various tongues ".

A curious memento of southern India's early foreign contacts
is a second-century papyrus manuscript of a Greek farce found
in Egypt. It has for its theme the adventure of a Greek lady
ship-wrecked off the west coast of India. A conversation in an
apparently unintelligible jargon between the " King of the
Indians " and some of his retinue is translated into Greek by
one of the characters in the play. Translated back again from
Greek, the mysterious language has now been found to be a
Greek attempt at recording Kannada.

Besides the Alexandrians, colonies of other strangers also

found their way to South India, as refugees or traders, in the early centuries of the Christian era. Syrian Christians and Jews, escaping from Roman persecution, arrived in the first century A.D. In the fourth century came Persian Christians, fleeing from persecution under the Sassanids. Arabs had already settled in considerable numbers along the Malabar coast from very early times, and their descendants form the Moplah community of today in the Malabar region of Kerala. A sixth-century work, *Christian Topography*, by the Greek monk Kosmos Indiko Pleustes, describes a visit to South India and Ceylon and comments on the progress of the early Christian communities he found settled there. According to Kosmos, they belonged to the Persian or Nestorian Church, and their dignitaries were all appointed from Persia. Old stone crosses with inscriptions in Pehlevi, or Old Persian, have been found fairly widely distributed from Malabar to Madras. Syriac remained the liturgical language of the Malabar Church until only the other day.

Jews, Syrians and Arabs have always borne a reputation for being shrewd traders. The time came when Indian commerce with Rome began to fall off, and these enterprising foreigners then gained control of the profitable spice trade. It was now diverted to the Persian Gulf, the pepper caravans then passing overland to Antioch and Constantinople, the eastern capital of the Roman empire, from where equally enterprising Italian merchants bought up the valuable produce and transported it by sea to Venice and Genoa.

Less familiar is India's extensive early pepper traffic with China. Cargoes for the China-India trade were carried both by Chinese junks and Indian sailing ships. A Sanskrit history of ancient Indian shipping mentions ten types of ships engaged in river traffic and fifteen types of seagoing vessels, each type bearing a name of its own. The large size of some of the ships is frequently referred to both in early Indian and Chinese literature. As late as the thirteenth century, the Venetian traveller Marco Polo says that ships were measured by the number of baskets of pepper they could carry, and that those carrying five to six thousand baskets of pepper required crews of two hundred sailors or more.

There seems to have been no time when South India was not in contact with a number of foreign lands, by way of the sea, but except for one or two retaliatory Sinhalese invasions, foreigners did not come as conquerors to disturb the normal life of the people of South India until the fourteenth century A.D.

This made possible a remarkably integrated cultural life, with no major break of any sort, and this is why the old traditions of Hindu culture are more vital in southern India today than in any other part of the country. The political history of the South, however, is the usual complicated narrative of the rise and fall of many rival dynasties.

By the beginning of the seventh century, the older kingdoms of Pandya, Chola and Kerala had all become subservient to Pallava overlordship. The Pallavas, whose very existence was unknown to modern historians before their early copper plate grants in Prakrit were discovered a little more than a century ago, emerged in the southern Deccan after the disintegration of Andhra in the third century A.D. From there they started on a conquest of the Tamil country. Chola was the first to succumb, and the old Chola city of Kanchi, close to Madras, had already become the Pallava capital by the third or fourth century. Under Narasimha-Varman I, in the seventh century, a Pallava naval expedition even took upon itself to interfere in the dynastic affairs of Ceylon, effecting the installation of a refugee Sinhalese prince who had earlier fled to Kanchi. From now on, however, the Pallavas entered into a long-drawn-out war with the powerful kingdom of the Chalukyas, which had recently emerged in the western Deccan. Exhausted by these wars, the Pallavas were unable to suppress a sudden revival of Chola power, and were finally annihilated by the Cholas in the last decade of the ninth century.

Lesser dynasties also fought their way to prominence in the southern part of the Indian peninsula from time to time. About the middle of the fourth century, the greater part of what is now Mysore State came under the rule of the Ganga dynasty. Though suffering eclipse during the expansionist period of Chalukyan rule, the Gangas again became powerful in the ninth and tenth centuries. An eastern branch of the Gangas also ruled in Orissa for nearly a thousand years, from the sixth to the sixteenth century.

Another minor dynasty was that of the Kadambas. They appeared in the fourth century but were extinguished by the Chalukyas in the sixth. The founder of this dynasty was a young Brahmin who had gone as a mendicant student to Kanchi, to complete his studies at one of the Vedic colleges there. Receiving some insult, real or fancied, from a Pallava horseman, the fiery youth fled away into the great Deccan forest and collected a resolute band of followers to attack the Pallavas. The Pallava king eventually made peace with him, even handing over to him a substantial little kingdom bordering the western sea, that part of India now known as the Konkan. The Kadamba capital was the ancient forest city of Vanavasi, one of those southern cities to which, seven hundred years before, Asoka had sent Buddhist missionaries.

After the disappearance of Andhra rule, the most powerful kingdom to arise in the Deccan was that of the Chalukyas. The origin of the Chalukyas is obscure. They are held by some to have been of northern extraction, but there is no proof of this, and all their early inscriptions are in Kannada. About the middle of the sixth century, they had imposed themselves as masters over the former Vakataka domain around the headwaters of the Krishna, in what is now Maharashtra, and soon spread out from there in all directions. Their earliest capital was Aihole, which they presently abandoned for Vatapi (Badami). The most formidable Chalukyan ruler was Pulakesin II (608-642). A few years after his accession, his great contemporary in northern India, Harsha Vardhana, attempted an invasion of the Deccan. The latter was roundly defeated by Pulakesin, whose resulting fame spread even beyond the borders of India. Khusru II, king of Iran, sent an embassy to the Chalukyan court in 625, and Chalukyan ambassadors also visited Persia.

Pulakesin's campaigns carried his victorious arms north into Malwa and Gujarat, as well as east into the Pallava domain. From the Pallava king Mahendravarman I (600-630), he wrested the province of Vengi, between the deltas of the Krishna and Godavari. Pulakesin's younger brother was then appointed viceroy of Vengi, but he soon revolted and set up an independent dynasty of his own. The eastern Chalukya dynasty of Vengi continued to flourish for five hundred years, until it was merged into Chola in the eleventh century.

The tide of war between the Chalukyas and Pallavas was really a struggle for the possession of South India. Pulakesin boasts in one inscription from Aihole that the Pallava lord was made to "conceal his valour behind the ramparts of Kanchi, enveloped in the dust of his armies." The next Pallava king, however, Narasimha-varman I (630-668), sent an army straight across the peninsula to besiege the Chalukyan capital, in revenge for the loss of Vengi. Vatapi was sacked in 642, and in this battle Pulakesin lost his life. The exultant Pallavas slaughtered most of the inhabitants of the city and destroyed everything they could lay hands on. Other Chalukyan kings were able later on to occupy Kanchi, at least briefly, at the end of the seventh century and again in the eighth, though a Pallava inscription claims that the invading Chalukyan king in the seventh century was driven off with " only a rag " left to cover himself.

About the middle of the eighth century, the western Chalukyas suffered a disastrous defeat at the hands of their former feudatories, the Rashtrakutas, and for the next two centuries it was the Kanarese-speaking Rashtrakutas who completely dominated the Deccan, ruling from Malkhed on the upper Krishna. A ninth-century Arab writer, Sulaiman, was so impressed by the power of the Rashtrakuta king that he called him one of the four great sovereigns of the world, the other three being the Khalif of Baghdad, the Emperor of Constantinople and the Emperor of China ! Toward the end of the tenth century, however, came a reversal of their political fortunes. A new Chalukyan dynasty arose and once more recovered the former glory of the Chalukyan House, and the Rashtrakutas disappeared from the scene. The dynasty of the Later Western Chalukyas, or the Western Chalukyas of Kalyana so known to distinguish it from the parent Chalukyas of Vatapi or Eastern Chalukyas of Vengi, lasted well into the twelfth century. Thus Chalukyan power, under one or another of its dynasties, was a formidable political force in the Deccan for altogether six and a half centuries.

Before the Chalukyan star finally sank below the horizon, the Tamil Cholas had already become supreme in the southern peninsula. After a long eclipse, in the ninth century Chola power reasserted itself at the expense of the Pallava and Pandya kingdoms. In the tenth century, however, came a disastrous conflict with the Rashtrakutas. Krishna III Rashtrakuta occupied Kanchi and the Chola capital of Thanjavur. The Cholas did not long have to endure the humiliation of this signal defeat, for with the accession of Rajaraja I (985-1014), the great period of Chola expansion was ushered in.

This ruler lost no time in creating a mighty Tamil empire, using both his armies and his fleet for the purpose. Rajaraja began by destroying the Kerala fleet of Malabar. He then sent his ships to Ceylon and annexed the northern half of that island, also capturing " the old islands of the sea, numbering 12,000 " — the groups known today as the Laccadives and the Maldives, in the south Arabian Sea. Next he proceeded to conquer the Ganga kingdom of Mysore. After these triumphs, he moved his armies northward and overran a good part of Chalukyan territory. Then he pushed on into Kalinga.

Rajaraja's son Rajendra I (1014-1044) continued his father's conquests. His first success was his annexation of the whole of

Ceylon. He then conducted a brilliant campaign in the north, carrying his triumphant arms as far as the Ganga. He subjugated Kalinga and parts of Bihar and Bengal. He is also credited with ambitious overseas expeditions. His ships crossed the Bay of Bengal to Burma, and on the way back the Andaman and Nicobar Islands were annexed. Rajendra and other Chola kings are mentioned in a contemporary Chinese work as having sent embassies to China, one of them consisting of seventy-two " ambassadors ", who were more probably enterprising Tamil traders.

As time passed, Chola kings found themselves increasingly embroiled with rebellions in one or another part of their extended empire, and they were also continuously in conflict with the Later Western Chalukyas. Ceylon, Pandya and other previously conquered territories began to shake themselves free. One of the Pandyan kings, Sundara Pandya I, took Thanjavur and made a prisoner of the Chola king who ultimately succeeded in regaining his liberty with the help of onetime feudatories of the Western Chalukyas, the Hoysalas, who had rebelled in the first half of the eleventh century and carved out a small kingdom of their own in Mysore. The Chola kingdom at last received its deathblow from the Pandyan king, Jatavarman Sundara (1251-1272), under whom Pandya assumed the dominant position in the Tamil country, which it maintained until Muslim armies from Delhi marched to Madurai, the Pandyan capital, in 1310.

Had it not been for the deeply rooted Indian institution of division of labour, it is difficult to see how through all this incessant warfare, a stable civilization could have continued to endure, century after century. Fighting was the work of professional fighting classes. Peasants, craftsmen and Brahmins were traditionally out of it. Nor were the Indian wars, it may be presumed, as destructive as those waged against India by outsiders. Villages and temples were spared, and victory was achieved when one side captured the royal city of the other. Even a defeated king was very often allowed to go on ruling, provided he acknowledged the victor as his overlord and agreed to pay tribute to him. This explains how, despite endless wars, literary, artistic and religious activities were carried on continuously, under Pandyas, Pallavas, Cholas, Chalukyas and Rashtrakutas, and many lesser dynasties of southern India and the Deccan, in a truly Indian tradition.

Pallava, Pandya and particularly Chola inscriptions tell of the efficient rural democracy and local self-government existing in South India in these times. Qualifications for election to a village assembly or committee were ownership of land, a good character and some knowledge of traditional Hindu law. Names of suitable candidates were placed in a jar and drawn by lot, and office was held for one year. Failure to render proper accounts or other misconduct justified removal from office. Women also could be members of these elected bodies. The Committees were responsible for managing nearly every department of the community life, social, religious and economic. Among committees whose names have been specifically recorded in inscriptions were those in charge of gardens, irrigation, fields, land survey, village servants, justice, fines, the collection and payment of taxes, money, temples and charities.

As Hindu temples began to replace the earlier Buddhist and Jain centres of learning in South India, they grew enormously in size, and temple management became a very complicated affair. Numbers of surviving temple grants give an excellent idea of the intricate problem of maintaining these huge temples. Lands, and sometimes whole villages, were assigned by kings and other rich donors for the support of temples. Gold, jewels and animals, as well as the revenue derived from such humble sources as a simple oil mill or a salt pan, were also bestowed by pious individuals. Contributions were made for the service of the particular deity enshrined within the temple, for the general upkeep of the establishment, and for charitable works maintained by the temple. Apart from its quota of Brahmin priests and its general manager, every large temple had its own treasurer. A regular staff of musicians, singers, parasol-bearers, lamplighters, washermen, potters, astrologers, cooks, gardeners, carpenters, barbers, actors and dancing girls also formed part of the temple institution. The custom had grown up of dedicating little girls — devadasis, servants of the Lord — to the service of the deity, and they were then trained to perform religious dances inside the temple. In modern times, the devadasis have been swept out of the temples by law, because of certain abuses which came along with them. Actors also performed religious dramas in the temple assembly halls. Sanskrit schools and colleges were frequently attached to Hindu temples and there were numerous charitable departments maintained by them for tending the sick and feeding Brahmins and destitutes. The number of persons fed might range from fifteen to a thousand, and the feeding might be a daily affair or take place on some stipulated occasion.

The most popular gift to a temple, judged by the number of inscriptions, was the maintenance of a lamp. This required a substantial donation of animals, from whose milk the *ghi* to be used as oil could be made. Ninety sheep or goats, twenty-five to thirty cows, five to six buffaloes, were essential to maintain one perpetual lamp. Some grants mention the donation of only enough animals to maintain half a lamp. Food to be offered to the deity and afterwards to be distributed as *prasad*, was another popular donation. Exact amounts of rice, curds, pulses, spices, vegetables, sugar, salt — even firewood to prepare the food — are mentioned in specific grants. There was, too, the bath of the deity, an important feature of the daily temple ritual. Though three pots of water might serve for ordinary days, upon occasion many more were provided. The bath might even consist of honey, ghi and curds, instead of water. Further requirements of the temple paraphernalia were flowers, incense, sandal paste, camphor, fly whisks, parasols and quantities of vessels. One inscription records a devotee's daily supply of one thousand lotuses. Another mentions a garland six spans long for daily presentation to the deity. Valuable ornaments were also given to the deities. A dedicatory inscription describes the gold crown of the deity of the famous Chola temple in Thanjavur, and states that it contained 859 diamonds, 309 rubies and 669 pearls.

In the first century B.C., thousands of Buddhist monks were living in the monasteries of Pandya, Kerala and Chola kingdoms. A few centuries later, they had almost everywhere fallen into neglect and ruin. Only at Kanchi was Buddhism still flourishing as late as the seventh century. Elsewhere in the South it was dying out. Jainism, on the other hand, was to maintain its hold in the South a little longer. Some of the early Pandyan kings seem to have adopted this religion, but in the eighth century a Pandyan king was converted to Hinduism. A vast religious conclave for debating the merits of the different religions is said to have been held in Madurai, and the eight thousand Jains who attended were utterly defeated, and according to one version, were even massacred. Driven out of the South, Jainism obtained temporary refuge in Mysore under the Ganga kings, and shortly spread to Gujarat, where it became firmly rooted. Yet by the twelfth century, Jainism, too, was a languishing religion in India.

The rather sudden popularity of Hinduism in the South was intimately connected with the appearance, in the seventh, eighth and ninth centuries, of numbers of saints who began to walk the Tamil country singing devotional songs in honour of Vishnu and Shiva. Theirs was an appeal to emotion, not to dry logic, and they achieved miracles of conversion. These Tamil singers came from every walk of life. Among them were kings, lowly outcastes and women. Minstrels of the Lord, touched by divine grace, they sang in Tamil, the common tongue of the people, praising God in the chosen form, pouring out their devotion for Him in ecstatic verses. The burden of their message was that the path of *Bhakti*, or devotion, is open to all. Complicated Vedic rites were never meant for the lower castes or for women. The path of *Jnana*, knowledge, and *Yoga*, disciplined meditation, were exceedingly hard to tread. But all might freely enter the path of devotion. Desire for liberation from material ties and loving self-surrender to the concept of a personal God were all the Bhakta needed. Tamil saints sang the praises of Vishnu or Shiva in almost identical words. Worshippers of Vishnu, in any of his divine incarnations, but more particularly Krishna, called themselves Vaishnavas, and worshippers of Shiva were known as Saivas.

The Vaishnava *Alvars*, or saints, were twelve in number. A collection of four thousand of their hymns and psalms, the *Prabandha*, is still recited as part of the regular services in the great Vishnu temples of South India. The greatest of these Vaishnava saints was Nammalvar. He was born in the Pandya country, of the farmer caste. A mystic from childhood, at sixteen he was already composing inspired poems. His four chief works are popularly called the four Tamil Vedas. Another of the great Alvars was a woman, Godha, or Andal, whose verses have deep emotional intensity. Refusing to marry, she spent her life in devotion to Krishna. Still another Vaishnava poet-saint spent his whole life in stringing garlands for images of the deity. Also numbered among Vaishnava saints was a king of Kerala, Kulasekhara, who renounced his throne and retired to live a life of voluntary poverty at the great Vaishnava temple of Srirangam, close to Trichinopoly. The last of the twelve Alvars was Tirumangai, who performed many charitable works. He set himself the task of collecting funds for the temple of Sri Ranganatha at Srirangam, and did not disdain to rob the rich he met on the road for this pious purpose.

The traditional list of the early Tamil Saivite saints or *Nayanmars* numbers sixty-three, among whom four in particular, Appar, Sambandha, Sundaramurti and Manikka Vachaka, are the great teachers, whose soul-stirring devotional songs won thousands of followers. Appar and his younger contemporary, Sambandha, both lived during the reign of the Pallava king Mahendravarman I, in the first half of the seventh century. They were close friends, and it was the young Sambandha who affectionately

bestowed on the elder saint the name of Appar, " Father ", by
which he was afterwards known. Appar was born near Kanchi.
He was first attracted to the Jain faith, but changed later into
an ardent devotee of Shiva. For this he suffered persecution
under the Pallava king, but his fortitude so impressed Mahendravarman that the king himself accepted Saivism. Appar chose to
live in extreme simplicity. His only garment was a loin-cloth,
his only possession a small tool for weeding temple gardens.

The child saint Sambandha was a Brahmin by birth. At the
age of three he is said to have been possessed by visions of Shiva
and Parvati, and to have begun to sing mystic songs. As a boy,
he started walking from village to village, moving all hearts with
his beautiful lyrics. Sambandha recognized no caste among the
devotees of the Lord. When an " untouchable " harp player and
his wife attached themselves to him, he gladly allowed them to
accompany him everywhere on his tours. When Sambandha
died at the young age of only eighteen, he had already composed hundreds of hymns of which three hundred and eighty-five
have survived.

Sundaramurti, third of the four great Saiva Nayanmars, was
born near Kanchi, like Appar. Although he came from a family
of Saiva priests, he was actually brought up in the Pallava palace.
Adopting a life of renunciation while still a youth, he began to
travel from place to place, singing his divine message that Shiva
was the Supreme Lord. Then a time came when he unaccountably fell in love with and married a non-Brahmin girl, only to
discover too late, that his bond of intimacy with the Lord had
been broken. Deserting his wife, he was suddenly afflicted with
blindness. This affliction he accepted as divine chastisement.
After suffering untold physical and mental agonies, he at last
regained his religious serenity, and tradition says that his eyesight
was also miraculously restored. Seven volumes of the hymns
of Appar, Sambandha and Sundaramurti have been brought
together in the collection of the *Thevaram,* which to Saivites is
what the *Prabandha* is to Vaishnavites.

The fourth great Saiva saint was Manikka Vachaka. His
great learning won for him the appointment of chief minister to
the Pandyan king of Madurai, but statecraft was not his true
career. He was sent to buy horses for the Pandyan army, but
chancing to meet on the way the individual who became his *guru,*
or spiritual teacher, he used the money he had been given to buy
horses for building a temple. Official disgrace followed, but
Manikka Vachaka wandered from shrine to shrine, debating with
Buddhists and Jains, losing himself in ecstasy and chanting

exquisite hymns. The theme of his hymns was invariably the soul's progress from ignorance to realization of God.

While Tamil saints were awakening an ardent religious sentiment among the people, Sanskrit scholars were encouraging literature and learning. Sanskrit authors found a warm welcome at the Pallava court. The poet Bharavi, author of the *Kiratarjuniya,* and Dandin, who composed the prose romance entitled *Dasakumara Charita,* or " Adventures of the Ten Princes," are both said to have received the patronage of Pallava kings. Throughout the Deccan as well, Brahmin teachers and scholars were writing voluminous and important works in Sanskrit. An eighth-century Chalukyan copperplate praises one Bhavasarman described as master of " three thousand branches of knowledge." Sanskrit works were in time translated into the Dravidian languages. The eleventh-century Telugu version of the *Mahabharata,* by Nannayya Bhatta, and the twelfth-century Tamil version of the *Ramayana,* by Kamban, were two important works produced under Eastern Chalukya and Chola patronage respectively. Aryan heroes and heroines of the ancient epics now became as much beloved in the South as in the North.

Southern India has the special honour of having produced the illustrious Shankaracharya, one of the world's outstanding intellects. Shankara was born in a Saivite family of Nambudiri Brahmins of Kerala, probably in the latter half of the eighth century A.D., at the little village of Kaladi. Tradition says he adopted an ascetic life from the age of eight, and that he completed his studies and began writing philosophic works in the form of commentaries in Sanskrit at the age of twelve. His teacher Govinda, who lived in a cave at Nasik, had been a pupil of Gaudapada and followed the Vedantic school of religious thought, but Shankara soon outstripped both. Later he travelled extensively about India, preaching, teaching, and debating with opponents in philosophical assemblies. He denounced degenerate Buddhism (but not the Buddha) and ritualism as such. He was the founder of four great Hindu centres for the religious Order of *Sannyasins.* These were at the four corners of India, Sringeri in Mysore, Puri in Orissa, Dwarka in Kathiawar, Kedarnath in the Himalayas. He is believed to have died at the latter place, while still only thirty-two.

Shankara's religious ideas deeply impressed India. Every educated Hindu of today, whatever sect he adheres to, owes something of his mental make-up to Shankara's doctrine of the *Advaita,* of ultimate Oneness. Shankara took his stand strictly on the *Upanishads,* and in his exposition of the *Brahma-Sutras* by

Badarayana, his commentaries on the ten major *Upanishads* and the *Bhagavad-Gita*, he made the earliest attempt to find a unified system of thought in these ancient teachings. Shankara was an out-and-out monist in his interpretation. Tolerating no idea of duality, no thought of Two, no reality of an external world, no God apart from the all-inclusive One, no " I " separate from That One, he taught that Brahman, or Atman, is the sole reality. All else is Maya, an illusive appearance. Brahman is without qualities, and cannot be defined by the limited mind. Brahman is neither He nor She. It is *Sat-Chit-Ananda*, Pure Being, Pure Knowledge, Pure Bliss. The individual soul is one with Brahman, but is ignorant of its true nature. When ignorance is removed, knowledge awakens, and the soul at last knows itself for what it is. It no longer makes the mistake of identifying itself with the body, the objects of the senses, the world as falsely perceived by them, and it becomes eternally free.

Shankara's interpretation of the *Upanishads* could not be ignored. It had either to be accepted or rejected. But the Bhakta did not want to argue. He simply wished to love God. The Saivas made a sort of compromise. Shiva, the object of their adoration, was meditated upon as a Great Yogi. He possessed nothing. He wore sacred ashes and matted locks. He frequented the burning ground. He was the God of Destruction, but essentially the destruction of Ignorance. The Saivas found little fundamental antagonism between their views and the Advaita system of Shankaracharya. Saivism henceforward gained many followers in south India, where Chola kings in particular became its zealous supporters. It also had many adherents in north India, and Kashmir developed its own special type of Saivism.

A new Saiva sect, the Lingayat, founded by Basava, sprang up in the western Deccan during the twelfth century. The Lingayats, still numerous in Mysore, are Shiva worshippers, but they oppose the whole Hindu caste system as a negation of the doctrine of fundamental unity.

The Vaishnavas were less able to come to terms with Shankara's Advaita. In the eleventh century, they found a great defender of their devotional dualistic form of faith in Ramanuja. He agreed with Shankara that the sole goal of life was spiritual knowledge, but he maintained that this depended on the grace of the Lord, and that the surest way to win his grace was by loving him. Ramanuja also based his teachings on the *Upanishads*, but differed from Shankara in his interpretation. He accepted God both with, and without, form, and held that God with form possessed positive attributes of love, kindness and mercy for his devotees. Everybody was entitled to share in the divine grace of the Lord, and he himself acknowledged as a teacher a saintly man who originally belonged to a low caste. He accepted the idea that in order to save mankind, Narayana (Vishnu) repeatedly took birth on earth under different forms. Ramanuja also believed that God, the world, and individual souls are all real, and that ignorance is the result of the contraction of the soul, as it were, from past bad actions. His system is called a philosophy of qualified monism, *Visishtadvaita*.

Ramanuja, as the ecclesiastical head of the Vaishnavas, made Srirangam his headquarters, but the antagonism of one of the Chola kings, a Saiva, compelled him to flee to Mysore, where he remained as a refugee for twelve years. Besides being responsible for many important philosophical works, Ramanuja organized seventy-four Vaishnava dioceses, or districts, in different parts of India, and appointed for each a pious householder as spiritual leader.

In art, as in literature, religion and philosophy, the Dravidian genius found ample scope for expression. Inspired by the earlier Buddhist cave temples, the Chalukyas, Pallavas and Rashtrakutas, between the sixth and ninth centuries, began to excavate similar Hindu rock temples dedicated to Vishnu or Shiva. The first Chalukyan rock-cut shrines are picturesquely located in the scarp of a hill overhanging Vatapi. They differ a little from Buddhist shrines in having an entirely open front and their oblong halls have a recessed cell in the back wall for enshrining an image. They are also smaller in size and less elaborate. Pillars sometimes show a purely southern " cushion " type of capital.

The most important Pallava cave temples of the Tamil country are practically contemporary with those of the Chalukyas. They are found near Madras at Mamallapuram (Mahabalipuram), the deserted sea-port of ancient Kanchi, and in various other parts of the ancient Pallava domain. Pallava rock pavilions, with their appropriate sculptures, were dedicated not only to Vishnu and Shiva, but to the goddess Durga as well.

In the middle of the eighth century, the new Hindu passion for cutting pillared halls out of solid rock reached its climax at Elura and Elephanta. What Ajanta means to Buddhism, Elura means to Hinduism. The Buddhists were the first to discover the suitability of the great Elura cliff of traprock for excavation. There are twelve Buddhist caves at this sight. By the middle of the seventh century, however, the construction of sixteen Brahmanical caves began in the same cliff, within whose shadowy depths magnificent images of Hindu gods were called into being. Later came five Jain caves.

At Ajanta, there is placid calm. Peaceful Buddhas sit in eternal meditation, and lovely Bodhisattvas, benign and compassionate, bestow blessings upon gentle worshippers. All human tempests subside in their presence. Everything echoes to the idea of renunciation. The world is unreal, only Nirvana is real.

How different the atmosphere of Elura! The vast walls thrust forth gigantic images carved in high relief. They are actors in crowded scenes drawn mainly from the Puranas. These Hindu gods are many-armed, many-eyed. They slay, they dance, they fight demons, they make love unabashed. They assume strange shapes, sometimes having the body of a man and the head of a boar, a horse or a lion. Never were these gods mortal. They are symbols of universal forces, of primal creation and ultimate destruction. They are abstractions, wearing the form of the particular. There is an immense vitality in the Elura sculptures, an originality quite indescribable. Here, nothing is still. The very shadows are restless, vibrating with hidden meaning. The beholder, of whatever race or creed, stands spellbound. Puny thoughts take wing. Nowhere in the world, perhaps, has the vision of the superhuman been so startlingly expressed in art form as at Elura.

It was one of the Elura temples which apparently supplied the direct inspiration for a beautiful eighth-century shrine of Shiva on the island of Elephanta, in Bombay harbour. Both have the same rather unusual plan of transverse halls, with three entrances approached by flights of steps guarded by lions. Both have the same massive " cushion " type of pillars. But the interior sculptures at Elephanta are its chief attraction. On the back wall of the main chamber are three square recesses, which frame these sculptures. The eastern panel presents Shiva in the form known as Ardhanari, the combination of male and female in one figure. The western panel enshrines Shiva and Parvati. But the commanding central panel holds a colossal bust with a three-faced head, intended to represent Shiva in three aspects of being, or it may be, the Hindu *trimurti* — Brahma the Creator, Vishnu the Preserver, and Shiva the Destroyer. The eyes in each face are meditatively closed. The full lower lip repeats the type found in the Ajanta frescoes. There is mysterious beauty and dignity in the vision of the unknown sculptor.

But the final expression of the rock-cut style of Indian temple architecture is the famous Kailasa temple of Elura, called by one authority " the most stupendous single work of art executed

in India ". A Chalukyan temple at Pattadakal, the Virupaksha
temple, built by a Chalukyan queen in 730 to celebrate her
husband's conquest of Kanchi, appears to have furnished the
plan for the Kailasa temple, though the Pattadakal temple in

The TRIMÛRTI

its turn employed a Pallava architect. In any case, the Kailasa
temple, begun by the Rashtrakuta king Krishna I, is double its
size, and the chief marvel is that it is not an architectural construction, like its Chalukyan predecessor, but is entirely sculptured from the solid stone. A copperplate inscription reads :
" Krishnaraja caused to be constructed a temple of a wonderful

form on the mountain of Elapura. When the gods, moving in their aerial cars, saw it, they were struck with wonder and constantly thought much over the matter, saying to themselves, ' This temple of Shiva is self-existent, for such beauty is not to be found in a work of art.' Even the architect who constructed it was struck with wonder, saying, ' Wonderful ! I did not know how it was that I could construct it ! ' "

The Elura artisans set to work with breathless daring to slice their temple out of the great Elura cliff. First they trenched out a stone island, 100 feet high in the centre, 100 feet broad, 200 feet long. Starting from the summit of this island, they cut and carved and sculptured their way down, finishing everything to the last detail as they proceeded. It has been calculated that at least 200,000 tons of rock must have been removed to create Kailasa — the name of Shiva's abode in the Himalayas — with its three tiered Dravidian tower, its pillared halls, its many small shrines and stairways and flying bridges. A double-storeyed pavilion stands in front of the temple, flanked by stone pillars fifty feet high. Two great sculptured elephants guard the courtyard, and a Nandi shrine is connected with the main temple by a stone bridge. Around the courtyard is a cloister with colonnades and side chambers, and the high plinth of the temple displays a bold frieze of elephants and lions. Although dedicated to Shiva, the Kailasa temple shows no exclusive sectarian spirit. Vishnu on Garuda and Krishna lifting Mount Govardhana are carved on its walls. There are also graceful figures of the river goddesses of Ganga, Jumna and Saraswati, and high up on the exterior are exquisite flying figures of celestial beings.

The oldest extant Hindu temples, as distinct from cave temples, are found in northern India, but little time elapsed before they had also made their appearance in the Dravidian South and the Deccan. The ruins of more than seventy early Chalukyan temples are located at Aihole, in the Deccan. Many have flat roofs like the earliest surviving Gupta temples of the North. Some are chaitya-shaped, with a rounded end. Two styles of towers rise above the shrines, both Indo-Aryan and Dravidian. In the first type, the lines slope upward with a slight outward bulge before converging in a narrow neck surmounted by a fluted stone ornament, the *amalaka*. Chalukyan towers of this type usually have a projecting flat band extending down the centre of each side. The characteristic Dravidian tower is usually described as a stepped pyramid. It rises from a square or oblong base, in horizontal receding storeys. The façade of each storey is deco-

the dance of shiva

e.e.

rated with little pavilions, chaitya windows and niches with overhanging canopies, architectural features obviously borrowed from the earliest style of the wooden Buddhist monastery.

While the Chalukyan rulers were building the Aihole temples in the western Deccan, their Pallava contemporaries of the seventh century had started work on some still more remarkable temples in the Tamil country. These earliest Pallava temples were monoliths, blocks or boulders of stone sculptured into architectural shape. Six monolithic temples of this type cluster along the seashore at Mamallapuram, not far from Madras. They are called *Raths* because they resemble the heavy temple cars used for taking out Hindu images in procession. They remain something of an enigma. Some were never completed, and it is doubtful if any of them was ever actually used as a place of worship. With the death of the Pallava king Narasimha, under whose order the work began in the second half of the seventh century, the chisels of the workmen fell suddenly silent.

The next great ruler, Narasimhavarman II Rajasimha, inaugurated a new architectural movement, of structural building with dressed stones. The earliest example of the new style is the so-called " Shore " temple of Shiva at Mamallapuram. It literally overhangs the sea, which has now been chafing and fretting at its base for twelve hundred years. Rising from the breakers directly in front of the shrine is a massive stone lamp-post, possibly a lighthouse to guide the many ships entering and leaving the harbour of Mamallapuram in the days of Pallava glory. Rajasimha was also responsible for other fine temples erected at Kanchi in the eighth century. Beside the early form of Dravidian tower, these Pallava temples have their own distinctive type of lion pilasters and pillars.

The Pallavas were also distinguished sculptors, and all their temples are handsomely carved. Near the Raths, a number of large granite figures of animals are finely sculptured in the round — a bull, a lion, two elephants — perhaps dedicated to Shiva, Durga and Indra. There is also a realistic group of monkeys, a female nursing her young, while the male, in monkey fashion, intently searches her head for lice. The temple sculptures of the Pallavas also include standing portraits of kings and queens, who are named in inscriptions. Amaravati, the ancient Andhra caiptal in pre-Pallava days, was a flourishing centre of Buddhist art at the time it passed into the expanding Pallava kingdom, and the influence of Buddhist Amaravati is clearly traceable in Hindu Pallava sculpture.

The most striking of all the Pallava sculptures is a unique

carving in relief on the side of a great whale-backed ridge at Mamallapuram. Though popularly known as "Arjuna's Penance", it represents the descent of Ganga from heaven. This sculptured picture is ninety feet long and twenty feet high. A natural cleft in the rock has been cleverly utilized to suggest the descent of the river goddess, indicated in the forms of a Naga king and queen. All creation greets the descent of Ganga with joyous adoration. In the upper air, gods and goddesses and bearded rishis dance ecstatically. In the forests, ascetics bow or stand with folded palms. One such remains poised on one foot, arms lifted above his head, in the time-honoured pose of the Brahmin ascetic. Emerging from behind rocks or looking out from the entrances of caves are delightful wild creatures, monkeys, lions, elephants, peacocks, rabbits, tortoises — all fearless, because they know they will suffer no harm from the holy men who have made their abode in the depths of the forest. A deer lying down and scratching its nose with a hind foot is charmingly realistic. There is also a cat hypocritically standing in an ascetic pose on its hind legs, while rats and mice play about its feet, illustrating an old Buddhist legend. At the base of the cliff two life-size elephants, accompanied by three young ones, move in a majestic procession.

After the ninth century, by which time the technique of building with separate stones had come into general use all over India, distinctive local styles in architecture arose in many parts of the country.

But it is to the Cholas and their successors, in the Tamil South, that credit must go for building temples on the grandest scale to be found anywhere in India. Rajaraja the Great erected a magnificent Saiva temple about the year 1000 A.D. at Thanjavur. Its walled courtyard measures 250 by 500 feet. In this temple the small tower of early Pallava times soars upward to a height of 190 feet. The single block of stone which forms the rounded dome has been estimated to weigh something like eighty tons. The feat of hoisting this into position commands unbounded admiration for the engineering skill of Chola builders. They also constructed remarkable irrigation projects. Rajendra Chola built a large artificial lake, sixteen miles long, and threw massive granite dams, or anicuts, across several great rivers in Chola territory. As sculptors, the Cholas likewise excelled, giving their distinctive imprint to all their creations. The exterior walls of the great Thanjavur temple have figures and scenes of exquisite finish.

In the twelfth century, after two hundred and fifty years of rule, the Chola empire in South India disintegrated, and the Pandyas reasserted themselves after a long period of quiescence. Since the style of Dravidian temples had become established, the Pandyas contented themselves with repeating and emphasizing all the well-known features. They built a series of great courtyards around the older temples, until they succeeded in evoking

The Tank of the Golden Lilies and a Gopuram Shiva Temple MADURA in South India

huge temple cities. Each quadrangular courtyard was surrounded by a high wall, and in the centre of each wall rose a massive gate tower, the *gopuram*, which completely dwarfed the *vimana* of the central shrine. As the height of the gate towers increased with each new addition, the outermost entrance towers eventually became the biggest of all. To support the great weight, the base had to be of stone, but the superstructures were now made of plastered brick, a medium which lent itself to excessively ornate and exuberant decoration, inferior in quality to the noble stone-work of earlier centuries. The tendency to over-ornamentation reached its climax in " thousand pillared " halls. In the famous Minakshi temple of Madurai, the pillars are a cavalcade of riders mounted on giant rearing horses, which seem to advance through the shadows to overwhelm and crush the puny spectator. Tunnel-like corridors of immense length, dwindling to a pin-point of light in the far distance, were added to the colonnaded cloisters. The corridors of the temple at Rameswaram, where Rama tradi-tionally worshipped Shiva after returning from Ceylon, accom-panied by the chaste Sita, extend nearly four thousand feet.

Kings and humble people combined their wealth and skill to construct and adorn the great Hindu temples of southern India. Wars for political domination were between kings who at least held a common faith. The victor usually signalized his victory by attempting to outdo his defeated opponent in temple-building, and some of these temples are places of worship and pilgrimage for millions of Indians to this day.

CHAPTER X

The Guptas and Harsha

FOR THE SAKE of simplicity, the broad outline of south Indian history and development of Aryan-Dravidian culture has been carried through consecutively, to a point much later than that at which the preceding account of north India was dropped. It is now necessary to go back and trace what happened after the fall of the Kushan empire in the third century A.D.

In its long history, India has many times been thrown into a chaos of rival states, bits of a jigsaw puzzle almost impossible to fit together in any orderly pattern, but it has also known long periods of brilliant and unified empire. Most of these Indian empires have rested on military conquest — yet with this difference. An Indian king, when he claimed to have conquered the Four Quarters, meant the Four Quarters of India. When political unity was achieved, it did not mean the riveting together of entirely unrelated and alien territories and peoples, as was the case with the Greek and Roman empires, or the British empire of the nineteenth century. When the Mauryan empire arose, sacred Vedic fires had long been sending up their smoke from all parts of India, even the Dravidian South. The Aryans, too, had absorbed many Dravidian ideas and raised them into abstract principles, incorporated into their own system of thought. Gods and goddesses were interchanged. A scheme of social organization based on colour and caste had broken society down into small units, but each unit, theoretically at least, was made to fit into the conception of a whole. Jainism and Buddhism, as they spread out from their original homes, added a feeling of brothership which cut across caste divisions. Brahminism and Brahmanical forms of worship, which gradually gave place to Hinduism, also flung out an all-embracing net, from North to South, and East to West. Different parts of India were constantly enriching one another, and making their individual contributions to the common store of religious ideas, customs, legends, literature and art.

One of the great unifying periods of Indian history came in the fourth and fifth centuries A.D., when the enlightened Gupta kings were able to bring all of northern India, and a good part of the Deccan as well, under their centralized authority. This they accomplished after a century of uncertainty in which many small weak powers had vainly struggled among themselves for an inheritance of the northern empire. The hundred and sixty years of Gupta rule which followed is often referred to as India's Golden Age.

Foreign influences had now been eliminated, and there was no immediate threat of danger to India from any external quarter. The Persian legions under their Sassanid kings were too busy defending Persia (and incidentally India) from the Romans to do more than occasionally nibble at India's western borders. China, midway between the Han and Tang periods of its history, was momentarily torn by internal strife. Distant Europe was about to be blacked out in the Dark Ages. Not for two and a half centuries was Mecca to see the birth of a little Arab boy who, when he grew up, would shake the continent of Asia in a tumultuous earthquake. Locust swarms of Huns were ominously gathering over the horizon in central Asia, it is true, but they were still afar off. It was during this interval of calm that northern India had the good fortune to be ruled by a line of extraordinarily intelligent and able kings. In the whole contemporary world of Asia and Europe, India under the Guptas ranked first in civilization and culture.

The founder of the dynasty was Chandragupta I, entirely unrelated to Chandragupta Maurya, six hundred years before his time. He was possibly descended from the family then locally ruling at Pataliputra, but shorn of its power. When he married Kumara Devi, a princess of the neighbouring Lichavi clan of Vaisali, which had been prominent in the time of the Buddha, he appears to have bettered his fortunes. Chandragupta I, obviously proud of the new connection, promptly issued a gold coin bearing not only his own but his queen's name as well. He now set about to acquire a respectable kingdom, which soon extended from Pataliputra (Patna) to Prayag (Allahabad). To mark his success he then called himself " King of Kings ", and had himself crowned at Pataliputra. The year was A.D. 320, the first year of the new Gupta era. Chandragupta could not long enjoy the privileges of a monarch, however, as he died shortly after.

Samudra, his son, was a born military genius, the real maker of the Gupta empire. He at once set forth on a career of conquest in all directions, and in a surprisingly short space of time had won an empire almost as extensive as that of Asoka. His long reign of nearly fifty years gave him plenty of time not only to consolidate his territories but to bestow on them the advantage of his enlightened rule. A follower of Vishnu (like all Gupta rulers), he nevertheless was liberal and just in his treatment of all religious faiths. He was also a generous patron of the arts and of learning. It seems strange indeed that in spite of his contributions, the very name of Samudragupta was long forgotten in India, and foreign scholars first disentangled it only a little more than a century ago, from old coins, occasional references in the Buddhist literature of Ceylon and China, and a single long inscription in Sanskrit verse and prose, engraved on one of Asoka's ancient pillars. This pillar, originally at Kosambi, was dragged forty miles and set up again in the Allahabad Fort by the Mughal Emperor Akbar, in the sixteenth century. The inscription was composed by Samudra's court poet and gives a grandiloquent account of his wars, in curious contrast to the half-obliterated message of Asoka carved on the same pillar, asserting that " The chiefest conquest is the Law of Piety ".

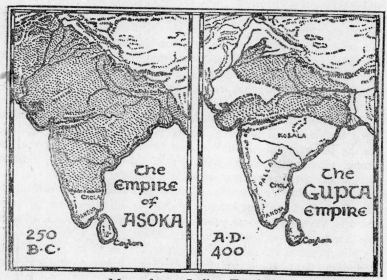

Map of two Indian Empires

As soon as Samudra ascended the Gupta throne, he marched west and north and pushed the boundaries of his realm as far as the Chambal River, a branch of the Jumna. Then he marched back east, subduing and once more reducing to a position of servitude the chiefs of the forest tribes of Kalinga. Without stopping to take breath, he continued his triumphal progress

southward, where he humbled the pride of eleven more kings.
He then swung westward, crossed the peninsula into Malabar,
and finally returned by way of the western Deccan plateau to
his capital at Ayodhya. In the three years of his southern campaign, he and his huge army marched altogether three thousand
miles, fighting their way the whole time through difficult country
against hostile forces. Yet nowhere does Samudra seem to have
suffered a single defeat.

In spite of his astonishing military successes, Samudragupta
made no attempt to incorporate the conquered southern kingdoms into his own empire. Permitting the humbled southern
kings to remain on their thrones as vassals and tributaries, he
was content to take home vast hoards of gold and jewels. On
his return, he celebrated the ancient Vedic rite of the Horse
Sacrifice with ostentatious pomp, as proof that he had become
a world conqueror. One of his gold coins shows the tethered
horse standing before the sacrificial altar. His fame was now
sufficiently great to make the frontier kings and chieftains of
Bengal, Assam, Malwa, Gujarat, the Punjab and the Himalayan
region see the wisdom of seeking subordinate alliances with him
and sending voluntary tribute in token of their submission. Even
the Saka and Kushan princes who still exercised some form of
attenuated authority in distant Kabul and in the region of the
Oxus, as well as Meghavarman, king of Ceylon, discreetly dispatched embassies and presents to the Gupta court.

This Samudra, " skilled in a hundred battles ", was also a
gifted musician and poet, according to his panegyrist. One coin
bearing his name shows him seated on a high-backed couch, or
throne, playing the *vina*. Samudra is also said to have taken
special delight in philosophical discussions, and the learned
Buddhist scholar Vasubandhu, brother of Asanga and co-founder
of one of the important schools of Mahayana Buddhism, is supposed to have spent some years as councillor at his court, though
it is hard to reconcile the known dates.

Chandragupta II, third and greatest of Gupta emperors, succeeded in 380. He is frequently known simply by the title he
assumed (also confusingly adopted by many other Indian kings)
of Vikramaditya, " Sun of Valour." Chandragupta II made it his
first business to undertake a few military campaigns, just to
round off the large empire he had inherited. Lustrous bits of
western territory still remained outside the Gupta orbit. Whoever controlled the western seaports and the ancient and distinguished city of Ujjain, capital of Malwa and chief inland distri-
buting centre for the Indian trade with Arabia and Egypt,

obviously controlled a valuable source of revenue. Chandra-gupta II wasted no time in attacking the Saka satrap still hanging on to this western territory. In the closing years of the fourth century, he defeated the opposing army and put the satrap himself, twenty-first and last of his line, to death. The whole of western India, including Malwa, Gujarat and Kathiawar, was then annexed to the Gupta empire. This notable victory probably was the incentive for Chandragupta to call himself "Vikra-maditya."

In the environs of Delhi, in the courtyard of a ruined mosque adjacent to the twelfth-century Kutb Minar, stands a curious Iron Pillar. The pillar, originally a shaft erected in honour of Vishnu, was removed from some unknown site and set up out-side Delhi in the eleventh century. It bears a long Sanskrit legend in early Gupta characters, detailing the military feats of one King Chandra, who conquered Bengal, and crossed the seven tributaries of the Indus. Although it is not certain that the Chandra of the Iron Pillar is really Chandragupta II, the time and style of writing generally fit into Chandragupta's period, and very probably the inscription refers to him.

The chief interest of the pillar, apart from the historical inscription, is that this marvel of the iron forger's art clearly dates from early Gupta times. The column is a foot and a half thick at the base and twenty-three feet high, and it has been estimated to weigh not less than six tons. It is forged in a single piece of pure rustless iron, and sixteen hundred years of exposure to every kind of weather has not affected the metal in any way. Another fourth-century pillar, unfortunately broken but originally even larger, lies at Dhar, an ancient city of Malwa. Europe, until the eighteenth century, could not equal India's metallurgical skill of the fourth century A.D.

During the reign of Chandragupta II, a sturdy Buddhist monk from far away China, the first of many such distinguished visitors, arrived in India to search for correct texts on monastic discipline. The traveller was Fa Hian, who set out from Chang-an, present-day Sian-fu, in the year 399, walked across the whole of central Asia and reached India six years later. Of the five friends who started out on the journey with him, two turned back, two died on the way and one decided to remain perma-nently in India. Fa Hian himself spent six years in India, visiting monasteries and making pilgrimages to places sacred to the Buddhist world. He learned Sanskrit in order to be able to copy the precious *Sutras* he wished to take back for the instruction of his brother monks in China, and he also made many drawings of holy images. Finally he returned home by way of the sea route from Ceylon. A friend, deeply impressed by Fa Hian's fortitude in braving countless dangers for the sake of his faith, begged him to write an account of his travels, which he did, on bamboo tablets and silk.

The author does not trouble to mention even the name of Chandragupta II, then the reigning king in northern India, but neither does he name any other contemporary king. Nevertheless he notes down observations about government and administration. He found the people generally prosperous and happy, and he was astonished at the absence of all those official restrictions and registrations so characteristic of his own land. " Those who want to go away, may go ; those who want to stop, may stop," he observes with obvious approval. Taxes were light. Members of the king's bodyguard received fixed salaries. Justice was administered with fairness and leniency. Corporal punishment was not ordinarily practised, and there was no such thing as a death penalty. Criminals were fined according to the gravity of their offences. For repeated attempts at treason, the offender was punished by the amputation of his right hand.

Fa Hian took it for granted that all Indians practised the same abstemious and controlled habits in regard to food that he found among the Buddhist communities. " Throughout the country," he asserts sweepingly, " no one kills any living thing, nor drinks wine, nor eats onions or garlic. . . . They do not keep pigs or fowls, there are no dealings in cattle, no butcher's shops or distilleries in their market-places. . . . Only the *Chandalas* go hunting and deal in flesh." The picture exaggerates, but obviously the religious and ethical doctrine of non-violence inherent in the Buddhist and Jain creeds had taken deep root in Indian life. Fa Hian's note about the Chandalas, however, shows the position of outcastes and also one reason why they were made to suffer social segregation. Their customs were held to be impure. As a result, they were compelled to live apart, and whenever they came into the towns or markets, they had to give warning of their approach by striking a piece of wood, so that others might not be contaminated by accidentally touching them. Fa Hian's testimony shows that " untouchability " was sadly established as a social custom by the beginning of the fifth century.

It appears that Buddhism was in a highly flourishing state, particularly in the northwest. In Gandhara and the Punjab, Fa Hian visited great monasteries housing many thousands of monks, belonging to both the Hinayana and Mahayana schools. When he reached Mathura, he counted twenty monasteries, and he was delighted to learn that once a year a great assembly was held there for the special purpose of expounding Buddhist doctrines. Even kings and Brahmins treated monks with politeness and respectfully made offerings to them. One type of meritorious offering took the form of gifts of lands and villages, with binding title deeds for the support of monastic institutions. As Fa Hian journeyed onward, visiting monastery after monastery, he was deeply impressed by the dignified ceremonial and courtesy observed in these establishments.

In Magadha, the Buddha's own land, the wayfarer from China found that the people were not only rich and thriving, but meritoriously emulated one another " in practising charity of heart and duty to one's neighbour." In all important towns and cities, free hospitals were maintained by the well-to-do gentry. Still more astonishing were hospitals for animals. There were also wayside resthouses, in which free lodging and food were available to travellers. Fa Hian scrupulously records that such charitable works were supported not only by Buddhists, but by many " heretical " sects as well. When he finally reached the old royal capital, Pataliputra, Asoka's ancient palace left him wonder-struck. It was built of huge blocks of stone, carved and inlaid with cunning designs. He naïvely decided that only super-human beings could have been responsible for such an architectural masterpiece.

A change in religious outlook, however, was beginning to manifest itself, in part a deep-seated reaction against a religion adopted and so widely popularized by Kanishka, a foreign ruler. One reason why Buddhism made such rapid progress outside India was that it set up no barrier of exclusiveness. The new undiscriminating democracy of Buddhism, which allowed foreigners and " untouchables " free access to sacred texts, came to be deeply resented by the orthodox elements in the country, especially those with a vested interest in the priesthood. Buddhist religion in the fifth century with its emphasis on morality, social helpfulness and faith tended to become an easygoing religion for laymen. At the same time, in loosening the ties of family and caste, it aroused the sleeping antagonism of powerful groups in many parts of the country.

As Fa Hian passed eastward from Mathura, the changing conditions became more apparent. He was informed that ninety-six schools of " heretics " flourished in the very heart of the old Buddhist homeland. Many sacred places had fallen into decay. Kapilavastu was nothing but wilderness. Gaya was deserted, though near the Bodhi tree were two monasteries of the Greater and Lesser Vehicles, housing six to seven hundred monks. The Hinayana monastery had been built by King Meghavarman of Ceylon in the fourth century, with Samudragupta's permission for sheltering Sinhalese Buddhist monks on pilgrimage to the Bodhi tree. At Sravasti, Fa Hian was depressed to find only a bare two hundred families scattered about the once prosperous capital of Kosala, where the Blessed One had spent twenty-five rain-retreats and preached most of his sermons. At Kusinagara, where he died, stupas and monasteries were seen, but the inhabitants were few.

It was at Pataliputra that Fa Hian, after repeated disappointments, at last succeeded in obtaining Sanskrit copies of the texts for which he had come all the long way to India. Paper, invented only in A.D. 105 by a Chinese named Tsai Lun, had not yet found its way to India even in the fifth century, and Indian manuscripts, whether of palm leaves or birch-bark, were fragile and costly. Students usually had to content themselves with committing to memory the texts as recited by their teachers. After obtaining the manuscripts, the Chinese visitor finally set sail from Tamralipti (Tamluk), the principal port of Bengal, and reached China, after fearsome storms and delays, in A.D. 414. He knew he was really home at last, he says, when he recognized all " the old familiar vegetables ". Thanks to Fa Hian's contemporary account, a picture of Gupta India has been preserved as that of a country in which laws were just, the people were generally contented and manners were refined and cultured. Within only a few years of Fa Hian's visit, however, India had to face a calamity more disastrous than any yet within her experience.

At about the same moment of history when Huns were overrunning Europe, another branch of the same mongrel race from the Steppes of Asia launched a devastating raid deep into India. They were a people of mixed Mongolian, Tatar, Turkish and Scythian blood. Some tribes bore down on China in the last quarter of the fourth century A.D. Others attacked the Slavs, crossed the Volga, and made their way along the northern coast of the Black Sea into Europe, where they spread out on both sides of the Danube in the country which still bears their name, Hungary. Under their wild leader Attila, burning, slaying and pillaging, they laid waste town and countryside. They demanded tribute from the trembling Emperor of the East, cowering in his palace at Constantinople. They struck terror into the heart of the Gothic tribes of northern Europe. Then one day in the year

451 they crossed the Rhine into Gaul. The fate of all Europe hung in the balance as the advancing swarm of stocky little men on a multitude of shaggy horses met a desperate army of West Goths, Romans, Burgundians and Franks, hastily assembled on the Plain of Chalons, in the valley of the Marne — but the Huns were beaten back, and Europe was saved.

Meanwhile, another tribe, or branch, of the same barbarous people, known to Indians and Iranians as Huna and to European classical writers as White Huns, or Ephthalites (because they kept flocks of white sheep and goats), began drifting about Asia on the lookout for new grasslands to conquer. When they reached the Oxus, they swam their horses across and galloped towards Iran. It was nearly a century before the Iranians finally succeeded in pushing the unwelcome marauders back. They then swarmed into Afghanistan and encamped at Bamian, and soon after they began pouring down through the mountain passes into India. China had a Great Wall, fifteen hundred miles long, to protect her frontiers against the barbarians. India had no such protection, and before the impetuous onrush, the lightly guarded mountain passes proved but a feeble obstacle. The Huns overran the Punjab, streamed southward into Rajputana, Kathiawar and Malwa, and made forays as far eastward as Bihar.

The great Chandragupta had died in about 415 A.D. He left behind him a rich and prosperous empire, at peace with itself and its neighbours, and his son Kumaragupta I was a worthy successor who, during a long reign of forty years, carried on Gupta traditions in the best style. When Skandagupta became emperor in 455, however, he was almost immediately confronted with flying columns of the Huna, pressing southward.

For a time, the hordes were held in check by the Gupta army, and an interesting memorial pillar was set up by Skandagupta at the town of Bhitari, describing how he came galloping into the courtyard of the palace at Ayodhya, to announce to his mother the defeat of the barbarians " just as Krishna, having slain his enemies, betook himself to his mother Devaki." But Skandagupta's first successes were only temporary. Led by their chieftain Toramana, by now firmly established in the Punjab at Sakala, former capital of the Bactrian Greek king Menander, the wild hordes moved onward like an avalanche. All efforts to check the advance were futile, and at this crucial moment of Indian history, Skandagupta himself died.

The mighty Gupta empire, already seriously weakened by the strain of trying to check the Huns, could not survive this latest blow. No master mind or military genius arose to direct the imperial armies, and the Huns swept down unimpeded into the plains of India.

There followed a century of unparalleled disaster. Previous invaders, whatever harm they had wrought, had always contributed something of their own to Indian civilization. The Persians organized a new system of sound administration. The Greeks bequeathed an artistic tradition which was absorbed by the Kushans. Out of the synthesis of Greco-Roman art and Buddhism, enduring cultural values took shape. But the foe with whom India now had to deal had nothing to give and everything to take. Mihirakula, the son of Toramana, though born in India and calling himself a follower of Shiva, far outstripped his father in cruelty and mad destructiveness.

At last, about 530, India rallied, and a revolt was staged against the invaders. Part of the credit goes to a king named Baladitya, possibly one of the late Gupta rulers of Magadha. The real hero, however, was Yasodharman, head of the independent Malwa clans. Mihirakula was taken prisoner, but was generously allowed to retire to Kashmir where he was offered an asylum by the Kashmir king. This courtesy Mihirakula repaid by killing the king and taking possession of Kashmir. There he collected his scattered hordes and, consumed by a passionate hatred for Buddhists in particular, set out to destroy Buddhism, root, branch and flower. He exterminated the ruling family in Gandhara and put thousands of innocent people to death. He deliberately burnt and broke to pieces monasteries, stupas and images, by hundreds and thousands. The work of senseless destruction continued until his death.

For a short time, the empire of the White Huns sprawled across a vast stretch of central Asia. At the height of its power at the beginning of the sixth century, it comprised forty provinces, of which the conquered Indian territory formed one. But history proved that though the Huns could conquer, they could not hold. Soon after the middle of the sixth century, a new power arose in Asia, that of the Western Turks. In alliance with Noshirwan of Persia, grandson of a king who had lost his life at the hands of the Huns, the Turks put an end to the Kingdom of the Galloping Horsemen. The Persians and Turks lost no time in dividing the Hun territory between them. Then the Turks ousted the Persians from their share and appropriated it to themselves. Weak, impoverished and dazed, India awoke from her long nightmare.

Scions of the Imperial Guptas still ruled over fragments of territory here and there, but the central power had collapsed, and royal treasuries were empty. A minor Gupta king sat on the throne in eastern Malwa. The Maukhari dynasty held sway at Kanauj (Kanyakubja). Thanesar was ruled by the Vardhana line. Sasanka had seized control in Gauda, or western Bengal, and the kingdom of Kamarupa, or Assam, further east, had become independent. The Maitrakas, of uncertain origin, held sway at Valabhi in Gujarat, where they founded a new dynasty. Northern India was thoroughly exhausted and the once great Gupta empire had fallen apart. Then, at the turn of the century, a new figure stepped onto the stage to play a brief but memorable role — the charming, warmhearted, romantic Harsha Vardhana.

Harsha was the younger son of the Raja of Thanesar, who ruled the small state lying west of Kanauj, in the Punjab. Harsha traced his descent through his father from the imperial Gupta line, but his mother was the daughter of that same Yasodharman of Malwa, who had inflicted a decisive defeat on the Huns. Two contemporary literary works have supplied us with a full-length portrait of Harsha. There are also three relevant inscriptions, one bearing Harsha's signature engraved in his own handwriting. Some of his royal seals and tiny silver coins, with his bust, have also drifted down across the centuries.

A long romantic biography, the *Harsha-charita*, or " Life of Harsha " was composed by Harsha's court poet, the Brahmin Bana. It gives a valuable record of seventh-century India, but unfortunately it covers only the early part of Harsha's career. In the ornate Sanskrit of the period, we are informed that Harsha's father was " a lion to the Huna deer, a burning fever to the king of the Indus land, a bilious plague to the lord of Gandhara, a troubler of the sleep of Gujarat, an axe to the creeper of Malwa's glory ! " The Malwas, in spite of marriage relations with the Vardhanas, are compared to " the hind clutching the lion's mane, the frog slapping the cobra, the calf taking the tiger captive." As for young Harsha, his royal toe-nails are said to be " rosy with the reflected light of the jeweled diadems of innumerable kings, bowing in obeisance at his foot-stool."

It seems that a late sporadic Hun raid into the territory of Thanesar occurred when Prince Harsha was fifteen years old. The old raja, who in his younger days had played a notable part in helping to drive the invaders out of India, was now too infirm to undertake a new campaign. The army was therefore dispatched under the leadership of Prince Rajya, Harsha's elder brother. Harsha accompanied his brother part of the way, but because of his youth was ordered to remain in the foothills of the Himalayas where he spent the time in hunting. While he was thus amusing himself, a messenger arrived in great haste to report that the old king had fallen dangerously ill. Harsha hurried back to Thanesar, arriving just in time to receive the dying king's injunction : " Succeed to this world ; appropriate my treasures ; make prize of the feudatory kings ; support the burden of royalty ; protect the people, practise yourself in arms ; annihilate your foes."

A series of domestic tragedies followed, no doubt reflecting the precarious conditions and the general disorder of the period. Swift camel riders summoned Prince Rajya, who had no sooner arrived than the news was brought that the ruler of western Malwa had assassinated the crown prince of Kanauj, husband of Rajyasri, the younger sister of Rajya and Harsha. Rajyasri herself was said to have been cast into prison and insulted by having iron fetters placed on her tender feet. Prince Rajya at once set off to rescue his sister and chastise the Malwa foe, but unknown to her brother, Rajyasri had already escaped from Kanauj and fled to a Buddhist hermitage in the Vindhya mountains. Prince Rajya was suddenly slain through treacherous intrigue, plotted by Sasanka, king of Gauda, an ally of Malwa. It was now the turn of Harsha to go in search of his sister, and with dramatic timeliness he arrived just as she was on the point of mounting a funeral pyre in grief and despair. After the safe return of Harsha and Rajyasri, and with the approval of the state ministers and counsellors, Harsha celebrated his coronation and ascended the combined thrones of Thanesar and Kanauj. This was in the year 606, afterwards chosen to mark the beginning of the Harsha era, which continued in use for several centuries over a large part of northern India and also in Nepal. Between this date and his death, in 648, Harsha made himself master of an empire very little smaller in extent than that ruled over by Chandragupta Vikramaditya. It stretched from the Punjab to Bengal and Orissa.

Most of Harsha's military conquests were made soon after he became king. We are told that for six years the royal elephants were never unharnessed nor the soldiers unbelted. Only on one single occasion did Harsha suffer a serious reverse. Acting on the unwise assurance of subordinate princes that " the Deccan is easily won at the price of valour," he set out with a huge army, bent on the conquest of the Chalukyan realm south of the Narbada. He marched into Maharashtra, and joined battle on the bank of the river with the Chalukyan king, none other than the proud and haughty Pulakesin II. Harsha's forces were thoroughly routed and had to beat a hasty retreat. Harsha never again attempted a trial of strength with his doughty Chalukyan rival, who remained the undisputed master in the Deccan as long as he lived.

Towards the end of Harsha's reign the most illustrious of all the early Chinese Buddhist pilgrims paid a prolonged visit to India. This was the famous Yuan Chwang (Hiuen Tsiang), who later wrote a fascinating account of his travels to India under the title of *Si-yu-ki*, or " Records of the Western World " — India being a " western " country from the Chinese point of view. Known as the Master of the Law, because of his great learning and scholarship, Yuan Chwang was one of the most distinguished men of his day, with a sensitive and intelligent mind, and he corroborates in a remarkable way much of what Bana has to say about Harsha in his more flowery biography.

Taken together, the two accounts portray Harsha as a benevolent and able ruler, a king of whom any country might well be proud. He assigned one part of the day to affairs of state and two parts to works of benevolence, but he was practical enough to maintain his military establishments in first class condition. He had inherited a substantial army of 5,000 elephants, 20,000 horsemen and 50,000 infantry, but this force he expanded to 60,000 elephants and 100,000 cavalry. The traditional fourth arm of an Indian army, the cumbersome war chariots, seems to have been discarded by Harsha. At least there is no mention of the use of chariots in any of his battles. Justice, according to current ideas, was considerately rendered by Harsha, and the people were not oppressed by heavy taxes. State revenue consisted mainly of the customary one sixth of gross produce from land. Out of this, Harsha devoted one fourth to expenses of government, one fourth to the endowment of public servants, one fourth to charity distributed among the various religious sects, and the remaining one fourth to rewarding high intellectual achievement.

In religious matters, Harsha followed the tolerant example of his predecessors. At his capital of Kanauj, there were two hundred Hindu temples and one hundred Buddhist monasteries. His father had been a devout worshipper of Aditya, the Sun, a deity greatly favoured in Hindu India during these centuries. Harsha's elder brother Rajya and his sister Rajyasri appear to have adopted Buddhism and Harsha himself was later converted to Mahayana Buddhism as the result of the persuasive eloquence of the Chinese scholar Yuan Chwang. He erected many stupas and monasteries, but continued to pay reverence to both the Sun-god and Shiva. After his acceptance of Buddhism, he promulgated a law forbidding under severe penalties the use of animal food throughout the length and breadth of his kingdom.

Like his great Gupta predecessors, Harsha was a liberal patron of letters. He was very fond of holding poetical contests at his court. Literary men would assemble there and recite before critical assemblies their poetical compositions. Harsha himself was a dramatist of no mean ability, and three of his plays still survive — *Ratnavali*, *Priyadarsika* and *Nagananda*. The latter begins with an invocation to Buddha and presents the story of the Bodhisattva Jimutavahana who saved the race of Nagas by offering himself in their place to Garuda, Vishnu's bird, mortal enemy of all serpents. The play is in five acts, and it was set to music and performed at Harsha's own court.

Asoka had set a pattern of royal benevolence which was followed by the Guptas, but Harsha outdid them all. Besides state hospitals and free resthouses for travellers and poor persons, he fed a thousand Buddhist monks and five hundred Brahmins daily from the royal kitchens, and whereas Asoka distributed his wealth three times over during his lifetime, Harsha made six such distributions. Every five years, an immense assembly was held at Prayag (Allahabad), and on each occasion Harsha gave away in charity to Buddhists, Brahmins, ascetics, the poor and the destitute, everything that had accumulated in the imperial treasury, except just enough to keep the army properly equipped. As a final act of grace, he even gave away his own clothes and jewels, the jewels being used to defray the cost of copying sacred manuscripts. What makes Harsha really unique, however, is the tenderness and sweetness which permeated his whole nature. It expressed itself in his deep affection for his father, his devotion to his elder brother, his love and respect for his widowed sister, his loyalty to friends. He is one of the last great kings of northern India who lived and ruled in accordance with the traditional ideal of Indian kingship.

Harsha owes his fame in generous measure to Yuan Chwang, the author of the most detailed and objective literary record existing of seventh-century India. Like Fa Hian two and a quarter centuries earlier, Yuan Chwang set out for India to search for authoritative Buddhist works and to steep himself in the fundamental truths and spirit of Buddhism. He left China in A.D. 629, at the age of twenty-six, already recognized as a scholar of high rank. China was then passing through a period of intense political turmoil. Tai Tsung, founder of the great

Tang Dynasty, had just succeeded in uniting many petty states into one great empire. But the outer territories were still in rebellion, and when Yuan Chwang applied for a passport to go to India, Tai Tsung refused, having no wish to risk the life of

Yuan Chwang

one of his most distinguished subjects by allowing him to under-take such a venturesome journey. Yuan Chwang was not to be so easily dissuaded from an enterprise on which he had set his heart. Having managed to reach the frontier, he slipped out secretly one night through the Jade Gate, and cautiously made

The White horse

his way, hiding by day and travelling by night, past the garrisoned Chinese watch-towers which extended far out into central Asia. Once he lost his way in the waterless desert and all but died of thirst. His old roan horse, too weak to proceed another step, lay down in the sandy waste. At this crisis, Yuan Chwang addressed a fervent prayer to the merciful Bodhisattva Avaloki-tesvara. " On this journey I covet neither riches nor praise nor fame. My sole aim is to go and seek the Higher Intelligence and the True Law! " Strength mysteriously surged back into his fainting limbs. The horse got up on its feet and without guidance miraculously found its way to water and grass.

Though the Master of the Law travelled to India in the earnest spirit of a humble disciple, India at once recognized his superior qualities. As he approached the capital of Kashmir, the king himself came out to meet and escort him. Roads were strewn with flowers and sprinkled with perfume. Yuan Chwang settled down in a monastery to brush up his Sanskrit and study Maha-yana philosophy. When the king of Kashmir learned of his desire to obtain authoritative texts, he placed twenty scribes at his disposal to make copies of all important Buddhist manu-scripts. Yuan Chwang in due course journeyed on to the world-famous Buddhist university of Nalanda, not far from Gaya. Two hundred monks, followed by a thousand laymen, came forth to meet him in a great procession, with parasols and banners, flowers and incense. The abbot Silabhadra could not restrain his tears at sight of him. He had dreamed of just such a monk from China arriving at Nalanda with the sole object of seeking instruction in Mahayana doctrine.

Yuan Chwang spent altogether five years at Nalanda copying out four hundred manuscripts of 500,000 verses and it was during this period that he received repeated royal summonses to visit Harsha. Yuan Chwang did not wish to interrupt his serious studies, however, and politely refused. A similar im-perative summons was also received from Kumara, also known as Bhaskara, Harsha's vassal in Assam. This invitation, too, Yuan Chwang felt compelled to refuse. When a third messenger arrived from Kumara with the warning that if Yuan Chwang did not come to Assam forthwith, Kumara would send an army and elephants and trample Nalanda into dust, Abbot Silabhadra prudently urged his guest to depart without delay.

Yuan Chwang has recorded that he did not find a single Buddhist monastery in this easternmost part of India, but he says the people, like their ruler, were earnest in study and possessed remarkably retentive memories. He also mentions that Kumara questioned him about certain Chinese songs cele-brating the victories of Tai Tsung as a prince, then popular in Assam. Later on Kumara sent a request to a Chinese ambassa-dor at the court of Harsha to procure for him, or have made for him, a Sanskrit translation of the *Tao-te-ching*, the famous work of the great Chinese philosopher Lao Tzu, of the sixth century B.C. Details like these throw an illuminating sidelight on early cultural relations between China and India.

While Yuan Chwang was still a guest of Kumara, Harsha learned that the Master of the Law was visiting his vassal. Kumara received a peremptory order to send on the priest from China at once, to which Kumara returned the spirited reply that Harsha might take his head, but certainly not his guest. " Send the head at once ! " was the next imperial command. Kumara then made prompt preparations not only to send Yuan Chwang to the emperor, but to accompany him himself. The cortège included a vast number of elephants and river boats. It set out from Assam and reaching Bengal, proceeded by way of the Ganga. The elephants moved slowly along one bank, while the boats progressed in midstream, until they reached Harsha's camp. Kumara then had a pavilion-of-travel set up for Yuan Chwang, and himself crossed the river to make his peace with Harsha.

A meeting between Harsha and the Master of the Law was arranged for the following day, but Harsha was too impatient to wait. That very same night, thousands of lighted torches were suddenly seen advancing across the river. There could be no doubt that the royal procession was on its way. Harsha's hundred music-pace-drums were soon solemnly sounding the beat in unison, at each step taken by the king. Harsha appeared before the Master, bowed low and touched his feet. After welcoming him in suitable language and appointing a second meeting for the next day, the king then politely withdrew.

The next day Harsha asked to examine a work of Yuan Chwang, supporting the Mahayana doctrine, and was at once converted. Then and there he decided to hold one of those great philosophic debates in which the Indian intellectual élite had always taken delight. Messengers were sent in all directions to summon leading scholars and religious men to the proposed assembly at Kanauj. The two Indian kings, Harsha and Kumara, marched along their respective sides of the river with their suites, Kumara along the northern bank, and Harsha, accompanied by Yuan Chwang, along the southern bank. It took them three months to reach the capital.

By the time they arrived, several thousands of Buddhist monks, representing both the Greater and Lesser Vehicles, and three thousand Brahmins and Jains had already collected. The eighteen vassal kings who were required to attend upon Harsha, together with their numerous retinues, were also waiting. The

assembly opened with a grand procession. A gold image of
Buddha was placed on the back of an elephant. Harsha walked
on the right, dressed as Indra, carrying a white yaktail fly whisk,
and on the left walked Kumara, dressed as Brahma, carrying a
costly parasol. Harsha scattered pearls and other precious stones
and silver and gold flowers along the route of the procession.
Yuan Chwang and other high dignitaries rode on state elephants.
The monk from China was invited to take the seat of
honour and preside. The theme of the discussion was announced,
and outside the gates a copy of the main points was hung up,
with a notice that if anyone could find any flaw in the argument
or refute it, Yuan Chwang would give his head. For five days
the discourse went on, and many of the audience, including
Rajyasri, who had previously favoured Hinayana, were converted
by Yuan Chwang's eloquence and lucid exposition. Brahmins
and Hinayanists were greatly discomfited, and a plot was hatched
to do away with Yuan Chwang, and even to kill Harsha, but
the king caught hold of the would-be assassin and disarmed him,
and the guilty persons were promptly banished to the frontiers.
These dramatic developments no doubt marred the concluding
ceremonies, which consisted of another grand procession, in
which Yuan Chwang was led about the town on an elephant.

Yuan Chwang's knowledge of India was by no means confined solely to the northern and eastern parts of the country.
In 639, five years before the assembly at Kanauj, he visited
the Pallava capital of Kanchi, where he found a hundred monasteries with ten thousand resident monks, mostly Mahayanists.
There were also eighty Hindu temples, and an unspecified number of Jain *bastis*. From Kanchi, Yuan Chwang crossed the
Deccan into the Chalukyan territory of Pulakesin II. The
Chalukyans struck him as stern, vindictive and relentless to their
enemies, though ever grateful to their benefactors, proud and
passionate, but esteeming honour and duty above all else and
caring nothing for death. They were also fond of learning and
sufficiently open-minded to study both orthodox and unorthodox
texts, that is, both Buddhism and Hinduism. Travelling northward, he paid a brief visit to the Maitraka kingdom of Valabhi,
in Gujarat, where the reigning prince was Dhruvasena, a son-in-
law of Harsha, who had also adopted the Buddhist faith. A
great assembly used to be held annually at Valabhi, after the
pattern of Harsha's quinquennial assemblies, during which dishes,
garments, medicines and jewels were freely distributed to the
monks, and so Yuan Chwang finally arrived back again at
Nalanda.

At last the time came when, against the entreaties of all his friends, Yuan Chwang decided to turn his face homeward. He had left China in 629, and it was now 643. Fifteen strenuous years had passed. He felt that the treasure of true knowledge garnered by him in India must now be shared with his Chinese brother monks. Before setting out on the long journey, he went to take leave of Harsha, who offered him gold and other valuable gifts as a farewell present. Yuan Chwang refused everything, insisting that he had no wants, but finally he accepted a fur-lined garment from his old admirer Kumara, as protection against the bitter winds he would have to face in the high northern passes and in the open wastes of central Asia. Harsha provided him an escort and royal letters (written on cotton cloth and sealed with red wax), to ensure his safety up to the confines of his empire. He also gave him an elephant for his personal use and arranged horse transport for his large collection of relics, pictures, statues and the 657 Sanskrit manuscripts which were the harvest of Yuan Chwang's sojourn in India. The two Indian kings, Harsha and Kumara, then accompanied the Master of the Law on the first lap of his journey, and bade him a regretful farewell with tears and sighs. This was not the final leave-taking, however. Three days later, mounted on fast horses and accompanied by a party of a hundred horsemen, Harsha and Kumara overtook Yuan Chwang, to say good-by once more, this time forever.

On Yuan Chwang's ultimate return to his own country, followed by his white horse bearing the manuscripts, he was feted and honoured, and the great Tai Tsung summoned him for an interview and bestowed on him his imperial blessings and patronage. He spent the remaining years of his life in the arduous task of translating his hundreds of manuscripts into Chinese, with the help of a qualified staff, and at the special order of the Emperor of China, he wrote down the account of his journey to India.

A few years later, in 647, Harsha Vardhana died, or according to one version was murdered, and his minister Arjuna usurped the throne. Just in the midst of the confusion, a Chinese mission from Tai Tsung arrived at Kanauj. Instead of being received with the customary courtesies, they were insulted and robbed, and thirty horsemen of the escort were treacherously killed. The leader of the mission barely escaped with his life, fleeing across the mountains into Nepal. Since Nepal at the moment was in subordinate alliance with Tibet, and the Tibetan king, Srong-tsan-Gampo, was on the friendliest of terms with the Chinese emperor Tai Tsung, who was indeed his father-in-law, Nepal and Tibet were persuaded to send a punitive army into India. It entered the country from the northeast, and some five hundred Indian walled towns and villages of Assam and Bengal were overrun, and large numbers of the population captured and beheaded. Arjuna was marched off in chains to China, and India saw and heard no more of him.

Harsha had no male heir, and his untimely removal was a signal for the usual disruption inherent in such a situation. The eighteen feudatory kings who formerly waited on him now felt free to go their own ways, and the imposing edifice of a paramount power in northern India came tumbling down.

CHAPTER XI

A House Divided

IN MAURYA AND GUPTA times, large parts of India, if never quite the whole of it, were brought under effective central administration. In Harsha's time, too, a loose imperial regime covered most of northern India, and Chalukyan territory in the Deccan was about equal in extent. After Harsha's death, however, many rival kingdoms quickly sprang up in northern India, all contending for the coveted position of supremacy. India became a house politically divided against itself. In the context of the period, it invited invasion, ending in eventual conquest from without.

In the opening years of the eighth century, Arabs under the command of the seventeen year old Muhammad ibn Kasim attacked Sind, on the pretext of a piratical act against one of their trading ships near the mouth of the Indus. Battles were brief and cruel, and Sind was annexed to the Omayyad Caliphate centred at Damascus. (Spain, in the far West, had already fallen in A.D. 710, two years before the attack on Sind.) The Indian territory was presently divided into the two minor principalities of Multan in the north and Mansurah in the south, and remained for three centuries under the rule of Arab princes only nominally subservient to the Abbasid Khalifs, now reigning at Baghdad. Finally, at the beginning of the eleventh century, Multan fell to the Turkish Muslim conqueror Mahmud of Ghazni, and Hindu rule revived in southern Sind.

The Arab conquest of Sind has often been called a mere interlude, of no political significance. In the light of recent history, this estimate no longer holds true. Under the long period of Muslim rule, large numbers of the inhabitants were converted to Islam, and when the Indian sub-continent was ultimately partitioned in 1947, the Muslim majority province of Sind passed over to Pakistan.

The next wave of foreign invasion came from a different direction, penetrated deeper into India, and had far more disastrous consequences. Mahmud of Ghazni, in the first quarter of the eleventh century, led a long series of looting raids down into the fertile Indian plains from his bleak little mountain kingdom in Afghanistan, founded in 962 A.D. by Alptigin, one-time Turkish palace guard of the Samanid ruler of Bukhara. Mahmud and his " army of the Faithful " — a motley array of fanatical central Asian converts easily lured to join him by the thought of destroying the infidels and enriching themselves at one and the same time — captured cities and towns, desecrated temples, robbed them of their gold and jewels donated by pious pilgrims over the centuries, slaughtered the inhabitants and carried thousands away into slavery. Systematic destruction like this India had never experienced before. Terror and despair swept over northern India.

Mahmud made no attempt to occupy and rule the Indian territory he overran, except the Punjab, where he appointed a governor at Lahore. Yet he clearly showed the road of future conquest to the Afghans of Ghur, a hardy mountain tribe occupying the region between Ghazni and Herat. When the Ghurs became masters of Ghazni in 1173, Muizz-ud-din, later to be known as Muhammad Ghuri, used Lahore as a springboard for his conquest of India.

The five hundred years between the conquest of Sind by the Arabs and the establishment of the Sultanate of Delhi in 1206 by Muhammad Ghuri's able ex-slave and general, Qutb-ud-din Aibak, might have been used by India to strengthen itself against danger ahead, but danger was scarcely foreseen. Nationalism had not yet been born anywhere in the world, and Indian kings were too busy fighting among themselves to be concerned about a distant frontier. There was no adequate preparation for united defence, no central command. When the lull of false security was at last shattered, defensive armies were hastily assembled, but it was then too late.

Accounts of kings and dynasties are only old dry bones of history, without flesh and blood, yet they are a skeleton holding history together after a fashion. Indian chronology is so extraordinarily confused and overlapping that only the dynastic inscriptions bring a little order and throw some light into the dark corners of uncertainty. Boundaries between kingdoms, however, were always fluid, and expansion or contraction depended on nothing more substantial than the presence or absence on a particular throne of a strong or weak ruler. It is also significant that most of the early medieval Indian kingdoms, as well as their inhabitants, are known only by the name or title of their ruling dynasty. In spite of regional variations in language and customs, the people were essentially Indians, sharing common values of life and common ideals. This is why

India could survive a thousand years of alien rule, and at last emerge free and independent.

In South India and the Deccan, throughout practically the whole of the period under review, the old traditional dynasties continued with varying fortunes of war, as already described in a previous chapter. The Pallavas of Kanchi, dominant for seven centuries, did not succumb to the Cholas till around the close of the ninth century. The Cholas ruled for two and a half centuries, but then went down to the Pandyas, whose period of revival lasted through the thirteenth century. In the Deccan, the Western Chalukyas supplanted the Rashtrakutas in the last quarter of the tenth century. When the Chalukyas collapsed at the end of the twelfth, the Deccan was briefly divided among their three former feudatories, the Yadavas of Devagiri, the Hoysalas of Dvarasamudra and the Kakatiyas of Warangal, or Telingana.

Very different were the winds of change north of the Vindhyas. Entirely new dynasties erupted here, from the eighth century onwards. Most of them called themselves Rajputs, and the Rajput kingdoms rapidly spread outward from that arid part of western India now known after them as Rajputana, or Rajasthan. By the eleventh and twelfth centuries, they covered the greater part of central and northern India as far east as Bihar.

Who were the Rajputs? The name Rajput, of course, means simply " king's son ". According to their own geneologies, they were descended from the illustrious heroes of Epic days, or even before them from Sun, Moon or Fire — whence their classification into Solar, Lunar or Agni-kula clans. Certain modern historians incline to trace the descent of some of them from Hunnish or other foreign chieftains who had invaded India during the fifth and sixth centuries, married the daughters of defeated Indian rajas, and settled down to make India their home. Their descendants took Indian names, became staunch Hindus and were finally accepted into the Indian social order as Kshattriyas, or warriors. In the distinctive Rajput clan organization, every male member of a clan was theoretically related by blood to the chief, or prince, and was bound to him by an oath of loyalty unto death. Land was held on a feudal basis, in return for military service in time of need.

Eventually thirty-six Rajput clans were recognized, though no two dynastic lists are exactly alike. Famous Rajput names still stirring proud memories of a by-gone age of chivalry are those of the Sisodias (Gahlots, or Guhilas) of Mewar, Paramaras of Malwa, Rathors of Marwar, Tomaras (Tuars) of Delhi, Chauhans of Sakambhari, Ajmir and Delhi, Yadavas of Jaisalmer, Solankis (Chalukyas or Chaulukyas) of Gujarat, Kalachuris of Chedi, Chandellas of Bundelkhand, and Pratiharas and Gahada-valas of Kanauj.

The real history of the Rajputs still lies shrouded in mist and legend, but India will always pay grateful tribute to them for their brave, though unsuccessful, effort to stem the Muslim advance. Attenuated Rajput lines even managed to outlive both the Muslim and British conquests. At the time of Indian inde-pendence, in 1947, these Rajput Princes rendered a last service to the motherland. They voluntarily surrendered all vestige of political power, and permitted their ancestral territories to become fully integrated with the Indian Union.

The first of the Rajput clans to rise to pre-eminence was that of the Gurjara-Pratiharas. One of the various Gurjara clans roaming around western India moved southward from central Rajputana about the end of the seventh century and established a footing at Ujjain, in ancient Avanti. The founder of the new dynasty was Nagabhata I. Early in his career he was confronted with the bold Arab attempt of Junaid, successor of Muhammad ibn Kasim as governor of Sind, to push on into Rajputana. Nagabhata at once put himself at the head of a coalition of local chieftains and petty princes, and the Arabs were thrown back. From this time on, the Pratiharas became their mortal enemies.

Nagabhata's rising star naturally attracted unwelcome attention from his contemporary, Dhruva Rashtrakuta, who looked upon Ujjain as part of Rashtrakuta territory. Dhruva attacked Ujjain, reducing Nagabhata to the position of a vassal. The name Prati-hara, " door-keeper ", perhaps originated at this time. The fourth in the Pratihara line, Vatsaraja, succeeded in greatly enlarging the territory under his control but he was finally driven out of Ujjain altogether by the Rashtrakutas. His son Nagabhata II, however, soon retrieved the fallen fortunes of the family. Enlist-ing support of several allies, he carved out a new Pratihara kingdom in the heart of Hindustan. His crowning achievement was the capture of Kanauj, Harsha's old imperial capital, in about A.D. 830.

For nearly two centuries, Pratihara kings ruled from Kanauj. Their empire extended at its zenith to the foot of the Himalayas and westward to the Arabian Sea, and in the first decade of the tenth century one of their kings even carried Pratihara arms eastward, annexing Magadha and temporarily overrunning north Bengal. Many lesser rulers acknowledged their overlordship and

paid customary tribute. But their supremacy was often challenged
not only by their old opponents, the Rashtrakutas of the Deccan,
who made frequent raids into the northern plains, but by the
Palas of Bengal as well. In the end, their downfall was achieved
by Mahmud of Ghazni, who took Kanauj in 1019, during one
of his whirlwind descents into India.

Another of Mahmud's early casualties was the Shahi kingdom
in the Punjab. After the collapse of Kanishka's great northern
empire back in the third century, Kushan princes had continued
to rule small principalities here and there, even under the Gupta
emperors. A branch known as the Kidara, or northern Kushans,
retaining the old Kushan title of Shahi, or Shahiya, ruled for
many generations over the Kabul valley in Afghanistan and in
Gandhara. These Kabul Shahis, though originally of Turkish
origin, had adopted Buddhism, and when the Arabs arrived in
Afghanistan, fought them intermittently for several decades, until
Kabul fell in 870. In the wake of disaster, Kallar, a Brahmin
minister of the last Kushan king, usurped the power. He was
soon compelled to retreat to the Indus, however, and there he
founded a new frontier Hindu Shahi kingdom, having a place
confusingly referred to as Udabhandapur, Waihind, Ohind or
simply Und, as its capital. In the following century Shahi kings
conquered most of the Punjab, but the misfortune of this kingdom was that it lay directly in the path of invasion from the
northwest.

Already before the end of the tenth century the Shahi king
Jayapal had come into conflict with Sabuktigin of Ghazni. When
the latter died in 997 and was succeeded by his son Mahmud,
the Shahis began to feel the full weight of Muslim pressure.
Twice defeated in battle, Jayapal was forced to sign a humiliating
treaty, but was unwise enough to repudiate its terms as soon as
he found himself safely back in the Shahi capital, now shifted
south to Bhatinda for greater security. This time, in spite of
generous aid rendered by Rajput and other neighbouring kings
of Hindustan, he suffered a third crushing defeat near Peshawar
in 1001. Unable to bear the disgrace, he handed over power
to his son Anandapala and committed suicide by mounting his
own funeral pyre. Anandapala was no more successful than
Jayapala in defending the Punjab. He and his successors fought
many losing battles against Mahmud, who had now vowed to
invade Hindustan every year and wage " holy war " against the
infidels. Mahmud did indeed raid India some eighteen times
before death at last put an end to his inordinate ambitions, in
1030. Thus, after a century and a half, Shahi rule was relent-

lessly obliterated, and the western part of the Punjab was annexed to the kingdom of Ghazni.

That adjoining Kashmir escaped a similar fate at the beginning of the eleventh century was due to its rampart of protective mountains and passes effectively snow-blocked in winter, the season favoured by Mahmud for all his Indian campaigns. Twice Mahmud attempted to invade Kashmir, but with little tangible result. Nevertheless, the very fact of its isolation gave scope for trouble within its own frontiers. Four separate dynasties succeeded one another, all but one of them as the result of rebellions, and the history of Kashmir in the early medieval period, politically speaking, was generally one of chaotic disorder.

Durlabha Vardhana, a contemporary of Harsha Vardhana, had become the founder of the Karkota dynasty in the seventh century. He himself was of lowly origin but rose from service as officer in charge of horse fodder for the army to become the son-in-law of the reigning king. Upon his father-in-law's death, he made himself king and established a new dynasty. It was Durlabha's grandson, Lalitaditya Muktapida, who proved to be the outstanding king of the Karkota line. He was born with an insatiable appetite for conquest. Choosing his own time to lead an army down through the mountain passes into the Indian plains, he attacked Kanauj in the eighth century and drove away or killed its ruler, Yasovarman. He then marched on across Bengal to the sea, turned south, and marched back again across the whole of the Deccan. Finally he returned to Srinagar, bringing with him eight times the treasure with which he had set out several years before. No sooner had he reached home than he set out once more for the north, with the intention of subduing the hardy border tribe of the Dards. From this wild adventure, he never came back. His war-weary soldiers, it is said, smothered him in his tent. Jayapida, his grandson, followed a similar military career, and in order to raise funds for the army exacted intolerable taxes from the people. He was succeeded by several weak rulers until, about the middle of the ninth century, the last of the Karkotas was overthrown by Avantivarman, founder of the Utpala dynasty.

Avantivarman is remembered as the greatest and best of all the Kashmiri kings. Inheriting an empty treasury, he sensibly decided to stay at home and devote his energies to the rehabilitation of the half-starved peasantry. He introduced schemes of irrigation and land reclamation and put down the haughty land barons, known as Damaras, who were creating disorder everywhere in the country-side. Unfortunately his successors were

weaklings, and a palace upheaval in 939 abruptly ended the
Utpala dynasty and brought in the dynasty of the usurpur
Parvagupta.

The next king died after a brief reign of only six years, and
his widowed queen Didda, a remarkable woman in many ways
but ruthless and intriguing, then ruled the kingdom of Kashmir
for half a century, first as regent in the name of her minor son
and after his death in her own name. On her mother's side
she was a granddaughter of the Shahi king Bhima, and on her
father's, of Lahara chieftains of the Poonch area. Just before
her death, in 1003, Didda nominated a Lahara nephew, Sam-
gramaraja, as her successor. One of his early acts was to send
a Kashmiri force under Tunga, a one-time herdsman who had
been elevated to the rank of a minister by Didda, to aid Trilo-
chanapala Shahi, son and successor of Anandapala, in the
continued fighting in the Punjab against the Muslims, but the
allies were scattered as usual.

For the next three centuries Kashmir was ruled by Lahara
kings, but many of them were incompetent, cruel and profligate,
and Kashmir was rapidly being reduced to a pitiful state. Turks
and other Muslim adventurers were increasingly infiltrating into
the mountain kingdom, sure of finding ready employment in the
army, and at length one of them staged a successful revolt.
Taking the title of Shams-ud-din, in 1339 he became the first
Muslim ruler of Kashmir.

The Shahi kingdom of the Punjab was now gone. Multan,
Mathura and Kanauj had been taken and ravaged. But still the
warning went unheeded. Former Rajput feudatories of the
Pratiharas, for some time past already restlessly trying to throw
off their compulsory allegiance to Kanauj, lost no more time.
They asserted their independence and then, each hoping to
augment his territory and fill up his treasury at his neighbours'
expense, plunged deep into wasteful wars with another. The
history of the eleventh and twelfth centuries becomes mainly a
monotonous story of their struggles, culminating in the fitful
emergence of some half dozen powerful new kingdoms.

The richest, on account of its valuable trading ports along the
western coast, was Gujarat. The Solanki dynasty of Gujarat
dates from the middle of the tenth century, at which time Mularaja murdered his uncle of the minor Chavada, or Chapa, line,
and made himself ruler of the territory around Anhilwara, fifty
miles north of modern Ahmedabad. One tradition says he was
the grandson of a Western Chalukya prince of Kalyana, who
had earlier gone to seek his fortune in Kanauj. The idea is

supported by the other name of the dynasty, Chalukya — or Chaulukya, as some prefer to spell it — of which Solanki is a local corruption. On the other hand, the Solankis themselves claimed to be Fire-initiated Rajputs, and were always accepted as such. In the early days, the Pratiharas were their overlords, but Mularaja strengthened his kingdom of Anhilwara by quickly annexing Kutch, Saurashtra and southern Gujarat, and thereafter seems to have paid little attention to Kanauj.

In 1025, Gujarat had to face a great disaster. Iconoclastic zeal and greed for riches inspired Mahmud and his Ghaznavids to march with great speed towards the temple of Somnath on the shore of the Arabian Sea, in Saurashtra. This temple was dedicated to Shiva as the Moon-God, and was one of the most famous temples of the time and a repository of untold wealth. Mahmud crossed the Rajputana desert in what was to be his next to last expedition into India, and presented himself suddenly before the gates of Anhilwara. Bhima I, the Solanki king, fled to Kutch, and Mahmud occupied the city, where he rested and re-provisioned his army, and then passed on to Somnath. For three days and nights, pillage and slaughter were carried on with indescribable fury. The vast treasure seized was loaded on camels, and the invaders set out for Ghazni by way of Sind. As soon as they had departed, Bhima returned and began the work of rebuilding Somnath.

It was some time after this catastrophe that Bhima, in alliance with the Kalachuri king Karna, launched a destructive attack on Malwa, which lay between Gujarat and Chedi, in southern Rajputana. Enmity between Gujarat and Malwa was of long standing, and it continued even throughout the reign of Bhima I's grandson Jayasimha Siddharaja (1094-1143), most powerful of Solanki rulers, and also during the reign of his successor Kumarapala. But Gujarat again became the object of attack by Muslims, in 1178. Muizz-ud-din, the future Muhammad Ghuri, then came down into India through Sind, for the first time. He was driven back and failed to occupy Anhilwara, but he did not forget his discomfiture. Twenty years later his general Qutb-ud-din Aibak succeeded, where he had failed, though he was unable to hold on to Anhilwara for long. Taking advantage of the growing state of disorder, a Vaghela feudatory of the Solankis seized power in the thirteenth century and established his own dynasty. It was in the reign of the third Vaghela king that Gujarat was once more invaded, this time by the imperial Muslim army of Delhi, and was finally annexed to the Sultanate in 1297. Thus ended Hindu rule in the kingdom of Gujarat.

The rise and fall of Malwa followed a similar pattern except that the Paramara chieftains, also Agni-kula Rajputs, ruled as Rashtrakuta vassals in the ninth century. Ujjain was situated in Malwa, and since this had been the original seat of Pratihara power, Malwa naturally became a bitter bone of contention between Rashtrakutas and Pratiharas, as a result of which the Paramaras were alternately vassals of one or the other, until Munja Paramara established its independence at the end of the tenth century.

The Western Chalukyas of Kalyana had by then taken the place of the Rashtrakutas as the leading power in the Deccan. Tailapa II Chalukya waged many wars to recover the lost territories of his predecessors. Munja found himself forced to fight a long series of southern campaigns, and at last, in an effort to end these Chalukyan wars, rashly crossed over the Godavari against the advice of his minister, was captured and was killed. After a short reign by a younger brother the great Bhoja succeeded in about A.D. 1000.

Bhoja is still considered an ideal Indian king. His fame rests on his many-sided accomplishments, including his reputation as a warrior. Incessant campaigns were carried on against all his neighbours, Kalachuris and Chandellas on the east, Chalukyas on the south and Solankis on the west, and he was one of those who also sent a contingent to fight Mahmud of Ghazni in the Punjab. His unfriendly relations with his contemporaries ultimately brought disaster upon him, however. The Solanki king Bhima I and the Kalachuri king Karna, as mentioned above, simultaneously attacked Malwa from both sides around the middle of the eleventh century. Bhoja's beautiful capital of Dhara was occupied, and in the midst of this melancholy campaign Bhoja himself suddenly died, leaving Malwa to be ruthlessly plundered. The allies presently fell out and a Paramara ruler got back his throne, but the old wars between Malwa and Gujarat broke out again in the twelfth century. One weak ruler succeeded another, and Malwa was repeatedly invaded. Eventually it was conquered by the Muslims in the early fourteenth century.

The Kalachuri kingdom of Chedi in central India lay along the upper reaches of the Narbada, in what now forms part of Madhya Pradesh. The Chedi capital was Tripuri, a few miles from present-day Jabalpur. The first known king of the Kalachuri dynasty was Kokkalla I, who appears to have flourished in the second half of the ninth century. After the break-up of the Pratihara empire, the Kalachuris, under their two most powerful leaders, Gangeyadeva and his son Lakshmi-Karna, became a powerful force to reckon with in the India of their time.

Gangeyadeva overran all the territory up to Banaras, and even raided Magadha and Bengal, though in 1034 he was unable to save Banaras from a looting attack by Nialtigin, Ghaznavid governor of Lahore. Karna continued the same expansionist policy of his father. He took Allahabad, led invasions into both western Bengal and Kalinga, crossed swords with Cholas and Chalukyas, and penetrated as far north as the Kangra valley. He also inflicted a humiliating defeat on Kirtivarman Chandella, whose kingdom lay just north of Chedi. It was he who invaded Malwa with Bhima I Solanki. Later the Solankis attacked and defeated Karna in his turn, and the Chandellas also won back all the territory they had been forced to yield. Towards the end of the eleventh century, Yasahkarna, Karna's son by a Huna princess, won a victory in the Deccan over the Eastern Chalukyas of Vengi. In spite of their military prowess the Kalachuris sank back into vassalage under the Gahadavalas some time in the twelfth century.

Another of the great medieval dynasties was the Chandella dynasty of Jejakabhukti (Bundelkhand, in Uttar Pradesh). In the ninth century its rulers were subservient to Kanauj, but by the following century they had grown strong enough to intervene in a Pratihara quarrel for succession between two half brothers. They were successful in placing their candidate, Mahipala, on the throne, and even helped him to recover Kanauj after its sack by Indra III Rashtrakuta. in 914. Before the middle of the century, however, Yasovarman Chandella boldly seized the strong fortress of Kalanjara, which guarded the southern flank of the Pratihara empire, and made his kingdom independent in all but name. Kalanjara, Mahoba and Khajuraho were then developed as the chief centres of the Chandella kingdom.

Yasovarman was outstripped in military aggressiveness by his son Dhanga. Dhanga first seized the eastern Pratihara territories, and afterwards made successful forays into Kosala and distant Bengal. He also annexed Gwalior, another strong fortress, whose Kachchhapaghata ruler was a Pratihara feudatory. Dhanga joined the other Indian kings who answered the Shahi king Jayapala's earliest call for help in his encounter with Sabuktigin, in 939. Like the rest, he suffered defeat on that occasion.

Early in the eleventh century he was succeeded by his son Ganda, and Ganda also sent a force to aid Anandapal, in 1008, in his fight with Mahmud. Chandella hostility towards the Muslim invaders remained active, and when a decade later

Rajyapala Pratihara handed over Kanauj to Mahmud, almost without a struggle, Ganda felt so enraged that he sent Vidyadhara, the Chandella crown prince along with his Kachchhapaghata feudatory Arjuna, to punish him. Rajyapala was overtaken in the forest to which he had fled and put to death on the spot. Mahmud, who now looked on Rajyapala as his protégé, retaliated by promptly marching against Kalanjara the next year, and now it was the turn of Vidyadhara tamely to submit. He paid a huge ransom, got back his fort and saved his life.

Later Chandella history records a number of serious defeats, not only at the hands of their Kalachuri neighbours, long a constant menace to them, but quite suddenly from a new quarter. Prithviraja III Chauhan, king of Ajmir and Delhi, seized Mahoba and other forts from Paramardi (Paramal) Chandella in 1182. Although Paramardi recovered them, his reprieve was short. Qutb-ud-din Aibak, now the master of Delhi, marched on to Kalanjara in 1202. In the face of overwhelming superiority, Paramardi capitulated, and for this act of cowardice, as he deemed it, his minister Ajayaseva killed him, but himself had to surrender the fort when the defenders ran out of water. A Muslim governor was installed, though Chandella rulers survived the disaster, and continued to exercise considerable power until as late as the fourteenth century.

The political pattern of the various Indian kingdoms in the north was now undergoing a notable change. As a result of the ever-shifting struggle for supremacy, the Chauhans of Ajmir and Delhi and the Gahadavalas of Kanauj had become the two most formidable powers in northern India by the middle of the twelfth century. At this time the Rajput Chauhans dominated the western half of India from Gujarat to Delhi, and the Gahadavalas the eastern part, up to Patna in Bihar. The Chauhans had been expanding from their original seat of Sakambhari, in Rajputana, for some centuries, but the Gahadavalas had arisen from obscurity only in the last quarter of the eleventh century, when they occupied Kanauj, and with this triumph laid claim to all the territory formerly belonging to their predecessors, the imperial Pratiharas.

Rivalry was greatly intensified when Vigraharaja IV Visaladeva Chauhan seized Delhi from its Tomara ruler a little after the middle of the twelfth century. Delhi at this time was only a small desert kingdom, which had been founded by a chieftain of the Tomara clan of Rajputs some two centuries before, but it had acquired strategic importance with its absorption of what was left of the Punjab after Mahmud's conquest, and the Gahadavalas held it rightfully theirs as a one-time vassal state of the Pratiharas. When Prithviraja III became king and made Delhi a second Chauhan capital, in addition to Ajmir, enmity between the two powers naturally increased (though Prithviraja and Jayachandra, the contemporary Gahadavala king, were first cousins, their mothers being two daughters of the last Tomara king). To make matters worse — if the romantic story is to be believed — Prithviraja now even had the audacity to attend un-invited at Kanauj the *svayamvara* of Jayachandra's daughter Samyogita, and to carry off the princess (with her willing con-sent) from under the very noses of his cousin the king and the assembled princes eagerly hoping for the garland of her choice.

A time of destiny was approaching, and India could ill afford to be divided and weakened by petty personal quarrels and irre-concilable ambitions. Muhammad Ghuri was now the undisputed master in the north, and he had made up his mind to conquer India. Gahadavala kings in the past had fought against minor Ghaznavid invasions, but on this critical occasion Jayachandra held back his huge army and did not join Prithviraja in the defence of the country. Perhaps he foolishly thought that if his rival were to be defeated, he himself would then become ruler of the whole of Hindustan.

Muhammad Ghuri advanced from Lahore and met the hastily summoned forces of Prithviraja at Tarain in the Punjab, eighty miles from Delhi, in 1191. In this first encounter, victory was with the Indians. Muhammad was seriously wounded by an arrow shot from the bow of the governor of Delhi and would have fallen on the battle-field if a Khalji foot-soldier had not jumped up onto his horse and, holding him from behind, galloped with him to safety. The whole Muslim army fell back in com-plete disorder towards Ghazni.

Instead of seizing the initiative and following up this victory by attacking the retreating enemy in full force, Prithviraja allowed his commander to waste a whole year in besieging the single fortress of Sirhind, previously occupied by Muhammad, while he himself returned to Ajmir. At the end of a year (which Muham-mad had utilized to reorganize and train a picked force of 120,000 horsemen), the Chauhan king received an arrogant letter advising him to embrace Islam and recognize Muhammad's supremacy, or face the consequences. This time Prithviraja collected a vast army, said to have comprised 300,000 horsemen, 3,000 elephants and innumerable infantrymen. He was also joined by one hundred and fifty princes and chiefs of Hindustan, but not by the Gahada-vala king, who probably commanded the largest army in northern

India at that time. The two armies, Hindu and Muslim, encamped at the same spot in the Punjab as before. The Hindus were falsely led to believe that no battle would actually take place until Muhammad had received a reply from his brother, the Sultan in Ghur, to the peace proposal submitted by Prithviraja. A surprise attack was then launched at dawn when the Indian army was off guard, and before the day was out a hundred thousand Hindus were either slain or had fled — among them Prithviraja. This was the second and decisive battle of Tarain, which took place in 1192.

Whether Prithviraja was overtaken in flight and killed, or led as a prisoner to Ajmir and executed there, is not of material importance. Muhammad and his generals captured all the strong forts on the way to Ajmir, and in the very same year Delhi also fell. Qutb-ud-din Aibak was appointed governor and viceroy in Delhi. The following year he marched against Kanauj. A battle was fought out on the plain between Etawah and Kanauj, in which Jayachandra Gahadavala lost his life. Aibak took Banaras and returned to Delhi. He had now cleared Hindustan — the heart of northern India — of opponents, and when his master, Muhammad Ghuri was assassinated by a vengeful tribesman on the bank of the Indus a few years later, he assumed the full title of Sultan, and in 1206 became the first independent Muslim ruler in India.

No mention has yet been made of the important eastern zone of India, spared by the early Muslim invaders for two long centuries. In Bengal chaos had followed Harsha's death, as a result of invasions from Assam and Tibet, and by Yasovarman of Kanauj and Muktapida of Kashmir, who had successively laid waste the land. In the eighth century, things had reached such a pass that the people, or more probably their leading chieftains, got together in desperation and elected one of themselves as king. The choice fell on Gopala, a Buddhist, and all the kings of his dynasty, which was to rule for nearly four centuries, added the suffix *Pala*, " protector ", to their names, and all remained faithful to Buddhism, long after it had begun to die out elsewhere in India.

Gopala contented himself with consolidating the little kingdom over which he had been invited to rule, Varendra in the north and Vanga, or Banga — whence Bengal — in the southeast. The next two kings, Dharmapala and Devapala, proved to be among the great military geniuses of the age, and under them the Palas energetically joined the triangular struggle with Pratiharas and Rashtrakutas for the sovereignty of northern India.

11

Dharmapala annexed Gauda, or western Bengal, and south Bihar, the ancient Magadha, after which the old Mauryan capital of Pataliputra became the new Pala capital. Kanauj, always a symbol of imperial prestige, was Dharmapala's next objective. After its capture, he placed his protégé Chakrayudha on the throne, but Nagabhata II Pratihara promptly drove Chakrayudha away, himself occupied Kanauj, and inflicted a serious defeat on Dharmapala in a pitched battle fought at Monghyr. According to Rashtrakuta inscriptions, both Dhruva and Govinda Rashtrakuta also got the better of Dharmapala at one time or another. Such reverses, however, did not prevent the Pala army from sweeping victoriously to the foothills of the Himalayas, and on through the Punjab and into Afghanistan. Eastern Rajputana, down to the Vindhyas, was also overrun. A great number of kings and princes of northern India hastened to acknowledge Pala supremacy and offer tribute, after this triumphal march.

Devapala turned his attention to the east and south. Assam decided that the time had now come to adopt the prudent course of bowing to Pala might, and so escaped without a war. Utkal, that part of Orissa touching Bengal in the south, was compelled to submit by force. Before the end of the ninth century, victorious Pala arms had been carried from the Brahmaputra to Rajputana, and from the Himalayas to the Vindhyas. Outside India in Tibet, Burma and Sumatra, the name Pala was identified with India itself.

In the eleventh century, when the rest of northern India was groaning under the attacks of Mahmud or of the Ghaznavid governors of Lahore, Bengal had its own troubles to face. In 1021, Rajendra Chola led his daring incursion into southwestern Bengal. Kalachuris and Chandellas in turn made extensive raids into western Bengal. Vikramaditya VI marched his Chalukyan army across Bengal all the way to the border of Assam, in 1066. Minor Chandra and Varman dynasties appeared in east Bengal, and in the north a dangerous revolt shortly broke out among the aboriginal Kaivartas. When Bengal had sunk to a low ebb, Ramapala came to the throne, and not only succeeded in putting down the recalcitrant feudatories and suppressing the revolts, but made aggressive attacks on Assam and Kalinga. Thus for a brief time in the twelfth century, Pala Bengal regained much of its former glory and power. About the middle of the century, however, the death-blow to Pala rule was delivered by the newly arising Senas.

The Sena dynasty ruled in Bengal for less than a century. On the basis of an inscription stating that Samantasena, the first known member of the family, performed valorous feats of arms in Karnataka in his youth, but later frequented the sacred hermitages along the Ganga, it is believed that the Senas came originally from the Deccan. They are called Brahmin-Kshattriyas in some of their inscriptions, indicating in all probability that they were Brahmins to begin with but, having taken to the profession of arms, changed caste and won recognition as warriors and kings. How Samantasena reached Bengal is unknown, unless he came along with either the Chola or Chalukya invaders and subsequently settled down there. At any rate, before the end of the eleventh century his son had acquired a small principality in Radha, or southwestern Bengal, and his grandson, Vijayalakshmansena, soon emerged as the destroyer of the Palas and the conqueror of Bengal for the Senas.

Lakshmansena, Vijayalakshman's grandson, came to the throne rather late in life, probably about 1180. He had earlier won many notable victories in the battle-field, including the defeat at Gaya of Jayachandra Gahadavala. This important success effectively arrested any further advance eastward by the Gahadavalas. An inscription records that Lakshmansena also planted " pillars of victory " both at Banaras and Allahabad. Besides the conquest of Bengal, the chief change brought about by the Senas was the restoration of Hinduism in this part of India. The Pala kings had all favoured Buddhism. The Senas were staunch Hindus. They were at first worshippers of Shiva, but Lakshmansena became a convert to Vaishnavism.

In his old age, while staying at Nadia, he and his dynasty suffered an irreparable calamity. The popular story, as told by a Muslim chronicler, Minhaj, is that Muhammad Bhaktiyar Khalji, a Turkish soldier of fortune, with a small advance guard of only eighteen men, arrived at Nadia, where they were mistaken for horse-dealers and so were allowed to pass unhindered into the city. Swift on their heels came the rest of the Muslim army of Muhammad Bhaktiyar. Fighting broke out in front of the palace, and the old king, who was taking his meal at the moment, hastily escaped by a back door and made his way eastward. He lived on for a year or two, and two of his sons exercised some sort of authority in east Bengal for a little while longer, but all real power of the Senas was broken. Bengal, too, only ten years after the second battle of Tarain, became part of the Sultanate of Delhi.

Only co-ordinated resistance could have saved India, and it has been amply shown that India in the centuries immediately preceding the Muslim conquest was politically divided, and therefore weak. Yet it is well to remember that the all-but-forgotten Indian kingdoms of early medieval times were larger and more populous, richer and more cultured, than their contemporaries in Europe, and that many of their dynasties, in spite of constant wars, lasted a quite respectable number of centuries. Each of the kingdoms made distinctive contributions to the civilization and culture of India as a whole, and these centuries were, in fact, centuries of extraordinary vitality and grace.

CHAPTER XII

The Wider Horizon

A MILITARY decision on the field of battle can make or unmake kings, but toppling dynasties do not necessarily mean the end of an epoch. The great classical traditions of the Gupta period remained the basis of Indian culture and civilization long after the Gupta kings were gone. There was exchange, modification, adaptation, rather than destruction. Not until India had lost its freedom to alien conquerors twice over, first to the Muslim invaders from the north and then to the British from over the seas, did the old patterns fade and change.

Information about ordinary people — in other words, most of the population — in early medieval times is mostly indirect. Legal compilations outline the customary rules of marriage and rights of Hindu inheritance according to various schools. Manuals of crafts lay down rules for the work of the artisans. Painted and sculptured representations depict the appealing charm of village life. Popular religious works, like the *Puranas* and the oft-repeated tales of the *Mahabharata* and the *Ramayana,* as well as enormous story collections, reveal the ethics and taste at the people's level. Most of the literary material of the age, however, is aristocratic in flavour. Sanskrit, widely patronized by the Guptas, but beyond the comprehension of the illiterate masses, remained for centuries the chief medium of intellectual expression. Authors composed their works in this language primarily for court circles, the city-bred and the learned.

The peasantry, one might assume off-hand, could have been reduced to nothing but a miserable sort of existence on account of the interminable wars of the medieval period. But armies were recruited from special castes and classes, and villagers were normally left alone. Soldiers marched along important roads and highways, with royal cities and forts as their objectives. The countless scattered villages, lying off the main highways, went unscathed. If by chance fields were trampled or crops seized, in another season they would surely grow green again.

The population being much smaller than today (perhaps only a hundred million, according to estimate) there was no scarcity of land and actual ownership was not a significant factor. Except in the emergency of a famine following serious failure of rains, the peasants normally had enough to eat, and more and of better quality than nowadays. Life was simple, and wants were few and easily satisfied. Village craftsmen and artisans supplied all the rural necessaries. Occupation (and hence caste) was traditionally limited by birth, but within each caste there was formal equality. No individual functioned in a total vacuum, or merely as a microscopic, helpless unit within a harsh competitive system. The group was a solid reality, from which the individual drew dignity and support. Whatever the obvious drawbacks of the Hindu caste system, it has to be acknowledged that it provided social and economic security for the majority of the population.

This security, however, did not extend downward to the so-called " untouchables " at the bottom of society. They suffered all the cruel injustice of an inferior status for which there was no human remedy, a condemnation all the more odious because the services of these unfortunates were indispensable to the rest of the community. They were the scavengers, hunters, butchers, fishermen, leather workers, burners of the dead, basket makers, potters, weavers and washermen. They lived in miserable hamlets on the outskirts of villages and towns, performing their unpleasant duties by day and returning to their own hamlets at night, shunned by respectable society. Hidden away in the jungles and forests were also unassimilated tribal folk having little or no contact with towns and villages.

The family unit, like caste, was a force for strength in medieval India. Within its all-embracing relationships, each member had a special place, but one that automatically changed with time and circumstance, thus introducing considerable variety. Both duties and privileges were flexible in the long run. Multiple little household ceremonies from birth to death, and endless festivals associated with religion, were an inexhaustible source of excitement and pleasure. Even the humblest home could feel the warmth of family life. Such social and spiritual values were real for the people of India, ignored as they may be by those who think only in terms of " economic exploitation " in the present day.

The basic prosperity of the country naturally rested on agriculture and the countryside, but cosmopolitan city life offered lucrative employment to very large numbers of non-cultivators. Superior craftsmen found ready markets among the well-to-do for their silks, brocades and fine muslins, their jewellery and beautifully worked metal dishes, and all kinds of luxury articles. Bankers, merchants' guilds and money-lenders financed, at good profit, trade and business, both within the country and abroad, and even lent money to the rulers to help pay for their wars. The maintenance of big armies required constant recruitment of foot-soldiers, cavalry, and those responsible for the camel corps and elephant divisions. A legion of fletchers, armourers, saddlers, weavers, tailors, tent makers, boat makers, carpenters, carters and wheel-wrights was needed. The commissariat departments offered substantial contracts to the grain-dealers and wholesale suppliers of food and fodder.

The well-known Arab traveller and merchant Sulaiman, who travelled widely in India during the first part of the ninth century, recorded that Devapala's army in Bengal numbered 50,000 elephants, and required the services of no fewer than ten to fifteen thousand washermen just to wash the clothes of the army.

Monarchical government was universal, as elsewhere in the contemporary world, but an Indian king was never a law unto himself. He was bound by ancient rules of kingship, well defined in the books of law and polity. The royal speech and conduct were to be restrained. In administering punishment, a king was expected to abide by the law. Whatever his personal religious preference might be, his duty was to give protection to the followers of all religions and sects, and to make grants impartially for religious purposes from the state funds. In war, he usually accompanied his army on the march, sharing its hardships and dangers. Civilized standards demanded that lives of Brahmins, women and children be spared, and the conquered were not carried away as slaves, nor were temples desecrated. If a defeated king acknowledged the overlordship of the victor and paid the stipulated tribute, he was usually allowed to retain his throne. It was ultimately the ruler of the kingdom who was responsible for the well-being, prosperity and happiness of his people, and tyrants, though they existed in medieval India, were the exception, rather than the rule.

In actual administration the king had the benefit of advice from his council of eight ministers, though he was not compelled to follow it. Governors ruled in the provinces, with subordinate officers appointed to look after districts or groups of villages, but hereditary headmen of villages exercised a good deal of weight in resisting any attempt at illegal exactions by dishonest or rapacious government officers. State revenues were derived from the customary tax of one-sixth of the gross agricultural produce (paid in kind or cash), fines, a share in the produce of mines and fisheries, income from the Crown lands, customs, tolls, ferry-dues, and numerous other minor impositions. Though there was no separation between the privy purse of the ruler and the income of the state, state establishments, including the maintenance of the army, public grants and patronage, and enterprises for the public good and the glory of the kingdom, accounted for the greater part of royal expenditure.

In intervals of peace, Indian kings vied with one another in beautifying their royal cities with palaces, massive walls and gateways, strong forts, artificial lakes and canals, and great temple complexes commemorating outstanding victories. Hundreds of thousands of workmen must have laboured on such enterprises. Often whole generations of sculptor-masons settled down to complete the construction of a single temple. A thousand years have since passed, and jungles and plains lie strewn with the gray ruins of the past, but many of the temples still stand, some even in actual use to this day. What eloquent testimony they bear, in their carved intricacy, to the patient skill of India's medieval artisans !

Every royal court, big or little, seems to have been a centre of refined cultural activity. Kings were often themselves authors of distinction, as also the chief patrons of poets, dramatists, musicians and scholars, and their munificence was imitated by queens and ministers, wealthy merchants, guilds and pious individuals. Even bad kings, like some of the Lohara dynasty of Kashmir, took boastful pride in inviting distinguished poets and scholars from all parts of India to their courts.

Sanskrit, from Gupta times onwards, was widely accepted as the language of administration, culture and commerce all over the country, and the classical modes of expression were now firmly fixed. Popularly associated with the " nine gems " of early classical Sanskrit literature is the name of Vikramaditya of Ujjain (possibly identifiable with the third king of the Gupta line, Chandragupta Vikramaditya II, who lived at the end of the fourth century A.D.) The nine luminaries could scarcely all have been living at the same time, since their activities certainly spanned at least two centuries, but the traditional constellation indicates the varied intellectual interests of the times — Varahamihira the astronomer, Brahmagupta the mathematician and astronomer, Vararuchi the grammarian, Amarsinha the author of a famous Sanskrit dictionary, Dhanvantari the physician, the architect Shanku, the astrologer Kshapanaka, Vaitalika a magician, and finally, Kalidasa, India's foremost poet and dramatist.

The fame of Kalidasa rests solidly on seven surviving works— two *kavyas*, or narrative poems, two lyrics, three plays. The kavyas, *Raghu-vamsa* and *Kumara-sambhava*, are mythological in subject. The two lyrics, *Ritu-samhara,* or " Cycle of Seasons ", and the well-known *Meghaduta,* or " Cloud Messenger ", present the many moods of nature against a background of human emotion, love in the one case, sorrow in the other. The three plays are *Malavikagnimitra,* " Malavika and Agnimitra ", with a plot laid in Sunga times in the second century B.C., *Vikramorvasiya,* " Urvasi Conquered ", based on a legend from a Rigvedic hymn, and *Sakuntala,* the elaboration of a charming tale embedded in the *Mahabharata.*

Unfortunately little or nothing concrete is known about the life of India's greatest poet, but it is generally assumed that Kalidasa belonged to the Maharashtra country and must have been living around the year A.D. 400. His name was widely familiar by the beginning of the seventh century. Those competent to judge are united in their praise of his lyrical genius, his skill in handling a wide variety of Sanskrit metres, his lucidity, his good taste, his sensitiveness to beauty, his tenderness and his happy choice of subjects.

Many imitators, lacking his originality and sincerity, tried to copy him in succeeding centuries. They went on selecting standard themes from the *Ramayana, Mahabharata* and *Puranas,* spinning them out inordinately in a highly ornate and artificial Sanskrit. Gradually a passion developed for clever word jugglery, with two, three or even more meanings all equally valid, so that different stories could be told at one and the same time. Verses were so constructed that they could be read forwards or backwards, or one line, read backwards, was identical with the following line, and so on.

Bharavi, of the sixth or seventh century, though he employed some of the above devices, produced one of the fine classical kavyas, *Kiratarjuniya,* describing Arjuna's fight with Shiva disguised as a hunter. Bhatti, in the seventh century, wrote a poem about the slaying of Ravana, whose real purpose, we are told, was " to illustrate the less common grammatical forms and figures of rhetoric." Kaviraja, around the beginning of the ninth century, was the author of a combined *Ramayana* and *Mahabharata.* Even as late as the twelfth century, Sandhykara Nandi of Bengal is found telling the story of the campaign of Ramapala against the rebellious Kaivartas and, in the same words, the oft-repeated *Ramayana.* Such word acrobatics obviously displayed an amazing skill and ingenuity on the part of India's medieval Sanskrit poets, even if the result was not necessarily poetry of a high order.

An outstanding kavya of a different type is the *Rajatarangini,* or " River of Kings ", a long metrical history of Kashmir, by

Kalhana.   Often acclaimed as the first real Indian history, it
begins with an account of fifty-two mythical kings of Kashmir,
but verifiable dates are given from the equivalent of A.D. 713
onwards, and it ends with contemporary happenings of which the
author had personal knowledge, in the middle of the twelfth
century.   Kalhana's critical objectivity makes his work invaluable
as a source of information not only about events and personalities
in Kashmir, but also about education and culture, and general
customs and manners, in the India of his time.

Lyric poetry in the same centuries also reached a high degree
of sophisticated perfection.   A favourite device of the Sanskrit
lyricists was the production of a " hundred verses " on some
given theme, very often love.   Mayura, Magha, Bhartrihari and
Amaru all composed such " centuries ", between the seventh and
ninth centuries.   Bhartrihari contributed three of them — one on
love, one on polity and one on renunciation.

Often classed as the last and greatest of all Sanskrit lyrics —
but a highly original work not fitting exactly into any conventional
category — is the famous *Gita-govinda* of Jayadeva, who lived
at the court of Lakshmansena, last of the Sena kings of Bengal,
at the close of the twelfth century.   His poem renders devotional
tribute, in very human terms, to the divine love of Radha and
Krishna.   One of its unusual features is the presence of a number
of *padas*, obviously intended to be sung, with specific melodies,
or *ragas*, noted down for each.   The *Gita-govinda* attained
instantaneous popularity, in spite of the political turmoil into
which the whirlwind of the Muslim conquest was just then
plunging the country.   The opening stanza was engraved on a
stone in Patan, in far-away Gujarat, shortly after the original
poem was composed, and by the thirteenth century the work was
already being quoted in Malabar, in the far South.

Sanskrit prose was susceptible to the same general literary
influences, and not infrequently took on the colour of poetry.
Dandin, who is thought to have resided for some time at the
Pallava court of Kanchi during the seventh century, was the
author of a standard work on poetics, but is better remembered
for his popular prose romance *Dasakumara-charita,* or " Adventures of the Ten Princes ".   Thieves, cheats, rogues, false ascetics
and courtesans all have parts to play in this unusual portrayal of
common life, but at the same time Dandin has tricks of supreme
word-skill.   He makes his hero tell his own story in the whole
of the twelfth chapter without the use of single labial, because
his mouth has become sore from too much kissing !   Bana enjoyed
Harsha's patronage at Kanauj in the same century.   His *Harsha-*

charita, more important for its social picture than as biography, and a long artificial prose romance, the *Kadambari*, are both characterized by high-flown and flowery language, typical of the kavya style.

Sanskrit story collections were another notable product of the medieval period, and the Indian tales soon spread far and wide. One of the earliest and best known of these collections is the *Panchatantra*, in mixed prose and verse. When and by whom it was composed is unknown, but a copy of the book was sent in the sixth century as a gift by some unnamed Indian king, along with a game of chess, to the Persian ruler Khusru I. Versions of Buddhist *Jataka* tales are included in this Sanskrit work, but they reappear shorn of any special Buddhist significance. What is left is a typical *niti-shastra*, witty instructions obviously intended for the benefit of the ruling class, in the art of practical life and worldly wisdom. The stories, in which the actors and speakers are all animals, clearly demonstrate the ill effects of vanity, greed, heedlessness, stupidity or cowardice.

The *Panchatantra* afterwards had a fascinating migration. Before the end of the sixth century it was translated into Old Persian, and then from Old Persian into Syriac and Arabic. The Arabic text, called *Kalilah wa Dimnah* (a corruption of the names of two jackals who are principal actors), was ultimately turned into Greek in the eleventh century, and into Hebrew, Latin and Spanish in the thirteenth. The Latin version, entitled " Aesop of Old ", gave the impression that it was the work of the ancient Greek author Aesop, of the sixth century B.C., who is credited with having written similar animal stories, though nothing of his has actually survived. A fourteenth century Greek monk of Constantinople next produced a new version, unblushingly called " Aesop's Fables ". Europe now had a new source of inspiration, and the *Gesta Romanorum*, Boccaccio, Chaucer, Shakespeare, LaFontaine, and the nineteenth century fairy-tale authors Grimm and Hans Andersen, all directly or indirectly drew upon this or borrowed from one another. Eventually some of the stories reached down to the nursery. They also wandered off as far as Iceland and China. In India, twenty-five different versions of the *Panchatantra* are known, the most popular being the eleventh or twelfth century *Hitopadesa*, or " Book of Useful Counsels ", by Narayana. This is still a favourite text-book for beginners in Sanskrit.

Other Indian story collections adopted the same device of a binding frame-work for a cycle of tales. The " Seventy Stories of a Parrot " (*Suka-saptati*), author unknown, is roughly assigned

to the seventh century. A certain merchant who does not trust
his wife too well finds himself compelled to go on a long journey.
He leaves behind a talking parrot, from whom he expects to get
a truthful account of what happens during his absence. By the
simple trick of telling the lady a story every evening, just as she
is on the point of going forth in search of adventure, the parrot
keeps her safely at home for the seventy nights her husband is
away. Naturally there is nothing to report when he returns. The
famous Arabian " The Thousand and One Nights' Entertainment "
has an exactly similar frame-work, very possibly imitated from
the " Seventy Stories of a Parrot." The " Twenty-five Stories
of the Vampire " (*Vetala-panchavinsatika*) and the " Thirty-Two
Tales of the Lion Throne " (*Sinhasanad-vatrimsatika*), both tied
up to the legendary Vikramaditya of Ujjain, are other collections
of the same class.

Kashmir in the eleventh century produced the *Brihat-katha-
manjari*, by Kshemendra, and a still vaster story collection, the
Katha-sarit-sagara, or " Ocean of Story ", by Somadeva, both
containing Sanskrit translations of part of Gunadhya's lost
Brihatkatha (said to have been written in the Paisachi dialect
in the first or second century A.D., by a minister of the Andhra
king Hala). Somadeva explains that his work was written for
the beguilement of king Ananta's queen, Suryavati, and many of
the stories end with the refrain, " The very stones laughed as
they heard these words." The age was a troubled one, and there
must have been plenty of need for beguilement. The Lohara
king, forced to surrender his throne to his wicked son Kalasa,
committed suicide in 1081, and the poor queen threw herself
into the flames of her husband's funeral pyre.

Another highly important achievement of Sanskrit culture,
mainly intended for sophisticated court circles, was in the field
of drama. A comprehensive work of Gupta times, the *Bharata-
natya-Shastra*, is the principal source of information about the
rules governing early Indian drama, which was inseparably
associated with dance and music. The somewhat later *Manasara*,
a text-book on architecture datable to between A.D. 500 and 700,
lays down minute directions for the construction of various kinds
of theatres and halls of music and dance, customarily attached
to palaces.

Of the ten types of Sanskrit plays, the two most important are
the *Nataka* and the *Prakarana*, the former having mythology,
history or political intrigue for its theme, the hero being either
a god or a king, the latter having an original plot and ordinary
people as characters. All the plays open with an invocation to

Shiva, Vishnu or Buddha, which is followed by a prologue between the stage manager and one of the actors or actresses, introducing the name of the author and briefly outlining the plot. The usual number of acts is five or seven, and rigid convention demands a happy ending. Sanskrit plays on the whole are romantic. Many metres, as well as passages in prose, are used. While the hero, important male personages and courtesans — whose profession obviously required cultured manners and speech — always speak in Sanskrit, women in general use Prakrit, and current variations such as Sauraseni, Avanti, Magadhi or Apabhramsa are the speech of appropriate characters.

Medallion with dancing figure from a 11th century Rajputana temple

The dramas of Kalidasa, all classical *Natakas*, have already been mentioned, but in the prologue of "Malavika and Agnimitra" Kalidasa refers to certain of his predecessors. One is Basa, whose work was unknown until one of his plays, *Charudatta,* suddenly turned up among twelve old Sanskrit manuscripts in the palace library at Travancore about fifty years ago. A better known and slightly later version of the same play is *Mrichchhakatika,* rendered into English as the "Toy Cart." In the prologue the work claims to be by one king Sudraka. As this king is otherwise unknown, the attribution is presumed to be fictitious, to give the play a royal stamp. The "Toy Cart" is an outstanding example of the *Prakarana* type of Sanskrit drama. The theme is the love affair of a noble-hearted courtesan, Vasantasena, and a poor Brahmin of Ujjain, Charudatta. The easy-going social life of an ancient Indian capital a thousand years ago is delightfully portrayed.

The *Mudra-Rakshasa,* or "Signet Ring of Rakshasa", by Visakhadatta (who probably lived a century or two after Kalidasa), is another important early play. It has a semi-historical plot, involving the struggle for the throne of Pataliputra between the last Nanda king and Chandragupta Maurya, and their respective ministers are assigned the leading roles. Harsha Vardhana was himself the royal author of three plays, and next in point of time came Bhavabhuti, again with three dramas to his credit. Of these, *Malati-Madhava* is the most outstanding. Bhavabhuti was one of the court poets of Yasovarman of Kanauj in the eighth century. Not nature's smiling face, but her terrible one, appealed to him, and he excelled in descriptive poetry of a grand and sombre style.

Bhatta Narayana, Rajasekhara and Krishna Misra, of the ninth, tenth and eleventh centuries, are other memorable names connected with medieval Sanskrit drama. Bhatta Narayana is remembered for his *Venisamhara,* or "Binding of the Braid of Hair", based on the *Mahabharata* story of Bhima's terrible revenge for Duryodhana's insult to Draupadi when he publicly dragged her by the hair. Rajasekhara lived at Kanauj under the imperial Pratiharas, receiving the patronage of both Mahendrapala and Mahipala. He has left four plays, including one in Prakrit. Of a different category is the *Prabodha-chandrodaya,* or "Rise of the Moon of Knowledge", by Krishna Misra, a protégé of Kirtivarman Chandella in the eleventh century. His play is an allegory pure and simple, glorifying philosophy through personification of abstractions such as Discrimination, Judgment and Knowledge.

An interesting evidence of the honoured place given to drama by medieval Indian kings is the discovery not long ago of fragments of three plays carved on stone slabs. Some of these contain portions of an eleventh century play by Bhoja Paramara, apparently originally incised on the wall of his famous Sanskrit college, the Bhoja Sala, at Dhar. They were found incorporated in the western niche of a mosque built from its ruins. Similarly, stone slabs engraved with portions of two other dramas have come to light in the Arhai-din-ka-Jhompra mosque, at Ajmir. One represents a play credited to the Chauhan king Vigraharaja Visaladeva, conqueror of Delhi in the twelfth century, and the other a play written in his honour by Somadeva, a contemporary.

Apart from pure poetry, drama and stories, the secular output in Sanskrit up to the end of the twelfth century was truly prodigious. Works on astronomy, mathematics, medicine, poetics, music, craft manuals, anthologies, digests of innumerable kinds, legal compendiums, encyclopedias, grammars and dictionaries are simply beyond enumeration. There was even a remarkable work on the science of love (or rather love-making), Vatsyayana's *Kamasutra*, belonging to about the fifth or sixth century. There were also a few semi-historical biographies of kings, but history, except for the *Rajatarangini*, was a neglected subject. India's early contributions in the realm of scientific investigations, however, deserve to be better known.

The father of scientific astronomy in India, as distinct from astrology, was Aryabhata, known to have been teaching astronomy at the age of twenty-three at Pataliputra, in the year A.D. 499. Without the use of a telescope or any modern instrument, Aryabhata was able to calculate by epicycles and eccentric circles the position and courses of the planets, and had reached the conclusion that the earth rotated on its own axis. A special section in his *Aryabhatiya* devoted to pure mathematics describes various original ways to perform mathematical operations, such as the extraction of square and cube roots and the solving of quadratic equations. In all his calculations he used the decimal and place-value systems of numbers, as well as zero, a practice adopted by every other Indian mathematician and astronomer after him, but not generally used in Europe until the sixteenth century.

Varahamihira, in the sixth century, contributed an important summary of five old astronomical works, or *Siddhantas*, two with names suggesting a Greek origin. It is clear that he was not only familiar with Greek astronomy but an admirer of their science. He quotes a saying to the effect that though the Greeks are barbarians, among them this science is duly established, and therefore they are to be honoured as *Rishis*. Another famous astronomer-mathematician, Brahmagupta, was a contemporary of Harsha. His *Siddhanta*, translated or adapted into Arabic under the title of *Sind-Hind*, exercised an important influence on Arabian astronomy in its most formative period. Bhaskara, in the twelfth century, was the author of the well-known *Siddhanta-siromani*, dealing with astronomy, arithmetic and algebra.

The arithmetic section is called *Lilavati*, and is sometimes romantically said to have been written for the benefit of his little daughter, later herself to become an accomplished mathematician. The eight hundred year old Indian arithmetic book cites model problems to be solved, such as : " Eight rubies, ten emeralds and a hundred pearls, which are in thy earring, my beloved, were purchased by me for thee at an equal amount, and the sum of the rates of the three sorts of jewels was three less than half a hundred. Tell me the rate of each, auspicious woman."

For the special study of Bhaskaracharya's works, an astronomical college was founded in the thirteenth century in Khandesh, then under the rule of the Yadava king Singhana. This king, it may be mentioned, was also the patron of Sarangadhara, who produced a highly valuable treatise on Indian classical music, the *Sangita-Ratnakara*.

Medicine and surgery, including veterinary science, received much attention in early centuries in India. Perhaps the oldest medico-botanical dictionary known is the *Nighantu,* by Dhanvantari. Though his date is largely guess-work, a copy of his work was extant at least as early as the eighth century. Long before Dhanvantari, of course, Charaka had already laid the foundations of medicine in India. The medical skill of Nagarjuna (not to be confused with the metaphysician of the same name) is often referred to in medieval Buddhist literature. The second Nagarjuna probably lived between the seventh and tenth centuries. He is credited with the discovery of the process of distillation and a method of converting mild alkali into caustic alkali for use as a disinfectant, and he is the first physician on record to have prescribed mercury as an internal medicine. Vagbhata, in the eighth century, made a popular summary of the ancient *Ayurvedic* system of medicine. The eight chapters of his work discuss treatment of sores, facial disorders including those of eye, ear and nose, bodily ailments excluding the head, mental diseases, children's diseases, antidotes for poisons, reputed means for lengthening life, and general hygiene and health. In the latter half of the eighth century, Indian doctors were being employed as chief medical officers in hospitals in Baghdad, and Indian medicine was highly respected even in China.

Veterinary science was mainly devoted to the study of elephants and horses, indispensable wings of the medieval armies. The *Hasti-ayurveda,* assigned to Gupta or an early post-Gupta period, treats in four sections of 160 chapters all the major and minor diseases of elephants, and gives instructions on elephant surgery. Salihotra was the traditional authority on diseases of horses and their treatment, and several *Asvasastras,* or medical manuals on horses, made their appearance in the middle centuries, cne reputedly by Bhoja. In contrast to medicine, the bright promise of surgery from the days of Susruta was gradually replaced by a dismal blank. *Ahimsa,* the doctrine of non-violence, preached by Buddhism, Jainism and Vaishnavism alike, discouraged animal sacrifices, a religious practice which had once served as a preliminary training school of surgery, through the necessary act of dissection performed by the priests, but it now rapidly fell into disrepute. In the end, its pursuit was left to the barber. Physicians also lost standing on the ground of ritual impurity associated with their profession.

If such, in bare outline, is a mere fragment of the enormous output of secular literature, reflecting the intellectual interests of the times, still more incredible is the outpouring of religious and philosophic works. Buddhists, Jains and Hindus defended their special views with subtle and elaborate arguments, reinforced by imaginative poetic biographies of their founders and their long lines of saints. Philosophers and thinkers speculated endlessly on the origin and evolution of the universe, trying to discover the relationship between Nature and Soul, or Nature, Soul and God. At the same time, inspired hymnists sang of their ecstatic love for the Lord.

As a result of all this churning tumult of questioning and thought, echoing and re-echoing from one end of the country to the other, no Indian could ultimately consider himself a stranger to any of his neighbour's beliefs. He was, in fact, remarkably tolerant of them. Was it not possible, after all, to worship at many shrines ?

By the end of the medieval period, a number of important religious developments had unfolded. Most of the old Vedic gods had moved into the background, and Shiva, Vishnu and *Shakti* had emerged as the principal deities in the new theistic form of Hinduism. Buddhism had practically disappeared, absorbed by Hinduism, and Jainism was more or less confined to the Deccan and western India. The concept of *Shakti* as the principle of dynamic creative Energy responsible for the world (whether the world was looked upon as real or illusory), had permeated to a greater or lesser degree all religious forms of belief, except Jainism. *Shakti* as an indivisible aspect of the Infinite was symbolically conceived as female and worshipped as a goddess, the consort, under different names, of every form of God, but more closely associated with Shiva. Like him, therefore, she had both a benign and a terrible aspect. Even the divine "sons" of Shiva and Parvati, Kartikeya (Subrahmanya, or Muruga) and the elephant-headed Ganesa, became objects of special cults. Out of the *Shakti* idea evolved the distinctive phases of Tantrik Buddhism and Tantrik Hinduism. Another doctrine of outstanding importance also arose among Vaishnavas. This was the conception of *Avatars,* repeated "Descents" of Vishnu, under various forms, for the compassionate rescue of mankind whenever evil was about to overwhelm the world. His two human *Avatars,* Rama and Krishna, captured multitudes of

12

hearts. And finally, image and temple worship rapidly acquired a new emphasis in these prolific centuries.

Buddhism, it will be recalled, had already separated into two main branches, Hinayana and Mahayana (the so-called Lesser and Greater Paths) before the beginning of the first century A.D. The principal difference between them was that Hinayanists, who took their original stand on the Pali canon, maintained that sainthood (*Arhatship*) and liberation of the self (*Nirvana*) were attainable through self-discipline, meditation and strict adherence to the Eightfold Path, as laid down by the Buddha, while Mahayanists chose as their goal, not personal salvation, but salvation for all. For them, the Bodhisattva, rather than Gotama Buddha, was the highest ideal. Each of the main divisions, however, broke up on the basis of what might now seem minor differences in dogma or practice into separate schools or sects, and each school produced an extensive philosophic literature, in support of its doctrines.

Of the Hinayana schools, the Theravada claimed to uphold "the doctrine of the Elders". Other splinter groups were the Sarvastivada, Sautrantika and Vaibhasika. In the fifth century A.D., Vasubandhu (younger brother of Asanga) was the chief exponent of Vaibhasika beliefs, before his subsequent conversion to Mahayana Buddhism, and wrote the outstanding textbook on this system. His pupil was the famous Dinnaga, who directed his sharp intellect to the refutation of contemporary Hindu logic. Dinnaga's work, in turn, formed the basis for no fewer than seven exhaustive compilations on Buddhist logic by Dharmakirtti, in the seventh century. Soon after this, Hinayana died away in India, but found a permanent home outside the land of its birth — in Ceylon, Burma, Cambodia, Thailand and Indo-China.

The oldest Mahayana texts are assigned roughly to the first three centuries A.D. They include the *Lalita-vistara,* a miraculous life of the Buddha, the *Saddharma-Pundarika Sutra,* "Lotus of the True Law", the *Mahaprajna-paramita Sutra,* "Sutra of Transcendental Wisdom", and the *Lankavatara Sutra,* or "Sutra of Self-realization of Noble Wisdom", all written in Sanskrit, by unknown authors. The first Mahayana writer actually known by name is Asvaghosha, who presumably lived around A.D. 100, when he converted to the new faith the great Kushan emperor Kanishka, who afterwards summoned the Fourth Buddhist Council to propagate the Mahayana doctrine and arrange for Sanskrit translations of the Pali canon. Asvaghosha was the author of the *Buddha-charita,* a popular poetic life of the Buddha on the model of the *Lalita-vistara,* and among his more important philosophic works, according to the Chinese tradition, was the *Mahayana-shraddhotpada-shastra*, or " Awakening of Faith in Mahayana."

All these early Mahayana texts were quickly translated into Chinese, and then into Tibetan, and were studied for centuries throughout the whole Buddhist world. By a strange twist of fate, when the Sanskrit originals were ultimately lost in India, they were restored, in modern times, through the medium of these foreign versions.

Like the Hinayanists, the Mahayanists broke up into several sects, of which the two chief ones were known by either of their twin names — Madhyamika or Sunyavada, Vijnanavada or Yogachara. The first was founded by Nagarjuna, born in the Deccan a century or two after Asvaghosha's time. His *Madhya-mika-karika*, or " Verses on the Middle Way ", presented the abstruse doctrine that nothing possessed any independent essence of its own, hence any real existence. The impression of unbroken continuity falsely held by the mind had no more reality than the circle of flame traced by a whirling torch. All phenomena were a fleeting illusion, and all that could really be said to exist was *Sunya, Void*.

The second school, Vijnanavada or Yogachara, was founded at Peshawar in the fifth century by Asanga, and received strong support from Vasubandhu after he had renounced his attachment to Vaibhasika. Starting from the position of Nagarjuna, Yogacharins went a step further. They reached the conclusion that reality was nothing but Pure Consciousness, the infinity of possible Ideas, the Dream of a Dream. Mystic apprehension of the essential nature of the dream was possible, not through logic or reason, but through introspection and meditation. Yet life had to be lived, and the moral teachings of the Buddha on righteous conduct for the individual, and the inspiring all-embracing compassion of the Bodhisattvas, persuaded Yoga-charins, like other Mahayana Buddhists, to pursue with diligence the " illusory emancipation from illusory bondage of illusory beings." This was the school of thought Yuan Chwang came all the way from China to India to study, in the seventh century.

Signs of Buddhist disintegration, however, were by now already beginning to appear within the monastic organization. In Bengal, under the Buddhist Pala kings, and to some extent in Kashmir, Buddhism survived in its Tantrik form, but with a new esoteric philosophy, new texts, new rituals, new types of cult images. It was this form of Mahayana Buddhism that passed on to Nepal and Tibet. After making an immeasurable contribution to the religious thought of India and to its civilization and art, for well over a millennium, Buddhism finally made way for other religious impulses surging through the country.

Jainism, meanwhile, followed a not dissimilar path of development and decline. Though it never took root outside of India, neither on the other hand did it ever completely lose its hold within India itself. The two original monastic divisions — Digambara, " sky-clad ", and Svetambara, " white-clad " — are still in existence, and the Jain lay community, numbering around two millions, remains a prominent element of the population. Though observing more lenient rules than monks, the Jain laity nevertheless is subject to notable restrictions. Its members do not take up military careers. They do not become agriculturists, lest their plows destroy life in the ground. In strict practice, they are not supposed even to walk at night, for fear of inadvertently crushing some insect. They are, of course, vegetarians. They maintain charitable institutions, especially hospitals and homes for sick and decrepit animals, and generously support the order of monks and nuns. Gandhi was born in Gujarat, a present-day Jain stronghold, and though not a Jain, was deeply influenced by Jain precepts in his youth. He not only adopted *Ahimsa,* non-injury, as his personal creed, but as all the world knows made non-violence the key-note of his political programme in the national freedom struggle.

The oldest part of the Jain canon is composed in an early Jain Prakrit, and is supposed to be a reconstruction of fourteen original *Purvas,* lost after the time of Mahavira, Gotama Buddha's elder contemporary, though this section is not recognized as authentic by Digambaras. The sacred texts as a whole were rearranged and settled at a council held at Valabhi, in Gujarat, in the sixth century. Jain writers continued to use various kinds of Prakrits, but in order to make their doctrines more widely known also adopted Sanskrit. Early Jain works also exist in Tamil, and from the ninth to the twelfth centuries Jain authors made significant contributions to the development of Kannada, the regional language of the western Deccan.

Translations, poetic commentaries, refined explanations of Jain metaphysics, hymns, collections of moral tales associated with sixty-three great Jain personages, resembling the early Buddhist *Avadanas,* or " Stories of Great Deeds ", and Jain *Puranas* extolling the twenty-four *Tirthankaras,* in imitation of the Hindu *Puranas,* were produced in great numbers. Of the Tirthankaras or Jinas, only the last two, Mahavira and his predecessor Parsava, have any known historical reality. Yet the stupendously conceived " Self-conquerors " of Jain tradition were presented as having

shown the way out of worldly entanglement and sorrow, through
ages past, for those groping in darkness. They taught that the
soul, linked by *karma* with matter in life after life, can be freed
only by right faith, right knowledge and right conduct. Jainism,
like Buddhism, had no place for the idea of God as creator of the
universe, and the Tirthankaras were never looked upon as gods.
Nevertheless their images were set up in Jain temples, where they
were worshipped just as Mahayana Buddhists and Hindus worshipped the images of their gods.

Jain authors by no means confined themselves to religious and
ethical subjects. They produced stories, dramas, anthologies,
works on poetics, logic, grammar and science, and also made
valuable studies in the Prakrit languages, which were in due
course to become the modern languages of northern India. The
most prolific and best known of the later Jain writers was
Hemachandra, who resided at the Solanki court of Anhilwara at
the end of the eleventh and beginning of the twelfth century, and
who converted Kumarapala, the Solanki ruler, to Jainism. He
was the author of no fewer than four dictionaries, including a
Prakrit lexicon, two grammars, a manual on poetics, an exposition of Jain ethics, a long poem on the " Sixty-three ", and a
poetic life of his patron Kumarapala, the last four cantos of which
were composed in four different Prakrits.

While Buddhism and Jainism were called " unorthodox ",
because of their refusal to accept the Vedas as revealed scripture
and their denial of any necessity to postulate a creator God, both
were highly ethical, enjoining upon their followers righteousness
in thought, word and deed. A very different school, going back
to about as early beginnings, was that of the Charvakas, or
Lokayatas, which continued to flourish long into the middle ages,
in spite of the fact that it set itself up against any form of religion,
and preached only crass materialism. Charvakas not merely
denied God and the infallibility of the Vedas, but totally rejected
karma and any idea of an after life. They poured ridicule on the
performance of age-old rituals and ceremonies. The only valid
source of knowledge about anything, they argued, was direct sense
perception. Hence body was the only reality, and enjoyment the
only aim of life. Eat, drink and be merry !

Of the original treatise of this school, ascribed to Brihaspati,
only cynical fragments survive in the form of quotations by later
writers. One familiar verse advises a man to go borrow money to
buy *ghee* (melted butter), for his feasting. The authors of the
Vedas are called rogues and buffoons. Priests jabber nonsense.
It was easy for followers of this sort of " philosophy " to slip into

unbridled licence, and they and their doctrines aroused the contempt of most serious thinkers and of society in general. Their
theories and assumptions were still being attacked as late as the
thirteenth century.

As a reaction to the sharp challenge of rebel religions and
thought-systems, what are known as the six orthodox schools of
Hindu philosophy took up a great deal of intellectual attention in
early medieval times. The six *Darsanas,* that is, " perceptions of
truth ", were philosophy, in the sense that they sought to establish a coherent and systematic approach to knowledge itself.
They were orthodox, in that they took their stand on the Vedas,
though each emphasized some different aspect of Vedic thought.
They tried to reinterpret and carry forward ancient ideas, mostly
derived from the Upanishads — about cosmic evolution, man's
place in it, what constitutes soul or self, means and methods of
attaining knowledge, the nature of moral duty, the ultimate unity
behind the bewitching diversity of world appearances. They were
not concerned with the idea of God, though *Isvara,* as agency of
the universe, is mentioned here and there. They were interested
in the methods and principles to be followed in the search for
spiritual knowledge.

The Six *Darsanas* are often grouped in complementary pairs :
Samkhya and *Yoga, Nyaya* and *Vaisesika, Purva Mimamsa* and
Vedanta (also known as *Uttara Mimamsa.*) The founder-
authors traditionally associated with the *Sutras* forming the basis
of each particular system are respectively Kapila, Patanjali,
Gautama, Kanada (Kasyapa), Jaimini and Badarayana. Three
are shadowy figures presumed to have lived between the sixth and
third centuries B.C. Patanjali is usually assigned to the second
century B.C. and Jaimini and Badarayana to the early centuries
A.D., though the date of the latter is quite uncertain. The ideas
they developed had been floating in the atmosphere from the time
of the Upanishads (eighth century B.C.), but the Sutras attempted
to systematize them into coherent doctrines. Sutras were strings
of extremely concise aphorisms, originally intended as memory
guides for advanced students receiving oral instruction from
competent teachers, and were an exceedingly popular form of
Sanskrit expression for several centuries. Because of their cryp-
tic brevity, however, they were difficult to understand, and endless
commentaries were written to explain them. This went on,
century after century, throughout the whole of the medieval
period. The concepts they put forward gradually permeated
Indian thought, and in differing degrees came to be more or less
accepted as part of Hinduism.

Samkhya was dualistic in outlook, maintaining that there were two eternal and separate realities, *Purusha* and *Prakriti*, cosmic soul and cosmic matter (or nature.) Individual souls were many, and *Prakriti*, which included mind, had three co-existing constituents, or aspects, called *Gunas* — illumination, energy and inertia (*Sattva, Rajas* and *Tamas*). The whole universe was an orderly unfolding of twenty-five principles. Discrimination between *Purusha* and *Prakriti* constituted knowledge.

Yoga concentrated on the method of perfecting the instrument of perception, through meditation and spiritual discipline directed to the control of body, senses and mind, leading to discrimination and direct experience of union with the object of meditation or devotion.

Nyaya dealt with the process of reasoning and logic, as based on perception, inference and comparison, with valid testimony accepted as an additional factor.

Vaisesika concerned itself with a logical analysis of the external world and the particular properties or essential differences distinguishing one thing from another, the cosmos being considered as the outcome of the action and interaction of nine eternal realities.

Mimamsa stressed *Dharma*, right action, as the only path leading to knowledge, but defined right action as the performance of beneficial rituals and sacrifices enjoined in the older portion of the Vedas.

Vedanta, meaning the end portion or conclusion of the Vedas, declared that ultimate reality was not two but one — *Brahman, Atman*, the Universal Self. The individual soul was one with *Atman*, not separate from it. When the veil of *Maya* was removed by knowledge, and world appearance was perceived as unreal in essence, then the soul would realize its true nature of *Sat-chit-ananda*, "truth-knowledge-bliss."

The Upanishads, the *Vedanta-sutra* of Badarayana and the *Bhagavad-gita* were the chief textbooks of the Vedanta school of philosophy, but the same texts gave rise to three different interpretations. Shankaracharya (8th century) was the great exponent of *Advaita*, non-dualism. *Visistadvaita*, qualified non-dualism, was taught by Ramanuja (11th century). *Dvaita*, or dualism, found in Madhava (12th century) its fervent spokesman.

Shankara, often described as the greatest mind India has ever produced, was so outstanding in his penetrating analysis that his name is practically considered synonymous with *Vedanta*. His fame rests on his great commentaries on the principal Upanishads, the *Vedanta-sutra* and the *Bhagavad-gita,* on a few independent philosophical treatises, such as the *Viveka-Chudamani,* " Crest Jewel of Discrimination ", and several magnificent *Stotras,* or hymns. With his razor-sharp intellect, he pointed out in his commentaries all the flaws in current doctrines, including Buddhist metaphysics, and did much to demolish them.

Biographical details of Shankara's life are disappointingly meagre. He was born in a Nambudri Brahmin family at Kaladi, in Malabar, towards the end of the eighth century. (There is no certainty, but his dates are usually given as A.D. 788-820.) He left home at an early age to join a Vedic school on the banks of the Narbada, where his teacher was Govindapada, chief disciple of Gaudapada. Gaudapada has sometimes been called the real founder of *Advaita Vedanta,* because he was the first to present a systematic elucidation of the Upanishad teaching of the *Atman,* in his *Mandukya-karika.* He did not find any antagonism between this teaching, however, and Mahayana Buddhist philosophy. Buddha, he said, was one who " by knowledge as wide as the sky, had realized that all appearances were vacuous."

The precocious pupil soon outstripped the teacher. Having completed his studies and adopted the life of a *Sannyasin,* Shankara first went to Banaras to gain acceptance from scholars there for his interpretation of the Upanishads. The rest of his short life was spent in wandering all over India and meeting countless opponents and refuting their arguments in open debate. He organized ten Orders of Sannyasins and founded four monastic centres on the four sides of India, Sringeri in Mysore, Puri in Orissa, Dwarka in Gujarat and Badrinath in the Himalayas. All are still in existence. The tradition is that he died in the Himalayas, while yet only thirty-two years of age. *Vedanta* took India back to the source of its ancient wisdom, and Shankara supplied Hinduism with a firm philosophic background.

All this literary and intellectual activity in India at a time corresponding to Europe's Dark Ages obviously indicated that facilities for education were fairly widespread. Many inscriptions recording grants, and the testimony of foreign travellers bear out this assumption. But education in the early medieval period meant mainly the study of Sanskrit. Boys of the higher classes normally began their studies in Sanskrit *Tols* and *Pathsalas,* in charge of Brahmin teachers. These were found in the larger villages, and were supported by the village itself or by public spirited individuals. There were also residential schools of the *Asrama* type, whose teachers frequently received royal grants. Children of craftsmen got their technical training " without tears ", and at no cost, at their father's knee. The superior among them mastered the *Shilpa-shastras* by heart. Traders employed private tutors to teach their sons writing and accountancy. Girls of well-to-do families were also tutored at home, and there are many literary references to their proficiency in painting, dancing and music. Girls of the martial classes even learned to ride horseback and shoot with bows and arrows. Since a number of Indian women are known to have distinguished themselves in early times as poets, philosophers and administrators, their formal education was certainly not totally neglected. It remained for the Buddhists, however, to introduce something like the first public educational system, with a curriculum extending beyond the Vedic learning traditionally imparted by Brahmins. Their monastic schools and colleges, moreover, were not limited only to Buddhists or to those intending to become monks.

The Chinese pilgrim I-tsing, who arrived in India in A.D. 673, has left an interesting record of primary education as carried on at a Buddhist monastic school at Tamralipti, in Bengal. Boys of six, he says, began by memorizing the forty-nine letters of the Sanskrit alphabet and their combination in syllables, in three hundred *slokas*. At eight they took up a simplified version of Panini's grammar, in one thousand *slokas*. At ten they were promoted to roots, cases and conjugations, and at thirteen they were ready for Panini's original work. On the completion of this, they were considered sufficiently advanced to make Sanskrit compositions of their own, in prose and verse. At fifteen or sixteen they proceeded to some higher institute of learning, usually, to specialize in logic or metaphysics.

The *Jatataks* refer to as many as 500 students, including a hundred princes, who used to flock to Taxila, in the far North-west, to study various subjects, including military and medical science. After the destruction of Taxila by the Huns in the fourth or fifth century A.D., Nalanda, in Bihar, rose to be the chief seat of learning in northern India. Other Buddhist centres of renown were Banaras, Valabhi, Somapuri, Odantapuri, Vikrama-sila, but there were many more. A copper-plate grant issued by Samudragupta (A.D. 330-380) and a coin of his grandson Kumaragupta (A.D. 415-455) are the oldest datable objects dug up by archaeologists at Nalanda. Fa Hian, at the beginning of the fifth century makes only a casual reference to " Nalanda village," but shortly after his time, under successive patronage of Gupta kings, Harsha Vardhana and the Palas, Nalanda became internationally famous.

Again, it is the Chinese pilgrim Yuan Chwang who has left an invaluable contemporary account of Nalanda university, where he pursued his studies for five years, in the first half of the seventh century. Thousands of students were then on its rolls, he states, and the needy among them received not only free tuition but free board and lodging, medicine and clothes. Standards of admission were stiff. Only two or three applicants out of ten were able to pass the entrance examination. (Yet the prestige of the Nalanda name was such that rejected candidates sometimes went about pretending to be graduates!) There were a hundred lecture-halls, and the day was never long enough, says Yuan Chwang, for asking and answering profound questions.

Though a stronghold of Mahayana Buddhism, all the eighteen different schools of Buddhism were taught at Nalanda, as well as Vedic literature and Sanskrit grammar, Brahmin philosophy, the agnostic *Samkhya* system, mathematics, medicine, and current literary works having nothing to do with religion. A special attraction of the university was its wonderful library of manuscripts, housed in three separate buildings known as the "Mart of Knowledge." Scholarship was generally measured by the number of Sutra collections a student had mastered. One thousand Nalanda students could explain twenty collections, Yuan Chwang informs us, five hundred could explain thirty, but only ten could explain as many as fifty collections. The distinguished visitor from China was one of the ten.

When Buddhism began to languish elsewhere in India, eastern India kept aloft the light of learning at the great Buddhist monasteries of Nalanda, Somapuri and Vikramasila, the last two, founded in the eighth century by Dharmapala, sharing the honours with Nalanda. The actual site of Vikramasila has only quite recently been discovered in the Bhagalpur district of Bihar, but it survived as a great university for four centuries. It is said to have had six colleges with 114 teachers, and it specialized in grammar, logic, metaphysics and ritualism. Graduates received diplomas and titles from the Pala kings, and portraits of famous alumni were hung in the college halls. The most distinguished scholar-teacher of Vikramasila was Dipankara Srijnana, better known as Atisa, who played an important part in the reformation of Tibetan Buddhism in the middle of the eleventh century.

Unfortunately, information about higher Hindu institutions in the medieval centuries is scanty. The Chinese visitors were not interested in Hinduism. Nevertheless, the *Agraharas*, exclusive Brahmin settlements where Vedic studies were earnestly pursued, served much the same purpose as the Buddhist colleges, though the traditional education was imparted to Brahmins only, on a strictly teacher-to-pupil basis. Hindu temples, like Buddhist monasteries, were associated with Sanskrit schools and colleges. The Pallava capital of Kanchi, reported by Yuan Chwang to have had as many as eighty temples in the mid seventh century, long occupied a position in regard to higher Hindu learning in the South corresponding to Nalanda in the Buddhist field in the North. But inscriptions, particularly from the tenth century onwards, give interesting details of many other Hindu establishments in Tamil-nad and the Deccan.

One, from the beginning of the eleventh century, mentions an endowment of three hundred acres by the local people for the support of 340 students attending a temple college at Ennayiram, in the South Arcot district of Madras. Here seats were reserved for different subjects, 75 for study of the *Rigveda*, 95 for *Yajurveda*, 20 for the *Chandogya Upanishad*, 25 for grammar, 35 for *Mimamsa*, 10 for *Vedanta*. Teachers received their food rations, plus an annual gift of gold, but the teacher of *Vedanta* received more than the others, and the teacher of grammar was paid in gold on the basis of each chapter completed by his class. Another inscription refers to a large college connected with a Shiva temple devoted exclusively to grammar. This institution was supported by its own village community with a fixed proportion of tax income, as well as a land endowment. A Chola grant makes special mention of a donation for the library of a college in the Tinnevelly district.

In the Deccan, a minister of Krishna III Rashtrakuta founded a Sanskrit college at Salogti, in Bijapur district, in the middle of the tenth century. It had twenty-seven student hostels, and the inscription mentions that the local inhabitants used to contribute for the upkeep of the college fixed sums on the occasion of every marriage and every sacred thread ceremony. In the next century, Bhoja Paramara's Sanskrit college at Dhar was famous all over India. It is abundantly clear that learning was highly prized in medieval India, and that scholars were looked upon as the jewels of a kingdom.

But time was fast running out. Though northern India must also have had numerous seats of Hindu higher learning, their traces were obliterated with the systematic destruction of Hindu temples, beginning with the disastrous raids by Mahmud of Ghazni in the eleventh century. The destruction of the Buddhist centres of Bengal followed in the thirteenth. Almost the first act of the fanatical Muslims of central Asia, who poured into northern India with fire and sword at the end of the twelfth century, was to raze to the ground the temples and monasteries of the " idolaters ". With them, of course, went the schools and colleges. Nalanda was senselessly burned down, and all the inmates who could not escape were put to death. Smoke from the burning manuscripts hung for days like a dark pall over the low hills. Nearly half a century later, writing from hearsay, the Muslim historian Minhaj described how Vikramasila, mistaken for a fort, and the shaven-headed Buddhist monks for hated Brahmin priests, was destroyed in 1203. When an effort was subsequently made to learn the contents of the large number of books found at this place, all those who might have explained them had been killed. Eventually it was discovered that what was supposed to have been a fortress and city was really a college.

CHAPTER XIII

India Finds Herself

THERE WAS ANOTHER side to the picture of scholarly and literary activity of medieval India, increasingly the monopoly, as time passed, of Brahmins and intellectual aristocrats. After all, philosophy, as such, did not touch the heart. Abstruse arguments were beyond the grasp of ordinary people, and the words were incomprehensible and dry. In the endless stories of the *Mahabharata,* the *Ramayana* and the greatly enlarged *Puranas,* however, were to be found exciting dramas of gods and demons, kings and sages, reflecting all the infinite variety of life itself, plus something more — a deep religious significance.

Passages from Sanskrit palm-leaf manuscripts had long been chanted by Brahmins and retold again, in comprehensible language, to enthralled village audiences, from one end of the country to the other. Gradually, as the regional languages began to assume literary shape, translations, adaptations and independent versions were made, and the old stories eventually were brought within the intimate reach of all.

Tamil, of course, was as old as classical Sanskrit itself, and references exist to a very early Tamil translation of the *Mahabharata,* now lost, going back even to the Sangam period. A Tamil *Skanda Purana* is also known from the eighth century. It was not until the great epoch of Chola supremacy, however, that the full impact of the Sanskrit Brahmanic tradition made itself felt in the Tamil speaking areas of the South. Three Tamil poets, all attached to the court of Kulottunga Chola (under whom the eastern Chalukyan kingdom of Vengi and the Chola kingdom of Tanjore were united in A.D. 1070) were mainly responsible for this development. Kulottunga set two of them, Kamban and Ottakkuttan, to making rival versions of the *Ramayana.* Kamban's was the masterpiece, and though a portion of Ottakkuttan's was eventually added to it, what is universally known among Tamilians as the "Kamba Ramayana" survives today as a great Tamil classic. The third poet, Pugalendi, reputedly sent by a Pandyan king to the Chola court as part of the dowry of a Pandyan princess married to Kulottunga, composed many poems on incidents drawn from the *Mahabharata,* especially a highly popular version of the Nala and Damayanti story. A century or more later, Tamil translations were retranslated into Malayalam, inspiring the famous Kathakali dance-dramas of Kerala.

The other two principal Dravidian languages, Kannada, spoken throughout Mysore and the western Deccan, and Telugu, the speech of Andhra, reached literary maturity in the tenth and eleventh centuries, and each, oddly enough, was also represented by a trio of poets. The earliest inscription in Kannada is engraved on a rock at Sravana Belgola, the ancient centre of Jain monasticism in Mysore, and belongs to the fifth century, but the Rashtrakuta king Amoghavarsha I was the first to define the principles of Kannada poetics in his *Kavirajamarga,* in the ninth century. The three Kannada " gems ", Pampa I, Ponna and Ranna, followed in the tenth century, all producing Jain Puranas in Kannada on the lives and legends of one or another of the twenty-four Tirthankaras, but Pampa was also the author of the *Vikramarjuna Vijaya,* afterwards known as the " Pampa Bharata." Ranna, originally a bangle-seller, was likewise inspired by the *Mahabharata* and wrote many poems based on it, the best known being his version of Bhima's great fight. Nagachandra, or Pampa II, turned out a " Pampa Ramayana " in the twelfth century, changing Valmiki's epic, however, to give it a thoroughly Jain atmosphere, to suit the temper of the western Deccan.

The same transitional process was anchoring Telugu in the neighbouring territory of Andhra to an all-India literary inheritance, around the beginning of the eleventh century. At the suggestion of Rajaraja Narendra, eastern Chalukyan king of Vengi, Nanniah commenced a Telugu version of the *Mahabharata,* but actually completed only the first two and a half cantos. Nearly two centuries later, Tikkana finished the remaining fifteen cantos, while Errapreggada (Errana) in the fourteenth century, finally completed Nanniah's third canto. The Telugu *Mahabharatam* shortened many descriptive passages, condensed or omitted much of the philosophic portion, and made the Andhra version into a beautiful popular poem within the grasp of the common people. Another Telugu poet who extended the Sanskrit influence through a translation of Kalidasa's *Kumarasambhava* was Nannichoda, probably living in the twelfth century.

Meanwhile, the various Prakrits of northern India, representing spoken modifications of Sanskrit, were also passing through a transitional stage, with Apabhramsa a half-way house on the road to the modern languages of today. The Sanskrit tradition in Aryavarta had always remained strong, and here translations were scarcely needed, but the religious fervour of the medieval period found a new powerful expression in regional languages spoken by the people.

In Maharashtra, Jnanesvar, or Jnanadeva, ostracized from the Brahmin community into which he was born because his father had returned to the married life after taking the vows of a Sannyasin, according to the legend, was the first of a long line of Maratha saints who helped to mould a vibrant Marathi literature. Jnanesvar completed his major poetic work, the *Jnanesvari*, a commentary on the *Bhagavad-gita*, in which the seven hundred slokas of the *Gita* were expanded into 10,000 Marathi verses, at the close of the thirteenth century. Namdev, a tailor by caste, was next in the line of the Maratha saints, with many *abhangas*, or short lyrics, to his credit. He propagated his passionate faith in Vithoba, or Krishna, whose centre of worship was the temple at Pandharpur, and on his death he was buried at the threshold of the temple, to become a symbolic stepping-stone to the Presence within. The period of the greatest of the Maratha saints, Tukaram, a Sudra grain-seller, lies further ahead.

On the opposite side of India, the earliest form of Bengali is found in a handful of forty-seven *Charya-padas*, or short poems of a mystic nature, by twenty-two different poets, contained in a manuscript (along with a Sanskrit commentary) discovered in Nepal half a century ago. The authors of the *Charyas*, including *Lui-pa* and *Kanha-pa*, are numbered among the eighty-four Siddhas known to Mahayana Buddhism, whose compositions were translated into Tibetan and preserved in the Tibetan *Tanjur*. Their dates have been variously placed, but may be rounded off to about 1000 A.D.

These Old Bengali *Charya-padas* are considered prototypes of the somewhat later Sahajiya *dohas,* Vaishnava *padas* similar to those introduced by Jayadeva in his Sanskrit *Gita-govinda* at the end of the twelfth century, and the Shaktas' hymns celebrating the Divine Mother in her multiple forms, especially Kali. As for the *Ramayana* and *Mahabharata,* they must certainly have been orally familiar all along, but were not adapted into Bengali until actually after the Muslim conquest of Bengal.

Hindi, the language now understood by the largest number of the people of India — and destined to become the official national language — was the last of the northern Indian languages to develop. The oldest Hindi work now known is the Prithvi Raj Raso of Chand Bardai, court poet of Prithviraj Chauhan, but it was the versatile genius of Amir Khusrau that first gave Hindi a truly literary status at the beginning of the fourteenth century.

Not till Akbar's time, in the sixteenth century, did Tulsidas appear on the scene, with his famous Hindi version of the *Ramayana*, the *Rama-charita-manasa*, which has since exercised a profound religious and moral influence throughout the Hindi-speaking area of northern India.

But it was in South India, after all, that an entirely new note was struck, one that went straight to the hearts of the people. Around the seventh century, at a time when the Pallavas were supreme in Tamil-nad, a large number of poet-saints suddenly began wandering about from village to village, singing in Tamil the glory of Vishnu or Shiva. Usual themes of Tamil poetry had been heroes and battles, secular love, the beauties of nature, the busy life of cities, and didactic worldly wisdom. Now, another vision unfolded. The theme was love of the Lord and loving self-surrender to Him, and the message of the saints was that Divine grace was to be won by sincere love, not by learning. The path of *Bhakti*, devotion, was open to all — to women, debarred for centuries from Vedic study and knowledge, to illiterates, to the humblest of men, to the outcast. A spark was lighted which in the course of the next few centuries set the whole of India aflame.

These inspired saints, flourishing between the fifth and ninth centuries, were themselves drawn from all ranks of society. Of the twelve early Vaishnava saints, or *Alvars* — mystics with direct perception of God — the greatest, Nammalvar, was an agriculturist by birth. Tirumangai had once been a robber. Perialvar was a Brahmin. Andal, a woman (also known as Goda) was his adopted daughter. Kulasekhara was a Chera king. Among the four chief Shaiva saints, called the *Nayanmar*, or teachers, the oldest, Appar, came from a Vellala, or agriculturist, family. Sambandha, Sundara and Manikka-Vachakam were Brahmins, but the boy saint Sambandha had as his constant companions a musician and his wife of lowly birth. The sixty-three Shaiva saints came from all sections of society, including a woman, and from all parts of Tamil-nad.

Four thousand surviving hymns of the *Alvars* were finally gathered together in the *Nalayira Prabandham*, under the direction of Natha Muni, in the ninth century, and their recitation introduced by him as a special feature in the great temple of Srirangam near Trichinopoly, dedicated to Vishnu under the name of Ranganatha. Afterwards other South Indian temples adopted a similar practice, and even the images of the *Alvars* were set up in temples and worshipped. Tamil had thus won for itself recognition as a sacred language, side by side with Sanskrit.

The *Prabandham*, particularly the section containing the poems by Nammalvar, became popularly known as the " Tamil Veda."

A time came when a reconciliation between Vaishnavism and the Vedas was considered essential, when a clear philosophic doctrine and canon had to be provided, and general recognition gained for Vaishnavism as an orthodox religion, in spite of its radical reforms. This work was accomplished by the Vaishnava Acharyas, of whom Natha Muni was the first and Ramanuja, born in the early part of the eleventh century, the greatest. The Vedas, *Ramayana, Mahabharata, Vishnu Purana* and *Bhagavatam* all lent authority for the worship of Vishnu, and some of the texts of the early sect of the Pancharatrins, mentioned in the *Mahabharata* as exclusively the devotees of Narayana, or Vishnu, were accepted as canonical. Theoretically 108 in number, but gradually accumulating to become a much larger collection, the Pancharatra texts claimed to be direct revelations of Vishnu, but later than the Vedas. They were classed as *Tantras*, or *Agamas*, suitable for all without distinction of caste or sex in the present age of the Kali Yuga. The Pancharatra *Samhitas*, the Vedas and the *Prabandham* were accepted as the sacred literature of Vaishnavas.

Ramanuja, a Brahmin and a great Sanskrit scholar, not only expounded a philosophy of reconcilation between Vaishnavism and orthodox religion, but justified Vaishnavism against other current forms of belief, especially the *Advaita* doctrine taught by Shankara. Using the same texts that Shankara had used, he too produced commentaries on the *Vedanta-sutra,* the Upanishads and the *Bhagavad-gita*. In his great *Sri Bhasya* on the *Vedanta-sutra*, he gave an interpretation in the light of the *Visishtadvaita* point of view, of qualified non-dualism, arguing that the world was real, the creation of Narayana the supreme personal deity, who possessed auspicious attributes, and who bestowed salvation through his grace on his devotees. Souls, though dependent on him, were separate, and continued to exist even after liberation.

Ramanuja became head of the Srirangam temple and monastery and also supreme pontiff of the Sri Vaishnava community. He travelled extensively, meeting opponents, teaching and preaching, renovating and building temples. He organized seventy-four Vaishnava dioceses, with pious householders as spiritual leaders of each, for the spread of Vaishnavism throughout India. He accepted non-Brahmin disciples, insisting that there was no caste among lovers of God. He granted all true devotees the right of initiation and permission to wear the Vaishnava mark on the forehead, and to study the *Prabandham*.

The story is told of him that when he himself was first taught the full meaning of the sacred eight-syllabled *mantra* of Vishnu, but was warned never to repeat it to any one else on pain of eternal damnation, since its potency was such that anyone hearing it, whether worthy or not, would attain the highest end of life, he immediately went into the street and told everyone he met to follow him to the Vishnu temple in the town, to receive a great treasure. Climbing to the top of the temple tower, in a loud voice he requested all men and women below to repeat after him three times the sacred *mantra*, and he blessed.

There came a time, however, when Vaishnavas suffered persecution at the hands of one of the Chola kings, and Ramanuja was forced to flee to the Hoysala domain. There he remained twelve years, making many converts from among the Jains, including the Hoysala king himself, who now took the name of Vishnuvardhana. The persecution having died down with the death of the Chola king, Ramanuja returned to Srirangam to end his life in peace.

Like the Vaishnavas, and with equal fervour and at the same time, Shaivas propagated their ardent faith in the All-Supreme Shiva. Woven into the fabric of Shaivism were many strands of belief, from many layers of consciousness. The *Linga,* phallic symbol of an ancient pre-Aryan fertility cult, became popularly linked with Shiva worship, and was set up in all Shiva temples. Also somewhere in the vicinity was a sculptured figure of the recumbent bull Nandi, Shiva's vehicle. The Vedic Rudra, god of storm and destruction, was transformed into the terrifying and awesome Bhairava, one side of Shiva. Another was the great Ascetic with matted locks, frequenter of cremation grounds, body whitened with the ashes of the fire in which all desires had been burnt, his only possessions the beggar's bowl and a trident. He was also Pasupati, Lord of creatures and of the flock of souls. He was the splendid Lord of the Universe, seated amidst the eternal snows on top of Mount Kailas in the Himalayas, with Parvati on his knee. He was Ardhanarisvara, one half himself, one half his *Shakti.* He was Mahesvara, the threefold god of creation, preservation and destruction in one. He was Dakshina-murti, the great Guru. He was a slayer of demons, and he it was who swallowed the poison churned from the ocean depths, to save the gods, and who caught Ganga in his matted locks as she fell from heaven to earth. He was Nataraja, annihilator of Time, destroyer of ignorance, dancing all the worlds into nothingness at the end of every *Kalpa.* He was Mahadeva, god of gods. Was there anything he was not?

The first Shaiva sect, that of the Pasupatas, (*Pasu,* soul, and *Pati,* lord), was founded by Lakulisa perhaps as early as the second century A.D. Followers of this sect meditated on Shiva's 1,008 names, and practised *Yoga* for liberation, bathed themselves in ashes and went about acting like madmen. Kalamukhas streaked their foreheads with a black mark, and their strange rites resembled those of another Shaiva sect, the Kapalikas. The latter carried a skull as a drinking vessel, wore human bones as ornaments, performed human sacrifices and ate the flesh of corpses to show their scorn of life. Around the sixth century A.D., these extremists began to disappear. Instead, Shaivas of a new type followed the Tamil saints, dancing in ecstasy and singing of Shiva as the one Lord, the supreme Reality. Love of him and service to his devotees was the path leading to blissful union.

Shaiva Tamil hymns were collected in about the year 1000 by Nambi-Andar-Nambi, and arranged in eleven sections in the *Tirumurai,* or sacred books. The first seven sections, the *Tevaram,* contain hymns of the three great saints, Appar, Sambandha and Sundara, and the eighth, called the *Tiruvachakam,* those of Manikka-Vachakam. The eleventh section, out of chronological order, represents the contributions of the earlier saint Tirumular, probably belonging to the sixth century. The rest is a miscellaneous collection. A final section was added later. This was the *Periapurana,* a work in 4,000 stanzas attributed to Sekkilar, giving a popular account of the lives and legends of all sixty-three Shaiva saints.

Besides the Tamil hymns, the Upanishads and the *Vayu* and other *Puranas,* twenty-eight *Shaiva-Agamas,* purporting to be the words of Shiva himself, constituted the Shaiva canon. As its philosophy developed, however, two separate schools, a northern and southern, Kashmir Shaivism and *Shaiva Siddhanta,* attained prominence.

The older of the two was the Kashmir system, also called *Trika* because of its triple principle of *Pati, Pasa, Pasu* (Shiva identical with *Brahman, Shakti* his creative and binding power inseparable from himself, and individual souls). The basic text of this school was the *Sivasutra.* As usual, this was supposed to be a revelation by Shiva, but was written by Vasugupta, a Kashmiri, in the ninth century. The object was to correct the dualistic interpretation of the *Agamas* then widely current, and reestablish a monistic doctrine. Vasugupta, his pupils Kallata Bhatta and Somananda, and Abhinava Gupta, the great commentator of the eleventh century, were the chief exponents of Kashmir Shaivism. This system was very close to Shankara's *Advaita Vedanta.*

The Tamil school of *Shaiva Siddhanta* recognized both Sanskrit and Tamil works as authoritative, but accepted only eighteen of the twenty-eight *Agamas*, and was naturally influenced to a greater degree by the *Tirumurai* and the *Bhakti* approach. The first attempt at a systematic presentation of the tenets of *Shaiva Siddhanta* was Meykandar's *Siva-jnana-bodham*, a short Tamil treatise composed in the first part of the thirteenth century, but the classic exposition of the subject was the *Siva-jnana-siddhiyar*, also in Tamil, by Meykandar's disciple Arulnandi. After a critical appraisal of the deficiencies of other religious systems, including Buddhism, Jainism and the Pancharatra doctrines, he triumphantly declared the superiority of *Shaiva Siddhanta* above all the others.

An interesting and important offshoot of the southern school of Shaivism was the Virashaiva, or Lingayat, movement, which spread throughout the western Deccan from about the middle of the twelfth century, and has remained vital and active to the present time. Basava, Brahmin minister of Bijjala, the Kalachuri usurper of the Chalukyan throne of Kalyana around 1160, was the organizer of this sect. Monasteries, community centres for religious discussions, and the creation of a special literature in the language of the people, Kannada, taking the form of *vachanas*, or brief pungent sayings strung together in series, were the effective means of propagation. Virashaivas acknowledged only Shiva as god, and in token of his worship wore a cord around the neck or arm to which was attached a miniature *linga*, whence the popular name of *Lingayat, linga*-wearer. The aspiring soul, taking the help of eight beneficial associations including a Guru, was to proceed by " six stages " on its spiritual journey towards realization of oneness with Shiva. Temples were not considered essential, and no images were worshipped. There were no restrictions on admission to the sect. Women were given equal status with men, widow remarriage was permitted, and child marriage forbidden. Respect for labour was upheld. Vegetarianism and abstinence from liquor were enjoined, and general morality was insisted upon.

Many-sided Hinduism, and Mahayana Buddhism also, were to find an intense emotional expression in *Shakti* worship, worship of the Divine Principle in the female form. The literature of the Shaktas, belonging to the *Agama* class, is specifically known as the *Tantra*. There were both Buddhist and Hindu *Tantras* — practical manuals of instruction, containing seed-*mantras* thought to be mystically related to inaudible spiritual vibrations, ordinary *mantras* consisting of mystic syllables associated with individual gods and goddesses, letters of the Sanskrit alphabet to be used for invoking the actual presence of the deities, *yantras*, or symbolic diagrams, as aids to concentration, *mudras*, or hand-gestures, the practice of breath control, helpful bodily postures, and above all the conscious effort to awaken *Shakti*, the spiritual power called the Kundalini, graphically portrayed as coiled up and asleep deep within every human being, until she is awakened and the current made to ascend through six planes of psychic consciousness, ultimately resulting in awareness of identity with *Brahman*.

But Tantrik rituals were of varied kinds, some involving methods of highly practical human experimentation of sex union and rites of a dubious nature. Whether these had a higher esoteric meaning, and were purposely advocated in a form to delude or repel the uninitiated, is really known only to those who have practised them. The " Left " path was only one form of Tantrik practice, however, and the " Right " path, chosen by the majority, had no such uncertain implications.

The roots of Tantrik worship go deep into India's past, starting with the pre-Aryan worship of the ancient Mother Goddess. The whole of western Asia once shared this form of worship, but the matriarchal family system of the Dravidians, in contrast to the patriarchal system of the pastoral Aryans, no doubt encouraged goddess worship. There were many local, tribal and regional goddesses, and kindly goddesses associated with seasonal festivals, as well as malevolent goddesses held responsible for diseases and calamity, who had to be propitiated by bloody sacrifices.

The Vedic Aryans also exalted goddesses in some of their earliest hymns, but all of them beneficent goddesses : Aditi, mother of the gods, Prithvi, the Earth goddess, the Dawn and Night goddesses, Gayatri, a personification of a very sacred hymn, Saraswati, first a river goddess and then the goddess of *Vachh*, (speech, or learning), Devi, most comprehensive of them all, and Sri or Lakshmi, goddess of grace, wealth and beauty, who made her first appearance in a late hymn appended to the *Rig-veda*.

By the time of the *Puranas*, goddesses had already come to occupy a very high and honoured place in the religious thought of the Indian people. A special cult had come into existence for the worship of the *Matrikas*, the Seven Mothers, in a single group. Ganga and Yamuna were now elevated to the rank of river goddesses associated with Varuna, the Ocean-god. The *Markandeya Purana* vividly fixed in the imagination of the people the picture of the goddess Chandi in particular, bestriding her lion and brandishing various weapons in her ten hands, as she fiercely fought Mahishasura the Buffalo-demon enemy of the gods, until she finally severed his head from his body.

Each of the principal Brahmanic gods acquired a consort, who as his divine " wife " shared his attributes. Brahma and Saraswati, Vishnu and Sri or Lakshmi, Shiva and Devi, were worshipped in pairs. Vaishnavas reverenced Sita along with Rama, and those who worshipped Krishna rendered devotion either to Rukmini or to Radha (embodiment of the ecstatic love of the Gopis.) It was the *Shiva-Shakti* philosophy of Shaivism, however, that lifted the principle of Shakti to its highest plane. Shakti was now looked upon as the source of the whole manifested universe, and Shakti, the Divine Mother, was the inseparable manifestation of Shiva, himself identical with *Brahman*.

By the tenth century, the chief centre of Tantrik worship in India was Bengal, and Buddhist and Hindu goddesses were increasingly exchangeable. Included in the Tantrik fold also, but neither wholly Buddhist nor Hindu, were the nine Naths and the eighty-four Siddhas, hard to identify historically, but the subject of innumerable legends. They are supposed to have originated in many parts of India, and beyond its north-western border, and in Tibet, and are presumed to have lived between the seventh and the thirteenth centuries. By their austerities and Yogic and Tantrik practices, they were believed to have obtained all sorts of miraculous powers, or *siddhis*, such as an ability to overcome gravitation, to fly through the air at terrific speed, to make themselves invisible at will, to control natural phenomena, to destroy enemies, to enter into the bodies of others, and to side-track death indefinitely. Gorakhnath, or Goraksha, was the most celebrated of these Yogis. He belonged to the thirteenth century, and the sect he founded still has followers in northern India.

Language and literature gave definition to philosophy and religion, and supplied the primary materials of a vast popular mythology and ethics. Temples and images were the visual expression of religion. Did any country expend so much wealth and skill and patience in erecting religious edifices as India, or where else have such streams of pilgrims travelled long distances on foot, often spending months or even years to reach the distant goal and bow down before a symbol or image of Divinity ? Europe built its beautiful cathedrals five or six hundred years later, but they were only a handful compared to the enormous number of Indian temples.

The first small Brahmanic shrines made their appearance in the Gupta period (A.D. 350-650). Foundations of a single Vishnu temple of the second century B.C. have been found at Besnagar, in Madhya Pradesh. They are adjacent to the inscribed Garuda pillar set up by Heliodorus the Bhagavata (Greek ambassador from Taxila to the Sunga court), but no other equally early Hindu temple is known. The earliest standing temples date only from the fourth century A.D., though large numbers of copper-plate grants indicate that temple building was more extensive than the existing remains.

Gupta temples are on the whole small and not very impressive, but are of a refined simplicity and dignity. They are generally experimental in plan, but already show features that were to persist. The most important part of the temple was the plain windowless *cella*, or cell, perhaps only eight feet square, where the image was enshrined. In front was a shallow porch with short heavy columns of a typical " vase and foliage " design. The frame of the doorway was sometimes beautifully carved, and in the lintel above, or later at the base on each side, the river goddesses began to appear, Ganga standing on her *makara*, or crocodile, and Jumna on her tortoise. No cement was used, and flat roofs were the rule, but here and there towers rose over the shrines — to develop before long into the tall rounded *shikaras* inseparable from the north Indian temple style.

The finest surviving Gupta temple is the little sixth century temple at Deogarh, in the Jhansi district of Uttar Pradesh. It has a finely carved doorway and three large recessed panels in the outer walls, exquisitely sculptured in high relief. One relief is a splendid four-armed Shiva, in the guise of a Yogi. Another depicts Vishnu as Narayana, asleep on the serpent of Eternity. At Bhitargaon, in Kanpur district, is a ruined brick towerlike temple seventy feet high, with a plain interior cell fifteen feet square. It has been described as similar in plan to the Buddhist temple of Bodh-Gaya, built during the reign of Samudragupta in the fourth century, but as the Bodh-Gaya temple has been so many times restored it is difficult to know what the original was like.

Far to the south, lies what is now considered to have been the true cradle of Hindu temple architecture. This was the Chalukyan temple city of Aihole, in the western Deccan. Here the remains of some seventy structures can be seen, the oldest going back to the fifth and sixth centuries. Between the Guptas in the North and the Chalukyas in the South, it is possible that the Vakataka dynasty served as a sort of bridge. There are flat roofs, northern Indo-Aryan *shikaras*, and stepped pyramidal Dravidian towers at Aihole. The square *mandapa*, or columned assembly hall in front of the main shrine, not found in Gupta temples, appears here for the first time. It is apparently an adaptation of the Buddhist *vihara*, or monastic dwelling. Simultaneously, examples of the long barrel-vaulted *chaitya* roof of the Buddhists, with gabled sun-windows at both ends, are found among Hindu temples of the early Chalukyas.

From such beginnings, fifteen hundred years ago, arose the prodigious temple industry of the Indian middle ages. Each of the different geographical areas, ruled over by different dynasties, eventually produced its own variations of the basic temple architecture, codified by the *Silpa-shastras*. Available materials, and especially the particular genius of royal architects entrusted with important works determined the distinctive regional styles.

The early form of excavated and rock-carved halls and abbeys (absurdly called " caves "), like the Hinayana Buddhist excavations at Ajanta and the Jain *gumphas* of Orissa, continued in favour with Mahayana Buddhists. Magnificent *chaitya*-halls and *viharas* were added to Ajanta in the fifth and sixth centuries, and more of them were chiselled out, from the seventh century, at Elura, or Ellora, barely fifty miles away. Here, Hindus and Jains also cut similar series of amazing rock-temples. In central India, too, at another Udaigiri in Madhya Pradesh, close to Besnagar and Sanchi, nine early Brahmanical rock shrines were cut, one of which bears an inscription of the time of Chandragupta II.

Chalukyas and Pallavas, in the sixth and seventh* centuries, began to produce their own type of rock-cut temples, or *mandapas*, at Vatapi (Badami) and Mamallapuram. They were on a comparatively modest scale, a pillared verandah seldom more than twenty-five feet across, with a shallow assembly-hall and a small shrine cut into the back wall, but they were distinguished by sculptured panels of very high artistic quality, and an intricate carving of pillars and ceilings. The " cushion " pillar appeared as the typical Dravidian mode. Last of the important excavated temples of India were the great Shiva temple on Elephanta island and the still larger Jageshwar temple on Salsette island, both in Bombay harbour. They were executed by Rashtrakuta builders, the first around the end of the eighth century, and the second early in the ninth.

The sculptured monolithic temple, cut from a single great block of stone, also made its appearance in the Pallava territory in the first half of the seventh century. The well-known *raths* of Mamallapuram, so-called because they apparently represent stone models of the heavy wooden temple cars used for carrying images through the streets on festival occasions, belong to this class. A whale-backed outcropping of granite some 250 feet long and fifty feet high was cut into isolated sections, and eight monoliths were sculptured into temple-like shapes, the largest forty-two feet in length. The final hollowing out of some *raths*, however, was never completed, probably on account of the death of Narasimha, the Pallava king, in A.D. 674.

The climax of the sculptured monolith was to come a century later, with the world-famous Kailasa temple of Ellora. Here was a great temple shaped out of a single giant stone block, two hundred feet long, one hundred feet wide and one hundred feet high. The general architectural plan was apparently borrowed from the structural temple of Virupaksha, just completed at the last Chalukyan capital of Pattadakal, before the dynasty was overthrown by Dantidurga Rashtrakuta, in the middle of the eighth century. It is to the imagination and munificence of the second ruler of the new dynasty, Krishna I Rashtrakuta (757-783), that the world owes a masterpiece which has no parallel.

The eighth century also saw the beginning of regularly constructed temples, of properly dressed stones, on a much larger scale than anything known so far. The new technique permitted very much more freedom and flexibility of design, and probably explained the sudden spontaneous explosion of temple-building all over India.

The earliest large-sized Hindu temple of the constructed type is the one found at the ancient port of Mamallapuram, not far from the monolithic *raths*. It was built in about A.D. 700, by Rajasimha, and now goes by the name of the " Shore " temple, because it stands directly on the shore, with the sea washing its feet. The Kailasanath and Vaikunta Perumal temples at the Pallava capital of Kanchipuram, and the Virupaksha temple at the Chalukyan capital of Pattadakal, followed almost immediately afterwards, besides countless others. In far-away Kashmir, Lalitaditya Muktapida was also already building his famous Sun-temple of Martand, as well as Buddhist monasteries and temples. To the eighth century, also, belongs the great ruined Buddhist temple of Paharapur (now lying within East Pakistan). This colossal structure was built of brick, since good stone was not to be had, and it has been identified as the remains of the famous Somapura *vihara* and temple erected by Dharmapala. All the great dynastic rulers were henceforth to erect magnificent temples, or whole groups of temples, in their respective territories, and these are the temples that astonish the beholder today, standing as wonderful symbols of all the rich and varied cultural traditions of medieval India.

Once the experimental period was over, temples grew larger and taller. The particular mode was already determined. It remained only to be elaborated and refined. When the Cholas replaced the Pallavas as masters of South India, towards the end of the ninth century, they naturally inherited the Dravidian style of Pallava architecture, but gave to it their own distinctive stamp. To commemorate his military victories and the might of the Chola empire, Rajaraja the Great built an enormous Shiva temple at Tanjore, assigned to the year 1000 A.D. Its massive *vimana* rises in thirteen elaborately sculptured stories to a winged cupola 190 feet above the base. Only twenty-five years later, his son and successor Rajendra Chola, in celebration of his northern conquests and successful crossing of the Ganga, built himself a new capital, which he called Gangaikonda-Cholapuram, in Trichinopoly district. Here a second huge temple was immediately erected, actually larger in plan than the Tanjore temple, though its tower was slightly shorter. Chola temples were more orderly than those of their predecessors, and they convey an impression of immense solidity and dignity. The panelled recesses and niches of the outer walls formed a splendid setting for single sculptured figures, half life size, of great beauty and vitality.

The Pandyas, in their brief period of revival in the thirteenth century, instead of building new temples, largely contented themselves with adding new features to old sacred shrines. Walled courtyards were enclosed within more walled courtyards, each pierced by enormous gateways (*gopurams*), which entirely dwarfed the central *vimana*. Endlessly long covered galleries were built around the courts, and *mandapas* now became fantastic halls of a thousand pillars, of overpoweringly lavish design. Typical of this late phase of the Dravidian temple style is the Minakshi temple at Madura, with twin shrines dedicated to Shiva and his consort, here called Minakshi, the " fish-eyed " one.

In northern India, the vertical Indo-Aryan *shikara* marking out the shrine remained the key-note of the temple design. Within a five hundred year period starting from the middle of the eighth century, Orissa under its Eastern Ganga kings became a great centre of temple-building activity. At least thirty temples rose up at Bhubaneswar, so close together that they seem like a gray petrified forest. The Jagannath temple at Puri, and the Sun-temple at Konarak, also belong to this period. The Orissa type of temple tower (called *deul*) rises vertically from the ground to about a third of its total height, and then curves inward slightly, to finish with a large round fluted *amalaka* stone, and a vase-shaped finial. The great Lingaraja temple, erected in the last years of the tenth century, still dominates everything else at Bhubaneswar. It is 160 feet high and incredible as it may seem, the shrine far below at the bottom of the hollow chimney-like shaft is only nineteen feet square. Though the interiors of all the Orissan temples are perfectly plain, the exteriors are elaborately carved, with an unbelievable amount of intricate detail. The typical device of a lion crouching on an elephant is found everywhere. Floral bands of exquisite beauty are delicately traced, and figures of infinite variety occupy every conceivable niche on the walls.

The Konarak temple, belonging to the middle of the thirteenth century, was built by Narasimha I. This Orissan king had already had a few encounters with the Muslim invaders by then over-running Bengal, but Orissa itself, known to the Muslims as " Jajnagar ", was not to be finally conquered for another three centuries. Conceived as a giant chariot of the Sun drawn on huge wheels by seven horses, the Konarak temple, even in its ruined state, has an indefinable grandeur of its own. The great superstructure over the main shrine has collapsed, but enough remains of the vast construction to justify the claim that here was one of the great temples of medieval India. Apart from the imaginative architectural plan, the sculptured decoration of the Konarak temple is an amazing expression of Orissan art, from the lively elephant frieze around the base of the high platform on which the temple stands, the minutely chiselled chariot wheels with sixteen spokes, ten feet in diameter, the multiple figures of Surya set in high niches, to the loving couples in every form of embrace (*mithuna*), carved all over the upper structure. Did the latter represent a frank Tantrik text-book of practices being secretly carried on by followers of the Left-hand path ? Why were these erotic figures associated with a Sun-temple ? No doubt because the sun is linked with the generating life force itself. Whatever the answer, Konarak has kept its secret for more than six centuries.

In something of the same tradition as the Orissan temples, but with a different grace and beauty, are the thirty or more Chandella temples of Khajuraho, in central India. They were all erected within a hundred years, between 950 and 1050, and nearly all are found within the radius of one square mile. They are of medium size, compact, and easily appreciated at a first glance. Each rests on a high individual terrace, and the various temple components of shrine, assembly hall and entrance portico are harmoniously united to give the appearance of a single building, instead of being strung out as separate units in a long straight line, in the Orissa fashion. Towers are more pointed, with miniature replicas and turrets of all sizes increasing the vertical effect. Interiors are splendidly sculptured, and charming female figures, fully sculptured in the round, drape themselves about the pillars in graceful sinuous compositions, with fantastic animals and grotesque dwarfs peering down from the capitals. At Khajuraho, temples of Shiva and Vishnu stand side by side, and a Surya temple and six Jain temples form part of the group.

Stretching across central India and Rajputana, and into Gujarat, are more and more temples, or fragments of temples — lonely pillars, broken towers, crumbled walls. In the village of Osia, near Jodhpur, are the remains of sixteen small Brahmanical and Jain temples, all strikingly different in design. Some go back to the eighth or ninth century, three of them dedicated to Harihara, the combined form of Vishnu and Shiva. Another Sun-temple is found here also, and a Jain temple is dedicated to Mahavira.

At Gwalior, three unusual temples, known by their odd local names as the Teli-ka-Mandir, " Oilman's temple " and the Sas-Bahu, " Mother-in-law " and " Daughter-in-law " temples, have survived from the eleventh century. The former is a high oblong shrine, with the old *chaitya* type of roof and sun-windows at each end. The " Daughter-in-law " temple is a smaller copy of the larger " Mother-in-law " temple, which bears a dedication to Vishnu in the year 1093. Only a large *mandapa* remains, however, which appears from the outside to have three stories, with numerous balconies opening out all around, but seen from within, is a single hall of great height, with four massive piers rising to support the framework of a roof once eighty feet above the ground level.

The further west the site, the more ornate and rich becomes the carving of the medieval Indian temple. What the famous Shiva temple of Somnath, in Kathiawar, was like before its ruthless destruction by Mahmud of Ghazni in 1025-1026, will never be known. Muslim writers characteristically speak with awe only of its vast treasury of gold and jewels. The roofless ruins of the lovely eleventh century temple of Surya at Modhera, however, reveal the extraordinary beauty and finish of contemporary Solanki temple sculpture, as also a characteristic elaboration of architectural plan, to include a large tank for sacred ablutions, with stepped and terraced sides adorned with many small shrines, and a handsome carved archway at the top of the stairs. But it is the Jain temples that represent the highest and richest achievement of temple building in the Solanki period, reflecting the great prosperity and wealth of medieval Gujarat, as also the zeal of kings, ministers and bankers newly converted to Jainism.

Jain temple cities still perch on the mountains of Kathiawar, at Satrunjaya and Girnar, near Palitana and Junagadh. The former, it is said, contains as many as 863 temples. At these centres the temples have been many times restored and rebuilt, and new ones added, so that now they belong to no definite period, but at Girnar a temple dedicated to the nineteenth Tirthankara, Mallinatha, was erected in the thirteenth century by the famous brothers Tejapala and Vastupala, ministers of Bhima II, the Solanki king of Gujarat between A.D. 1178 and 1239.

In spite of the wake of devastation left behind by the Ghaznavids, temple building obviously went steadily on in Gujarat for another two and a half centuries, and the most famous of all Solanki temples are the two Jain temples of Dilwara, on Mount Abu, in Rajputana, belonging to the eleventh and thirteenth centuries. The earlier of the two, built in 1031 by Vimala, an officer of Bhima I, was dedicated to Rishabha, the first Tirthankara. The second was built by Tejapala, and was dedicated to Neminath, the twenty-second Tirthankara. Both temples are very similar in style and execution.

Enclosed within an outer wall is a colonnaded cloister, lined by rows of cells containing identical seated images of the Tirthankara for whom the temple was built. Within the entrance of Vimala's temple are ten statues of Vimala and members of his family on the backs of large sculptured elephants, seated in solemn splendour, a rather unexpected personal note in a temple otherwise dedicated to a high abstraction. A pillared *mandapa* with an octagonal space in the centre, set off by eight columns, leads to the shrine. The brackets of the eight columns support a circular canopy of concentric rings, with a great pendant hanging down like a beautiful jewel from the apex, surrounded by fretted festoons. The dome itself consists of several bands of sculptured dancers and animals, ornamental borders and mouldings, and sixteen *Vidyadevis*, the Jain goddesses of learning, spanning the lower part of the canopy. All the interior is of white marble, brought from the Makrana quarries, and the perfection and delicacy of the carving of pillars and ceilings beggars description. It is most often compared to lacework.

When a similar technique was transferred to a fine greenish-blue stone, on an even more lavish scale, but at the same time with far greater vitality, the final stage of the medieval Indian temple was reached. No direct connection existed between the Jain temples of Mount Abu and the Chalukyan Hoysala temples of Mysore, of the twelfth and thirteenth centuries, but with the Hoysala temples the sculptured temple art of Hindu India had moved full circle, back to its starting point eight or nine hundred years before.

Hoysala chieftains, beginning as feudatory rulers of the western Chalukyas of Kalyana, became independent at the end of the twelfth century and their kingdom, corresponding to the greater part of Mysore, lasted for just a little more than one century, before it was overrun by Malik Kafur and Muhammad Tughlak, Sultan of Delhi, early in the fourteenth century. Within this brief period, the Hoysala style was brought to perfection, with some eighty temples to its credit.

The Hoysala style is, in effect, a blending of southern and northern traditions, though basically Chalukyan elements are retained. The towers, which are comparatively low, carry up all the contours of every rhythmic projection and indentation in the so-called star-shaped angles of temple and plinth below, so that the vertical lines of the towers produce a fluted or almost corrugated appearance. Many temples have double, triple, or even multiple shrines, with all the parts exactly duplicated, but they are unified by a broad sculptured frieze of superimposed bands, sometimes running to a total length of 700 feet, carried around the entire outside of the building, including shrines and *mandapas*. In many instances the towers, for reasons not very clear, have entirely disappeared, with the result that the temples look rather like flat jewel-caskets, as someone has aptly put it. And it is, indeed, the endless jewel-like carving, covering almost every foot of space on walls, pillars and ceilings, both within and without, that is the special Hoysala distinction.

The principal temple at Belur, eleven miles from the old Hoysala capital of Dwarsamudra (now known as the small town of Halebid), is the Vaishnava temple of Kesava, constructed early in the twelfth century by king Vishnuvardhana shortly after he had been converted to Vaishnavism by Ramanuja. The horizontal frieze at the base of the temple starts with a band of elephants, above which are superimposed bands of lion-masks, scroll-work, small figures in ornamental niches, more delicately carved figures between pilasters, and finally a band illustrating stories from the *Mahabharata* and *Ramayana*. A series of twenty large perforated stone screens adorn the walls of the assembly-hall. Half of them are of geometrical design, while the other half are sculptured panels depicting Puranic legends of Vishnu. Many little Vishnus are flanked by Hanuman and Garuda, or Vishnu is shown with his consort Lakshmi. He is represented in all his various Incarnations, and there are scenes of the churning of the ocean by the gods and demons, the story of Prahlad, the killing of Kamsa by Krishna and Krishna playing his flute. The minutely carved monolithic pillars of the *mandapa* are all different, except the four central ones. One which goes by the name of the Narasimha pillar was so cleverly contrived that originally it could actually be made to rotate on its base. Among the carved figures the guides love to point out is a tiny bull, the size of a pea. The four central pillars display enchanting female figures which stand boldly forth from the capitals, and three of them are signed by the sculptors who made them. One holds a parrot on her hand, another is a dancer, one is dressing her hair. The ceiling they hold up has another *Ramayana* frieze, and on a lotus bud depending from the centre Brahma, Vishnu and Shiva are carved together.

The Hoyasalesvara temple of Halebid, dating from the middle of the twelfth century, is the largest and most impressive of the Hoysala temples. It is a double temple, enshrining two separate Shiva lingas, but the mythological frieze around this temple contains not only scenes connected with the Bhairava aspect of Shiva, Shiva and Uma enthroned, Nandi, Ganesa and his mouse, and Kartikeya (Subrahmanya) and his peacock, but many episodes from the *Mahabharata* war, the Krishna and Prahlad legends, and, once more, scenes from the *Ramayana*. In the great slab of the lintel twelve feet long above the entrance, an eight-armed Shiva dances the dance to end the worlds, a faint smile on his lips, while musicians accompany him with drum and cymbals.

Such, then, are a few of the great temples of medieval India. How many more perished? When Mahmud destroyed Mathura, the holy city of Krishna, in 1018, he gave orders that all the temples should be burnt with naptha and fire, and levelled with the ground. In the middle of the city was a temple larger and finer than the rest which the Sultan himself conceded must have taken two hundred years to build, and which, as the contemporary historian wrote, "can neither be described nor painted." Five idols of red gold, with eyes formed of priceless jewels, were so large that they had to be broken up and melted down, before the gold could be carried away. When Prithvi Raj was king of Delhi, twenty-seven temples ornamented the Chauhan capital. An inscription states quite matter-of-factly that the twenty-seven

" idol temples " were demolished to provide materials for the Qutb Mosque, erected by the first Sultan of Delhi, Qutb-ud-din Aibak, in the first years of the thirteenth century. In the mosque cloisters, three rows deep, are 240 carved pillars, each made up of two superimposed Hindu temple pillars, or a total of 480 pillars originally. The second building to be erected in India after the Muslim conquest was the Arhai-din-ka-Jhompra mosque at Ajmir, also attributed to Qutb-ud-din Aibak. Here nearly a thousand old pillars were used, three for each new pillar, indicating the destruction of about fifty Hindu temples to build the mosque.

Images (Buddhist, Jain or Hindu) were of course installed in all the shrines and temples as symbols of the deity, or deities. Thousands upon thousands of such images were turned out, in stone, metal or clay. Mahayana Buddhist and Jain texts, the *Puranas, Agamas* and *Tantras*, supplied necessary descriptions, and artisan manuals provided technical instructions. Vast workshops came into being, sometimes directly attached to great religious centres, like Nalanda, or more usually developed as informal studios at the actual sites where temples were being built, over long periods of time. Though the superior artist or craftsman could, and did, give his work the stamp of his own genius, faithful adherence to accepted tradition was the rule, and originality and self-expression were never the aim. Images of the gods were anonymous.

Just as different schools of architecture grew up in different parts of the country under dynastic patronage, various styles in sculpture also evolved, with their own clear conventions. The classical Gupta style, as an expression for both Buddhist and Hindu themes, continued into the Pala period, but was lost in the elaborate Sena transformations and the exuberant outpourings of Orissa. Tantrik Mahayana Buddhist figures, characteristic of the last phase of Buddhism in India, survived mainly in the form of small metal images of goddesses, not easily distinguishable from Tibetan and Nepalese types. Orissan and Chandella sculptures strongly reflected Hindu Tantric concepts. The Pallava style, passed on to the Cholas, became formal and mature, but lost something in spontaneity. Chalukyan and Pandyan sculptures, almost disconcertingly animated, possessed an extraordinary vigour, and Hoysala sculpture, as just indicated, was a long narrative scroll of the whole of Hindu mythology. Yet in medieval India, Hindu iconography spoke a common language, everywhere understood.

Jain images, on the other hand, were intended to symbolize a complete dissociation with worldly life, and the rows of Jinas remained forever calm, remote, identical. One exception is the famous colossus of Sravana Belgola, fifty-eight feet high. This statue is a representation of Gomatesvara, or Gommata, saintly son of the first Tirthankara. It was fashioned from the top of the granite hill of Indragiri, by the order of Chamundaraya, minister of the Ganga king Rajamalla, in 983 A.D. There Gommata has stood for nearly a thousand years, silently contemplating infinity. Sculptured termite-nests rise around his feet and vines entwine his arms and legs, eloquent testimony to his serene indifference to passing time.

In a country of such vital artistic imagination as India has displayed, it is strange and regrettable that little of any early Indian painting has survived. Painting was almost as evanescent as music or dance, though these, too, were indispensable in temple ritual. There are many references to painting, including portrait-painting, in the Sanskrit classics, but all are gone — apart from the treasured frescos of Ajanta. Only fragile fragments may still be found on pillars, walls or ceilings in a few of the rock-cut halls and early temples, such as have been located in the early Hinayana Ajanta excavations (200 B.C.-A.D. 200), in the Bagh cave-shrines near Gwalior (A.D. 500), in a Brahmanical *mandapa* at Badami (6th century), on a wall in a passage of the Kailasa-nath temple of Kanchi and the ceiling of the Kailasa temple at Ellora (8th century), in the great Brihadisvara temple of Tanjore (11th century). But the large paintings at Ajanta, though badly damaged by time and ancient neglect, show how painting was also once a great religious art in India.

The Ajanta masterpieces are assigned to the late Gupta-Vakataka period, that is, the sixth and seventh centuries. They are naturally Mahayana Buddhist in inspiration, though they vividly reflect contemporary life. The artists who laboured in the cool dark halls of Ajanta managed to fix on the rocky walls all the animated world from which the yellow-robed monks had run away. The subject matter, to be sure, is the familiar story of Buddha's life, the noble examples of his self-sacrifice, as told in the *Jatakas*. There are, too, those mysterious and deeply moving Bodhisattvas gazing down compassionately upon their devotees. Whoever has seen the great " Bodhisattva of the Blue Lotus " on the back wall of Vihara Number One must remember him forever. But like the ancient sculptors of Sanchi, the painters of Ajanta, in exactly the same way, used the vivid contemporary pulsing world as a setting for the Buddhist ideas of renunciation. At first sight — but only at first sight — the art of Ajanta seems oddly secular.

14

The scenes crowd into one another, alive with intense blues
and many shades of green, soft reds, ochre and brown, cream
and gray, black and white.   Kings and queens attended by their
retinues hold court within lovely palaces.   Shaven-headed Buddhist monks in yellow robes and Brahmin ascetics in white with
twisted topknots, misshapen dwarfs, mothers and children, watch-
ful attendants waiting upon their lords and ladies, bearded
foreigners in fur caps on unknown missions from the cold north,
all meet on the Ajanta walls.   Noble processions of elephants
tread their way out of city gates.   Vijaya Sinha goes ashore in
Ceylon.   Canopied pleasure-boats rock on lotus lakes, sea-going
masted vessels carry Indian merchandise to distant ports.   Animal
life is everywhere.   Monkeys scamper over terraced roofs, peacocks preen themselves or drag behind them their silken trains.
Birds and deer and elephants disport in flowery jungles.   A snake
charmer charms his cobra.   Decorative friezes and panels frame
cockfights and bullfights, lovely lotuses and birds.   But all this
antique pageantry had but one message for the Buddhist brotherhood of Ajanta. It was the lesson book of selflessness taught by
the Master, renunciation of what is for the dream of a perfection
that yet may be.

Did the gods rejoice in the sculpture and painting, music and
dance, poetry and drama, associated with Indian temples?   So
it seemed to the Indian mind.   All the arts were employed in
the creation of the temple and its rituals, and fortunately sculpture,
the most enduring, was given first place.   Centuries passed and
temples were weighed down with incredible sculptured detail,
the handiwork, it might appear, of goldsmiths or carvers of
sandalwood or ivory, rather than workers in stone.   This gigantic
effort to add splendour to exterior walls, where the ever-changing
patterns of light and shade under the strong Indian sun were a
ceaseless delight for all to see, were understandable.   But what
of dark interiors where almost nothing was visible?   Even here,
often with still more lavish expenditure of energy and time, the
same infinite patterns of beauty were created, not for the benefit
of human beings, but as an offering to the all-seeing gods.

No machines could duplicate this work again, nor would the
modern world, preoccupied with its pressing utilitarian needs,
harried by time, and dreaming (if it dreams at all) mainly of how
to reach the moon, consider as anything but futile the creation
of " useless " beauty. The challenge thrown down by the medieval
Indian artisans is one that cannot be heard except in the realm
of spirit.   But the achievement was more than they themselves
knew.   By giving visual expression to the vast mythology, the

fundamental religious ideas and the intense devotion of their age, they helped to strengthen the spiritual and cultural unity of India. When the foreign invaders arrived, and India went to pieces politically, it still clung to its own soul.

CHAPTER XIV

Indian Culture Beyond the Seas

FOR WELL OVER a thousand years, from the centuries immediately preceding those of the present era up to the twelfth or thirteenth century, India radiated to adjacent islands and neighbour countries the civilizing influences of her material greatness and spiritual achievements. Rarely, during this long period, did she act the part of an aggressor. Merchants, sailors and missionaries, but seldom soldiers, set out from the shores of India. Traders carried with them the varied produce of the Indian soil and the much-prized articles of Indian craftsmanship. Others preached an illuminating message of peace and spiritual values more lasting than worldly blessings. Sometimes, too, petty Indian rulers fled abroad for refuge, after suffering defeat at the hands of some powerful rival. Gathering supporters around them, they ended by founding new dynasties in the lands of their adoption.

The Indian colonies which began to grow up all along the periphery of the motherland were essentially cultural, religious or economic, rather than political or racial. They owed allegiance to no Indian emperor, were obedient to no Indian imperial policy. Yet they spread Indian influence outward, like a tidal wave. It passed south to Ceylon and beyond to the remote islands of the Pacific. It inundated Burma, Malaya, Thailand and Indo-China (Viet-Nam). It overwhelmed Nepal and Tibet. From Afghanistan, it passed along to central Asia and China. It lapped at the far shores of Korea and Japan. Indian religious ideas and literature, Indian conventions of art and architecture, Indian legal codes and social practices, even, upon occasion, the peculiarly Indian institution of caste, all took root in these outer territories.

India held a strange and irresistible attraction for the whole of Asia in the first millennium A.D. People in the most primitive stage of development, as well as the Chinese with a civilization as ancient and illustrious as India's own, acknowledged Indian supremacy in the realm of spirit. Yet the civilization of India, transplanted abroad, did not have a deadening effect, suppressing or stifling native genius, as imposition of a foreign culture very often does. On the contrary, it called out the best that others had to give. As a result of India's fertilizing influence, new and distinctive types of culture everywhere arose, and each new centre was able to create and contribute fresh treasure to add to the great Asiatic heritage. How Indian religions and Indian culture blossomed anew in foreign environments and endured for many centuries, is a fascinating and little appreciated chapter of Indian history.

Seventh Century Indian Colonists sailing to Java

For a long time Indians seem to have held the monopoly of maritime commerce in both the southern and eastern seas of Asia. They possessed large ocean-going vessels, in which they first ventured to Ceylon, Burma and Malaya. Gradually they extended their journeys to Java and Sumatra, and then to southern China. Not until the second and third centuries A.D. did Persian and Arab mariners appear on the scene, and not until the seventh century did China take an active part in maritime trade with southern Asia. Tamralipti in Bengal, Palura on the coast of ancient Kalinga, and the Ganga river ports of Banaras and Champa (Bhagalpur), were the oldest Indian sailing ports for the East. In the seventh century, Mamallapuram, the Pallava port, became the chief point of embarkation in southern India.

Many of the early Indian settlements, planted at favourable points along the trade routes, later developed into independent states or kingdoms. Their history today has to be reconstructed from chance inscriptions, architectural and sculptural remains, manuscripts or ruined cities — materials lost for centuries in the tropical forests of southeastern Asia, buried under the drifting sands of the central Asian deserts, hidden away beyond reach in the inaccessible mountain fastnesses of Nepal and Tibet. Scholars have had to ransack endless documents, pursuing clues and disentangling evidence, bit by bit, collected from Sanskrit, Pali, Tamil, Chinese, Arabic, Javanese, Malay, Burmese, Siamese, Nepalese and Tibetan sources, as well as such unfamiliar or dead languages as Mon, Pyu, Khmer, Kuchan, Khotanese and Sogdian. To add to the difficulties, ancient cities and kingdoms of Asia were known by many different names at different times to different peoples, and names were also transferred, with disconcerting casualness, from one place to another. No wonder the thrilling story of the great outward movement of Indian civilization has only just begun to make itself vaguely known !

The island of Ceylon was the first of all the outer lands to open its heart to India. It was a natural stepping-stone between India and both East and West, and Indian merchants who went there were followed by refugees and Buddhist monks. Ceylon adopted Buddhism in the third century B.C., and for fifteen hundred years Buddhism continued to mould the life and culture of the Sinhalese people. It is still there today.

Indian and Sinhalese sources both agree that Indians who first settled in Ceylon were not Tamils, as one would naturally expect, but Aryans from the north. Proof seems to lie in the fact that the Sinhalese language belongs to the Aryan family, and not to the Dravidian. The ancient Sanskrit epic of the *Ramayana*, though scarcely history, has fixed in the minds of countless millions of Indians and Sinhalese the story of Rama, Aryan prince of Ayodhya, making his way south to Lanka as Ceylon is known in Sanskrit literature, where he defeated Ravana, the island king, and rescued Sita. The *Dipavamsa* and *Mahavamsa*, the two great Pali Buddhist chronicles of Ceylon, of the fourth and fifth centuries A.D., ignore the story of Rama and Ravana, but treat the island history as commencing with the arrival of another north Indian prince, Vijaya Sinha of Bengal.

This exiled prince, following the sea route of the traders, supposedly landed in Ceylon with seven hundred followers in the fifth century B.C., on that very day and at that very hour when Gotama Buddha, far away in the north, entered into Nirvana. Subduing the primitive Veddahs, Vijaya Sinha made himself king of the island and named the newly conquered country Sihala or Sinhala — whence Ceylon — to commemorate an old myth that his grandfather was a lion. He then sent suitable presents to Madura on the Indian mainland, according to the story, and obtained the hand of a Pandyan princess who brought over with her seven hundred maidens to become the wives of Vijaya's seven hundred followers, and a thousand families representing the eighteen guilds of Indian craftsmen. Rice cultivation was introduced, and all the typical Indian arts and crafts began to be practised in Ceylon, such as music, drama, dancing, metalwork, building and sculpture. Immense masonry reservoirs were constructed, and great buildings followed.

But the monks of those early days were to place the whole world in their debt, when, with unparalleled zeal, they set to work transcribing and translating the sacred texts brought over from India. The literary language of Magadha of the Buddha's or Asoka's days was retained, but a new script was adopted to render the language understandable to the Sinhalese. Both language and script came to be known as Pali. After a few centuries, when the original Buddhist works unaccountably got lost in India itself, the oldest existing version of the Buddhist Canon, in the Hinayana tradition, was found to be that preserved on the palm-leaf manuscripts of monastic libraries in Ceylon. Thither Buddhists came from many parts of Asia, including India, to study the doctrine anew.

The Pali Buddhist chronicles of Ceylon have preserved the detailed story of how Buddhism was first carried to the island. When Devampiya Tissa succeeded to the Sinhalese throne at Anuradhapura in the northern part of the island about the middle of the third century B.C., he sent courtesy gifts to his contemporary, the great Asoka of India, whose sphere of influence had reached the Tamil country just across the straits. Asoka sent return gifts and exhorted Tissa to seek the incomparable treasure of the religion of the Buddha. When the Sinhalese king asked for further enlightenment, Asoka despatched members of his own family as the first Buddhist missionaries to Ceylon. The chief of the little mission was his son Mahendra, or Mahinda, who had taken his monk's vows twelve years before. Mahendra was accompanied by four other monks and Asoka's young grandson, Sumana. A little later Asoka's daughter, the nun Sanghamitra, followed her brother to Ceylon to initiate the royal ladies in the Buddhist faith. Tissa and all his people accepted Buddhism with eager hearts. Precious relics arrived from Asoka as a reward for this conversion, and Tissa and the long line of Sinhalese kings who came after him emptied the royal treasury again and again to build stupas and monasteries more magnificent than any in

India. Ruins of many of them still survive in the vicinity of the early Sinhalese capitals.

Utmost reverence has always been paid by the Sinhalese to the sacred relics and traditional places associated with the first Buddhist missions from India. These are inextricably intertwined with legend, art and history. Most precious among the treasures was a rooted branch of the Bodhi tree under which Gotama Buddha attained enlightenment. Cut off by Asoka himself, it was brought to Ceylon by sea in a golden vase carried by Sanghamitra. Tissa received it personally at the port and accompanied it on the fourteen days' journey to Anuradhapura. There it was planted with solemn ceremony outside the southern gate of the capital, and for twenty-two hundred years, successive generations of its offspring have flourished at Buddhist sites all over Ceylon. Tradition also says that Asoka sent the Eating-bowl of the Blessed One, filled with bodily relics, which included the especially sacred relic of his right collarbone. Tissa erected the Thuparama stupa at Anuradhapura, the first stupa in Ceylon, for preserving this precious memento. The bowl he kept in the palace and worshipped daily, but after his death many vicissitudes befell it. It was said to have been carried away to India, to Peshawar, to China, to Iran, and to Afghanistan. Fa Hian was convinced that he had seen it in Peshawar, early in the fifth century. " It holds perhaps over two pecks and is of several colours, chiefly black," he wrote. " It is about one fifth of an inch thick, of transparent brilliancy and of a glossy lustre. Poor people throw in a few flowers and it is full ; the very rich may throw in ten thousand bushels, without ever filling it."

The equally famous " tooth relic " became the centre of another remarkable series of legends. After the Nirvana and cremation of the Buddha, his four eyeteeth traditionally passed to Indra, to the Nagas of the Underworld and to the kings of Gandhara and Kalinga. The Kalinga tooth, preserved for eight hundred years at Dantapura, " City of the Tooth " — usually identified with modern Puri — was secretly carried away to Ceylon by a Kalinga princess, about the beginning of the fourth century A.D., perhaps during the period of Samudragupta's military conquests. A special tower was built for it in the precincts of the Sinhalese royal palace, and the actual remains of this structure were discovered and identified by an inscription only in this century. Whenever the kings of Ceylon shifted the capital, the tooth went with them, and a new tooth temple was built to enshrine the sacred relic. Its possession, indeed, came to symbolize the right of sovereignty. In the sixth century, the Greek monk Cosmos, while visiting Ceylon, wrote that above the tooth temple he saw a priceless ruby fixed, " as large as a great pinecone and fiery red."

At last, in 1560, the Portuguese invaders of the island somehow got hold of the sacred relic and bore it off to Goa, the seat of their government in Asia. The reigning king of Burma, a devout Buddhist, offered to ransom it from the Portuguese for a huge sum, but his offer was spurned, and in the presence of the Portuguese viceroy, the archbishop of Goa solemnly pounded it to bits, cast it into a fire and threw the ashes into the sea, to destroy forever the heathen heresy of its worship. But presently a whisper arose that the Portuguese had never gained possession of the real tooth, only an imitation ! The original, it was maintained, had never left Kandy, the medieval fortress capital in the heart of Ceylon. Hidden away during times of trouble, brought out again when the clouds passed, it was all along carefully preserved in the island. Today, a piece of darkened ivory two inches long rests on a lotus of beaten gold within the white Temple of the Tooth at Kandy. Every August it is placed on the back of an elephant and is taken out in a great procession, while crowds lining the streets reverently pay homage to what they believe to be the Buddha's own tooth.

Rock inscriptions engraved in Asokan Brahmi of the second or third century B.C. — the oldest inscriptions in Ceylon — point to the historical relations between the two countries. Most of them briefly record pious donations to Buddhist monks or monastic institutions. Architectural monuments of brick and stone date from the same early period. King Tissa, builder of the first stupa, also built the first monastery in Ceylon. He erected it on the hill of Mihintale, eight miles east of the old capital of Anuradhapura, to commemorate the place of his meeting with Mahendra. Pilgrims still flock to see the cell, with its narrow couch of stone, where Asoka's son, the royal monk Mahendra, lived and died.

The great period of building in Ceylon, however, begins with the close of the second century B.C., when King Dutthagamani defeated a Chola invasion and re-established his unified rule over the island. Dutthagamani's most famous construction was the Ruanweli Degaba, which enshrined all the precious body relics previously sent from India, together with an incalculable treasure of gold and pearls. Thousands of Indian Buddhist monks were invited to the Sinhalese capital for the dedication ceremony. During another Chola invasion, however, the stupa was rifled of all its treasures. Another of Dutthagamani's famous buildings at Anuradhapura was a nine-storied, thousand-chambered monastery, known as the Brazen Palace, because it was roofed with copper. Sixteen hundred stone pillars twelve feet high, the foundation of this monastery, still stand in forty parallel rows. Size had a strange fascination for these Buddhist king-builders of Ceylon. The giant Abhayagiriya Dagaba, begun by King Mahasena at the end of the third or beginning of the fourth century A.D., is 300 feet in diameter and rests on a platform extending over eight acres. The Jetawanarama Stupa is of the same huge dimensions.

It was far easier for India in the past, as it still is today, to have direct contact with Burma and Malaya by way of the Bay of Bengal than by land routes passing through dense jungles and over jagged mountain ranges thousands of feet high. The Pali Jatakas contain the earliest references to eastward voyages undertaken by Indians, probably as early as the fifth century B.C. Such voyages usually had Suvarnabhumi, the " Gold Country," or Lower Burma, as their objective. . A vague acquaintance with eastern countries and islands is also discernible in early Sanskrit literature. Suvarnadvipa, " Gold Island," and Javadvipa, " Barley Island," are mentioned in the *Ramayana* when Sugriva orders his monkey battalions to search for the lost Sita even in such distant places as these, beyond the seas. The name Suvarnadvipa, at first loosely applied to the whole of Malaya, was later more closely identified with Sumatra. In the same way Javadvipa, used at one time or another for various localities in Malaya, and also for both Sumatra and Java, was confined to present-day Java only as late as the ninth century.

The climate of Lower Burma has not been kind to ancient remains. Concrete traces of Indian contact go back only to the first few centuries of the present era. The inhabitants of this region were Mons (or Talainas), definitely related in speech and very probably in stock also to the Khasis of Assam and the Mundas of central India. They are different from the Arakanese and the Burmese proper, the latter being of Mongolian descent. Wide-scale Mon migrations certainly took place in prehistoric times, but whether from east to west, or west to east, is still a matter of conjecture. The ancient Mon capital of Thaton lies on the Gulf of Martaban, not far from the modern Moulmein, a port easily accessible to ships from India. Medieval chronicles of the Mons, written in Pali, Mon and Burmese, all testify that Buddhism had become established in Thaton by the first centuries of the present era. Confirmed in their faith in the fifth century, after a visit from the great Buddhaghosa — Indian translator and commentator of the Pali texts — the Mons adopted the Pali Buddhism of Ceylon.

Another small Mon kingdom of southern Burma, partly contemporary with that of the Mons of Thaton, was the Pyu kingdom of Old Prome, in the Pegu district, west of Thaton. Despite the reckless use of Old Prome's archeological treasures as ballast for the Prome-Rangoon railway line, ruined stupas and other ancient objects going back to the sixth century A.D., have come to light in the vicinity in considerable quantities. One stupa is a majestic structure rising above five superimposed terraces. The intact relic chamber of another was found to contain a votive offering of a miniature silver stupa with Buddha figures in relief and a mixed Pali-Pyu inscription. A manuscript of twenty gold leaves with extracts of the Pali Canon, inscribed in Pyu characters, was also found in Prome. This Pyu writing is strikingly similar to the early Kannada-Telugu script and obviously was a direct importation from India. Royal funerary urns with legends in Pyu show that kings of the seventh and eighth centuries in southern Burma also bore such familiar Indian titles as Varman or Vikrama. Buddhism of the Greater Vehicle as well as Pali Buddhism and Hinduism had their votaries in Old Prome at this time, as is proved by discoveries of clay tablets, inscribed plates of gold and silver, and sculptures in stone and bronze.

About the middle of the eleventh century, the Burmese king Anawrata, who had made himself master of Upper Burma, conquered the old Mon kingdoms of Thaton and Pegu. In Upper Burma, the first Buddhist king had reigned some nine hundred years before, and Mahayana Buddhism was well established there. Anawrata had never seen copies of the Pali scriptures, however, and on being informed that thirty sets of the three *Pitakas*, and many sacred Buddhist relics, were to be found at the ancient city of Thaton, he demanded a share of them. When Thaton refused, Anawrata, bent on conquest, set out (as the Burmese *Glass Palace Chronicle* picturesquely states) " with eight hundred thousand boats and four-score million fighting men." What happened after the victory is related thus : " The king brought away the sacred relics which were kept in a jewelled casket and worshipped by a line of kings in Thaton ; and he placed the thirty sets of Pitakas on the king's thirty-two white elephants and brought them away. Moreover, he sent away in turn the mighty men of valour and all the host of elephants and horses. Thereafter he sent away separately, without mixing, such men as were skilled in carving, turning and painting ; masons, moulders of plaster and flower-patterns ; blacksmiths, silversmiths, braziers, founders of gongs and cymbals, filigree flower workers ; doctors and trainers of elephants and horses ; makers of shields, forgers of cannon, muskets and bows ; men skilled in frying, parching, baking and frizzling ; hair-dressers, and men cunning in perfumes, odours, flowers and the juices of flowers. Moreover, to the noble Order, acquainted with the books of the Pitakas, he made fair appeal, and brought them away. He also took King Manuha and his family, and returned home."

Thus, with the Burmese conquest of the Mons in the eleventh century, Pali literature, monks to interpret it, the Pali language and script, and representatives of all the crafts from India, passed on to Upper Burma.

Though Anawrata tolerantly continued to allow all forms of worship, including the Tantric Buddhism of Bengal, then at the height of its popularity, under his royal patronage the Pali Buddhism of Ceylon rapidly supplanted the other forms of religion and became dominant throughout the whole of Burma. With the help of the master workmen brought from southern Burma, Anawrata and his successors set about making the Burmese capital of Pagan one of the proudest cities in the world. It is said that thirteen thousand pagodas and monasteries at one time lifted their golden spires above the city. The ruins of eight hundred of them, many in a fairly good state of preservation and some in actual daily use, may be seen in Pagan even today.

Anawrata and his son kept in intimate touch with India. They maintained the friendliest of relations with the neighbouring Pala kings of Bengal and Bihar, and gained great fame for themselves by paying for the reconstruction of the Mahabodhi Temple at Bodh-Gaya, which had fallen into disrepair. Indian Buddhists invariably received a warm welcome at Pagan. When Muslim invaders of northern India, in the opening years of the thirteenth century, compelled the monks to flee from their monasteries in great numbers many hurried to take refuge in the Burmese capital. A fresh influx of Indian ideas came with them, revivifying the Burmese civilization and strengthening the ties with India.

Limited researches in the Malay Peninsula have yielded some twenty Sanskrit inscriptions, ruined brick stupas, deserted Buddhist caves and a number of images of Indian gods, in stone, bronze and brass. By the third or fourth centuries A.D., Indian colonists had settled at points of vantage all down the western coast of Malaya as far as Malacca, and some had already crossed over the narrow Kra Isthmus from the port of Takuapa to the Bay of Bandon, on the eastern side of the peninsula. From there they trekked on into Thailand and Indo-China. The fertile valleys and plains of this region invited an agricultural type of settlement, in contrast to the tin-mining activities associated from earliest times with interior Malaya, or the busy trade of the ports.

Malaya received its Indian colonists from both northern and southern India, and during the first centuries A.D., the Brahmanic faith and both types of Buddhism flourished among the settlers. From a ruined shrine in Kedah, said to be the oldest surviving building in southeast Asia, has come a stone slab with a fourth-century Buddhist dedication. Four Sanskrit inscriptions in northern Malaya, of the fifth century, contain the name of the " great sailor " Buddhagupta, of Bengal, and mention certain donations by him. His religious faith is evident from the outline tracing of a stupa above one of the inscriptions. The most impressive ancient monuments in Malaya, however, are in the Thai strip, at Chaiya and Nakhon Sri-Thammarat. The Chaiya ruins consist of Buddhist brick temples built according to the square plan of the earliest Gupta temples of northern India, though one has a roof in receding stories suggestive of Pallava style. Nakhon Sri-Thammarat boasts a great bell-shaped stupa surrounded by a sculptured gallery a hundred feet long on each side. Some fifty smaller temples and shrines and hundreds of little votive stupas, besides 171 seated stone Buddhas, are scattered about the great courtyard of the main temple.

Chinese annals refer to embassies arriving in China from different kingdoms of Malaya from the sixth century onward. These historical records give an idea of the distinctly Indian character of some of these states at that period. The " History of the Liang Dynasty " (A.D. 502-556) records the arrival in 515 of an envoy from the king of a state in northern Malaya called Lang-ya-su, already established for more than four hundred years, where, it was stated, " the precious Sanskrit " was generally known. At that time kings with purely Indian names ruling in Malaya were enlightened enough to employ state historians, who accompanied their embassies to China.

Indianized kingdoms arose about the same time in Further Asia. Once more, thanks to the Chinese histories, accounts of them have been preserved. A Brahmin named Kaundinya landed in Cambodia by sea from Malaya in the third century A.D. He must have arrived with supporters, for he is said to have defeated the naval forces of Queen Willowleaf, sent to oppose him. He made up for his conquest by chivalrously marrying the queen, and it was he who founded the first Indian kingdom in Indo-China (Viet-Nam), called Funan by the Chinese. The primitive inhabitants were taught to wear clothes, and foreign merchants, skilled craftsmen and learned men began to frequent the chief cities. A Chinese official historian reported that " More than a thousand Brahmins reside there. People follow their doctrines, and give them their daughters in marriage. They read their sacred books day and night."

In the fifth century, the first Chinese mission visited Funan, and one of its members wrote a book. Not long before, an Indian merchant had arrived in the country and had deeply stirred the king of Funan by his glowing description of the Indian motherland.

" How long does it take to go there ? " asked the king.

" The journey there and back takes a good three years, or it may be four," replied the merchant.

The king at once decided to send an embassy to India, headed by one of his own relatives, and the Chinese mission met the members of this expedition just after their return to Funan, and saw with their own eyes four Yuechi horses, sent as a present to the king of Funan by the king of India.

The Chinese annals record that a second Indian Kaundinya, with the personal title of Jayavarman, became ruler of Funan in the fifth century. He had heard a mysterious voice of command announcing, " You must go and reign in Funan." He set out from Pan-pan, in northeastern Malaya, and when he arrived in Funan " The whole kingdom arose with enthusiasm, came to meet him and chose him as their king. He changed all the rules according to the customs of India."

The ruins of some sixty brick Hindu temple towers have been found in ancient Funan, and it is evident that its early Brahmin kings generally favoured Shiva worship, though in the fifth century King Gunavarman installed Vishnu footprints for perpetual worship, according to a Sanskrit inscription. In spite of royal favour extended to Hinduism, Buddhism also had its votaries in Funan. An Indian monk living there, Sakya-Nagasena, was twice chosen to accompany embassies from Funan to China. On these occasions he took as presents for the Chinese emperor miniature ivory stupas and coral and sandalwood Buddhas, besides some tame elephants. Buddhist monks also went from Funan to China to make some of the early Chinese translations of Buddhist scriptures.

A second Indianized kingdom, Dvaravati, arose in the Indo-Chinese peninsula in what is now Thailand. Mons from Lower Burma had drifted eastward as early as the second or third century, carrying their Hinayana Buddhism with them, and there they founded the independent kingdom of Dvaravati which lasted until the eleventh century. Dvaravati kept up continuous relations with India, both by way of the trade route across the Kra

Isthmus and by a northern pass to the Gulf of Martaban. Bronze Buddhas like those of Amaravati, if not actually imported from there, and Gupta type images, ruined stupas and monasteries of an archaic Indian type, and tablets with the Pali Buddhist creed in south Indian Pallava characters, are clear proof of the early contact between Thailand and India.

When the Mongolian Thais, ancestors of the present-day inhabitants of Thailand, overran the country in the thirteenth century, they in turn were converted to Buddhism and the new Thai king built a Buddhist temple at his capital of Chiengmai, on the Mekong, which was a copy of the Mahabodhi temple at Pagan, itself a copy of the famous Bodh-Gaya temple in India. As the Thais rapidly extended their power southward into Malaya, they came into touch with another stream of Buddhist influence emanating directly from Ceylon. A king of Ceylon sent one of the Thai rulers a much-prized Buddha image, with a flamelike emblem rising from the crown of its head. This image, still cherished in Bangkok, inspired an individual school of Thai sculpture characterized by slender Buddha figures with flame-crowned oval faces and a strange all-pervasive smile. Thailand also developed its own distinctive type of pagoda, or *wat*, charming but fragile, often made entirely of broken bits of Chinese porcelain.

Indo-China also saw the birth of a third Indianized kingdom towards the close of the second century, the seaboard state of Champa, destined to survive for nearly fourteen hundred years. This colony undoubtedly took its name from Champa in Bengal — Bhagalpur of today — from which presumably the original Indian immigrants came. The earlier inhabitants of Champa were of mixed Malay and Polynesian stock, and their wealth was chiefly derived from the lucrative practice of piracy, which they carried on with great zeal all up and down the coast of the China Sea. They also waged frequent wars with their neighbours, especially the Annamites of the north. When the Annamites finally threw off the Chinese yoke, which had long bound them, they began to exert pressure on the Chams. The latter were forced to withdraw farther and farther south, but no retreat could save them. They suffered defeat and political extinction in A.D. 1471.

Ruled by Hindu, or Hinduized, dynasties for centuries, the primitive Chams were slowly tamed. With their inborn vigour, they were able to create remarkable sculptures and a highly original type of brick temple architecture, the earliest surviving examples of which are contemporaneous with the first temples constructed by the Pallavas in south India. The Cham temple, unlike the later Indian temple, never developed into a vast architectural complex. It always remained an isolated structure, consisting of a square shrine with plain interior topped by a huge ornamental tower. But such temples were sometimes grouped together into impressive temple cities, as in India. The two best-known Cham temple groups, Mi-song and Dong-duong, both lie within twenty-five miles of the little port of Tourane. At Mi-song no less than sixty ruined shrines, ranging in date from the seventh to the twelfth centuries, cluster together. A little to the southwest is Dong-duong, whose temple remains date from the ninth and tenth centuries. Though Buddhism never competed successfully with Shaiva Hinduism in Champa, the largest temple at Dong-duong was Buddhist.

Cham figure sculpture, in its earliest phase, closely followed Gupta models, not only in subject matter but to a great extent in technique also. It was simple and natural, and it possessed striking dignity and power. Brahmin priests from India probably supervised both temple-building and image-making in Champa during this period. At Mi-song, engraved Sanskrit letters appear to have formed the numbering system for assembling the separate stones of one well-carved pedestal, bearing a date in the Indian Saka era equivalent to A.D. 657. Ultimately, however, a strong Further East or Polynesian tendency to subordinate sculpture to decoration triumphed in Champa. As Indian influences weakened and the Gupta ideal of restraint vanished, Cham art began to grow heavier and coarser, and later Cham art, in which the Polynesian element predominates, bears a strong resemblance to Peruvian, Mayan and Aztec art, far away on the other side of the Pacific.

All the kingdoms of Indo-China, ancient or modern, Hindu or Buddhist, pale to insignificance before the marvel of the fourth and last of the Indianized states of the peninsula — the Cambodian kingdom of the Khmers. Pearl-laden Khmer princes, half sacred during their lifetime and wholly deified after their death, struck terror into the hearts of Chams, Annamites, Burmese and Thais alike, for the better part of eight long centuries.

Fortunately for posterity Cambodia did not lie on any main highroad of the world. After its destruction by the Thais in the fourteenth century, the ruins of the wonderful Khmer cities and temples remained locked in a silent death struggle with the all-enveloping jungle, unknown and forgotten. Once, in the sixteenth century, a lonely French priest passed that way. Then another Frenchman officially rediscovered Angkor, in 1861. The district

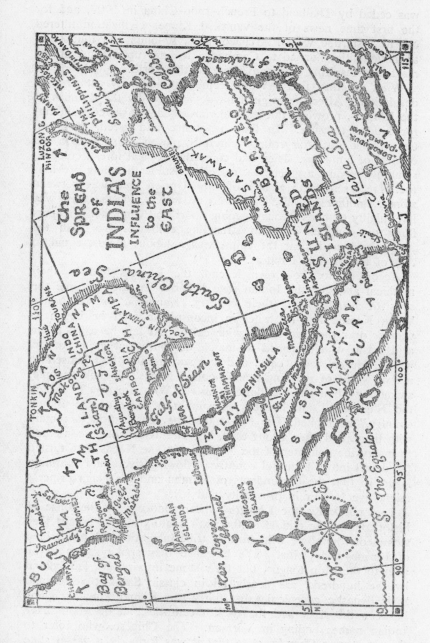

was ceded by Thailand to French Indo-China in 1907, and for the first time news of the vanished Khmer civilization filtered out to a startled world. Archaeologists, scholars and tourists of all nationalities hurried to Cambodia, to gaze upon some of the most awe-inspiring ruins anywhere in the world.

What did they find? What seemed at first only catastrophic desolation! After the original havoc wrought by the enemies of the Khmers, prowling thieves had ransacked the sacred buildings for hidden treasure. In their ignorance and greed, they had even pulled out iron cramps carefully placed to strengthen the corners of buildings. Then had come the tropical forest, creeping stealthily up like a green sea, more irresistible than any previous foe. Trees sent forth giant roots which pried their way between stones, smothered walls, clambered up towers, twisted their way like mighty pythons through gaping doors and windows. Creepers flung out sinuous arms in strangling embrace. To push the jungle back and clear the ruins, was a labour almost equal to that of the original builders.

According to their own legend, the Khmers had as their mythical ancestor the Indian sage Kambu. So they became the sons of Kambu, and their country, Kambuja, or Cambodia. When Kambu lost his wife, in inconsolable grief he began to wander over the face of the wide earth. At last he came to an arid waste which seemed to match the burnt-out crater of his heart. He entered a cave, and was surprised to find himself in a dim world of writhing many-hooded Nagas, or snake people, swimming about in the dark pools. "Who are you?" asked the Nagas. "I am Kambu Svayambhuva, king of the Indian country," he replied. The Nagas then begged Kambu to remain with them, and after a long time, his grief assuaged, he consented to marry the daughter of the Naga king. The Nagas then turned the desert into a beautiful country of flowing rivers and charming lakes, so that the descendants of Kambu and the Naga princess might live forever in prosperity and joy.

Less poetically, the Khmers appear suddenly on the stage of history about the middle of the sixth century A.D. Perhaps they stemmed from some wild frontier tribe inhabiting the borderland of Burma and China. The language they spoke seems to be akin to the Mon tongue, but their stone inscriptions, left behind by the hundreds, are nearly all in classic Sanskrit verse, and their dynastic genealogies list thirty-two Khmer kings, reigning between the sixth and the twelfth centuries, all of whom have Indian names ending in Varman. The Chinese, who refer to the country as Chen-la, state that it was formerly a vassal state paying tribute to Funan, in the south. After the conquest of Funan before the end of the sixth century, intermarriages between Khmer chiefs and the Brahmin-descended royal families of Funan took place, and Indian civilization spread northward from Funan into Cambodia.

Alternately Hindu or Buddhist, the great kings of ancient Cambodia vied with one another in warlike exploits to extend the boundaries of their kingdom. In the twelfth century, Cambodia reached from the China Sea to the Bay of Bengal. Using the natural wealth of the land and the inexhaustible supply of labour furnished by their prisoners of war, the rulers created magnificent cities and temples which, even in their present state of ruin, stir the beholder to dazed wonder.

Scattered through the mountains and jungles, more than six hundred ruined Khmer monuments are still to be counted — temples, palaces, city walls, gates, terraces, reservoirs, bridges. A number of early capitals have been traced, but for five centuries the most glorious of Khmer cities was Angkor Thom — a corruption of the Sanskrit *nagara*, " city ", and the Khmer *damma*, " great ", thus literally meaning, " Great City." The site was happily chosen by King Yasovarman, in the ninth century, in the very heart of Cambodia. It was conveniently close to a large lake, which gave anchorage for the Khmer navy, at the same time allowing easy access to the sea through the Mekong River. The finest Khmer buildings are all to be found in or near Angkor. The huge gray temple of Prah Khan lies like a sunken galleon on the floor of the orchid-hung forest, five miles north of the city ramparts. Ta Prohm and Banteai Kedei, nearly as large, are the same distance away on the east. Angkor Wat, hugest of all, rises from the open plain a mile to the south.

Angkor Wat, exceeding in size and grandeur all other Khmer monuments, has the distinction of being actually the largest temple in the world. It was built in the twelfth century by Suryavarman II as a tomb temple, to contain his own ashes and to be dedicated to himself, after death, in his deified form of Parama-Vishnuloka, identified with Vishnu. Except that it faces west instead of east, as the most accessible approach from the city, Angkor Wat is typical of all other Khmer temples of the great period of building in ancient Cambodia.

A raised causeway of flagstones leads from the main road across a broad moat to an entrance gallery, or portico. This portico, a thousand feet wide, forms the front part of the outer temple enclosure. The causeway re-emerges on the other side of the portico and continues in a straight line, through a park filled with palms, to the main entrance of the temple. From road to temple, it traverses a distance of two thousand feet. The moat is six hundred feet wide, and the surrounding wall has a length of nearly three miles.

The temple itself rises steeply in the form of three concentric rectangular galleries, each doubling in height the preceding one. The galleries are connected by precipitous stairs and intervening open terraces. The innermost of the three galleries is reached by twelve flights of steps, three flights on each side, and is crowned by a cluster of five tall domes. The lotus-bud pinnacle of the great central stone tower dominates the green plain below from the magnificent height of 213 feet. The holy of holies, where the ashes of king Suryavarman must once have lain, is a small dark empty chamber at the very top of the building, directly beneath the central tower.

All this vast edifice, from top to bottom, has been chiseled into endless beautiful designs and patterns, as if it were soft wood instead of hard stone. Broad window openings are barred with slender stone colonnettes, precisely imitating wooden ones turned on a lathe. The high plinths have row upon row of carved bands and borders. Miles of roof stones have been grooved to fit together like tiles. Square columns supporting the narrow stone vaults of the galleries are covered with flower-and-bird medallions and ornamental niches framing an endless variety of little figures. Everywhere are troupes of sacred dancers. Within the first gallery is a whole half mile of sculptured bas-reliefs. Even the outer walls are sculptured. Maidens, linked arm in arm and wearing three- or five-pointed tiaras, jeweled necklaces, girdles, floating angular scarves and long skirts peer into sunken stone tanks or pools at their feet, as if to catch a glimpse of their subtle charm.

In contrast to these accentuated reliefs, the sculptured story-book of the first gallery of Angkor Wat is delicately and lightly executed, scarcely a half inch in depth. The Khmer artists who carved these vast panels, ninety or a hundred yards long, must have given their lives to the work. Nowhere in India are there sculptures on anything like such a grand scale. The themes of the bas-reliefs are taken straight from the *Ramayana* and the *Mahabharata*. Vishnu, as might be expected in a temple built by one who claimed to be his earthly representative, occupies chief place in the decorations — whether as the Tortoise upholding the world, as Narayana sleeping on the serpent of eternity between the cycles of creation and dissolution, or as Rama or Krishna. Though Vishnu reigns supreme at Angkor Wat, other

Indian gods also have their place. Shiva dances his cosmic dance, fights his mighty battle with Arjuna, in the guise of the wild hunter, reduces Kama, god of love, to ashes for disturbing his meditation, overwhelms Ravana for daring to shake his palace on the summit of the Kailasa mountain, thus frightening Parvati.

The Khmer Smile
XII-XIII Century

The southern wing at Angkor Wat has reliefs of another sort. One long historical panel shows Suryavarman II himself as " His Majesty Parama-Vishnuloka ".   Two short inscriptions in the Khmer language, written in an alphabet derived from India, leave no doubt about the identification.   First he is seen seated on a throne on a hilltop, surrounded by Brahmins, engaged in giving orders to his various ministers for assembling his troops.   Later he is shown again, standing on his mighty war elephant, fourteen royal parasols held aloft around him by his parasol-bearers. The ensign-bearer in front grasps a pole on the top of which appears a little image of Vishnu, mounted on Garuda.   Along the base of the panel, a march-past of the Khmer infantry takes place, and behind the Khmers come Thai levies, in their own distinctive dress.   The great procession includes Brahmins carrying an ark with the " sacred fire " of Vedic worship, Dancing buffoons and musicians, and royal ladies in litters and palanquins, attended by female servants plying long-handled fans, also form part of the long cortège.

Another panel in the same gallery is designed to impress upon the beholder the lesson of good and evil actions, inseparable from the Indian doctrine of rebirth. Men and women advance in line to the judgment seat, presided over by Yama, god of death, who is assisted by Chitragupta, keeper of the fatal records. Here the panel divides to show heaven above and hell below, and brief inscriptions explain the various scenes. Those who insult the gods, spiritual preceptors or Brahmins suffer appropriate punishment in the hell of worms ; the untruthful find themselves hanging from thorny trees ; those who wilfully damage the property of others have their bones crushed ; those who betray a trust are sawed in two ; those who steal or who do not pay their just debts are thrust upside down into boiling cauldrons or roasted alive on pans of burning coals. There is no doubt of the fate in store for evildoers. Righteous Khmers, on the other hand, ascend to heaven, where in small pavilions with looped-back curtains they are shown placidly enjoying the bliss of family life, with plenty of good things to eat spread out before them.

The religion of the Khmers, at the time when Angkor Wat was built, was a curious mixture of the distinctive cult of a Royal God, and of Tantric Hinduism and Buddhism, then scarcely distinguishable. A king might personally favour Buddhism or Hinduism, but he did not fail in his support of all the great temples, whatever the deity to whom they were dedicated. Some idea of the nature of the Khmer temple establishment is revealed in a remarkable inscription of 145 Sanskrit stanzas set up in 1186 in the Ta Prohm temple just outside Angkor Thom, by the Buddhist king Jayavarman VII.

Ta Prohm was dedicated to an image of the king's mother in the form of the Mahayana Buddhist divinity Prajnaparamita, or " Holy Wisdom." It also contained 260 other images, including one of the king's royal preceptor. Altogether 79,365 persons were on the temple registry, of whom 12,640 had the right of lodging within the temple precincts. The privileged persons included 18 chief priests, 2125 ordinary officiating priests and 615 temple dancers. Menial services in connection with the temple were performed by Cham and Burmese prisoners of war and by innumerable slaves who formed the lowest division, or caste, of Khmer society. Armed guards protected the temple treasures, which consisted of 40,620 pearls, 35 diamonds, 4540 other precious stones (such as rubies and cat's-eyes), many cauldrons of gold, great numbers of gold and silver utensils used in the temple services, quantities of ordinary utensils made of copper, bronze, tin or lead, 965 Chinese mosquito curtains of silk gauze, and 523 silk parasols with handles of gold, carried in temple processions. The same inscription informs the reader that Jayavarman VII fostered all the pious works of a good Buddhist. He fed daily from his palace 489 " saints " and supported 970 students residing with their teachers. He maintained 102 hospitals throughout his realm for free treatment of patients, without regard to caste. For their upkeep, the services of no fewer than 81,600 men and women were required.

Jayavarman's versatile genius was also responsible for the most important building enterprises at Angkor Thom, the Khmer capital. These were the great stone causeways over the moat, the tall city gates, and the many-towered Bayon, in the centre of the city, a temple second in size only to Angkor Wat, and with an equally wonderful series of bas-reliefs. Colossal kneeling figures representing the gods and demons of Indian mythology, fifty-four stone giants in each row, once lined both sides of the five causeways over the moat, grasping in their arms the body of a huge Naga, which formed a magnificent parapet. Many of the petrified giants were later thrown down, and heads and broken limbs still strew the ground, but French archaeologists have repaired the damage as best they could. Massive gates sixty feet high, pierced the city ramparts. They were flanked by three-headed elephants of stone, lazily swinging delicate clusters of water lilies in their trunks. The passage was just wide enough for a single chariot or elephant to pass. High overhead, forming the dome of each gate, were four huge faces, or masks, framed by pendant earrings, each face eight feet from brow to chin. Forbiddingly stern, they glared at the four cardinal points.

These same strange faces of the gates of Angkhor Thom also look down from the fifty ruined towers of the Bayon. Etched by centuries of rain or bleached by the burning tropical sun, festooned with gray lichens or with grass or trees sprouting from their lotus crowns, like green hats, the two hundred huge faces appear to weep or smile, open their eyes in amazement or shut them in remote isolation, stare down gloomily or with sinister animosity, at puny man, or throw at him a look of benign haunting compassion. The broad straight mouths are traced with double outlines. The straight heavy brows meet in the middle. In the centre of the foreheads a third eye is placed vertically. At first the great faces of Angkor were taken for a representation of four-faced Shiva, but later researches indicate that the God of the Bayon, and of the city gates, is in reality Avalokitesvara — the omnipresent, all-seeing, all-merciful Bodhisattva of Mahayana Buddhism — in the guise of a portrait statue of Jayavarman VII, with the king's own heavy features.

Fighters, builders and inveterate temple-goers though the Khmers were, they were also saturated with Sanskrit learning. Asramas — forest retreats and schools — of purely Indian type were numerous in Cambodia. Under guidance of Brahmin pundits, Khmer princes were taught the ancient Vedic rites and studied Indian astronomy, grammar, logic and literature. The Khmer inscriptions often quote from, or mention by name, the Vedas, Puranas, *Ramayana, Mahabharata, Harivamsa,* Yoga and Nyaya philosophical systems, Manu, Panini, Patanjali, Susruta, Gunadhya, Mayura, Vatsayana and Kanada. Tantric texts are also named, manuscripts of which were recently discovered in Nepal. Sanskrit technical treatises, too, were familiar to the Khmers. Sanskrit names of thirteen musical instruments are given in descriptions of the martial music to which Khmer armies marched out to battle. The thoroughly Indian institution of public recitation, without interruption, of the great Sanskrit epics was very popular, and pious donors made gifts of sacred books to the temples. All the great Khmer temples had libraries well-stocked with Sanskrit manuscripts. The ruined stone libraries remain, but the manuscripts, alas, were irretrievably scattered and lost during the Thai invasions of the fourteenth century, which destroyed the Khmer kingdom.

Indian colonies and kingdoms arose and fell, likewise, in Indonesia. Sumatra had its great Buddhist kingdoms, Java its Hindu ones. Some lasted until after the discovery of America.

Sumatra was certainly visited by Indian ships and received Indian religious missions from very early times. Archaeological exploration here is far from complete, but ancient remains have been discovered under thick deposits of ash, from volcanic eruptions. Ruined stupas have been found in many parts of the island, as well as Indian types of images and a few important inscriptions. Some day, perhaps, the early history of Sumatra will become better known.

The more easily accessible island of Java is singularly rich in ancient treasures, and Javanese chronicles and early Javanese literature throw considerable light on the past. A legend still cherished in Java is of the Rishi Agastya, supposed to have come from India and settled in the island. Inscribed statues of the ancient Indian sage indicate an Agastya cult in the eighth and ninth centuries. That Indians arrived in the eastern archipelago at some very early period, however, is beyond question. Four stone posts inscribed in Sanskrit, in an archaic writing of the Pallava Grantha style and probably belonging to the fourth century A.D., have been found in distant Borneo. They record that one King Mulavarman, third in the dynastic line, performed a great religious sacrifice accompanied by a gift of 20,000 cows to Brahmins. A cave in eastern Borneo has also yielded twelve primitive sandstone images of Buddhist and Brahmanical deities. A gold *linga*, recovered from a river-bed, and a small gold figure of a four-armed Vishnu are other evidence of early Indian settlements in Borneo.

Inscriptions so far discovered in Java are later than those from Borneo. The earliest are assigned to the fifth century, and come from western Java. Like the Borneo inscriptions, they are in Pallava Sanskrit. They give the information that a king named Puranavarman, whose footprints are said to have resembled those of Vishnu, reigned in Taruma. He and his father constructed two canals, called by the names of two Indian rivers, Chandravaga and Gomati. Puranavarman, upon the completion of his canal, paid a fee of a thousand cows to the Brahmins. Since kings with Indian names acquainted with Sanskrit and following Indian religious customs were already ruling over part of Java in the fifth century A.D., it may be assumed that the first Indian colonies there go back another century or two.

The medieval Javanese chronicles assert that 20,000 Indian families arrived in Java from Kalinga in the second century A.D. No explanation is offered for this formidable exodus from India, but the immigrants are said to have prospered and multiplied, to have built cities and towns, to have promoted trade and industry, and to have taught the primitive inhabitants all the civilized arts. Another five thousand Indians are said to have arrived at a later date, this time from India's west coast, in six large ships and a hundred small ones. The second party included soldiers, craftsmen, cultivators, physicians and poets, and was led by Prince Aji Saka, who had obeyed his father's orders to sail away as his own country was about to be overwhelmed by some unnamed enemy. The refugees were not only received with great friendliness by the Javanese, but were permitted to invite another two thousand of their countrymen, including sculptors and metalworkers to join them in Java. These invasions do not appear to have been considered at all hostile by the Javanese.

The later Han Annals of China (A.D. 25-220), mention that in 132 an envoy arrived at the Han court from a Javanese king named Devavarman, and that the Chinese emperor was pleased to send him as a present a golden seal and a purple ribbon. The first dependable account, however, comes from the pilgrim Fa Hian. On his way back to China from India and Ceylon in A.D. 414, Fa Hian encountered a terrific storm, which blew his ship far off its normal course, and it finally took shelter in a Javanese port. Here Fa Hian had to wait five months before another ship was able to take him the rest of the way home. In the enforced interval of waiting, he learned all he could about Java, and as a pious Buddhist, records his disappointment at finding that the people generally favoured Hinduism. "Heresies and Brahmanism are flourishing," he wrote in disgust, "while the faith of the Buddha is in a very unsatisfactory condition."

Indians who had gone to Java up to this time were chiefly Hindus, but ten years after Fa Hian's brief visit a distinguished Buddhist monk from Kashmir, or possibly Kapisa, in Afghanistan, landed in the island. This was the royal monk Gunavarman, who had refused to accept a throne and had chosen instead the life of a Buddhist monk. Imbued with true missionary zeal, he first went to Ceylon to study the sacred scriptures, and then journeyed on to Java, where he converted the reigning king and queen mother to Hinayana Buddhism. It was he who dedicated the first Buddhist monastery in Java. Later he went to China, built more monasteries there, founded the first Order of Chinese Buddhist nuns and died in China in A.D. 431. Hinduism thus amicably made room for Buddhism, and without quarreling the votaries of each religion erected their respective temples side by side.

After a period of obscurity, a new great centre of Buddhism arose in southeast Asia. Attention shifts back to Sumatra, and again the principal witness is a Chinese pilgrim, I-tsing. I-tsing, on his way to and from India in the latter half of the seventh century, spent altogether eight years in the Sumatran kingdom of Sri Vijaya. More than a thousand Buddhist monks resided in the capital at that time, and it was under their tutelage that, on his outward journey, he diligently studied Sanskrit, and on his way back, again with their help, translated some of the four hundred manuscripts he had collected at Nalanda. "They study and investigate all the subjects that exist, just as in India," he wrote. "The rules and ceremonies are not at all different. If a Chinese priest wishes to go to the West in order to hear and read, he had better stay here one or two years and practise the proper rules, and then proceed to India." The Buddhist colleges of Sri Vijaya were long held in high repute, and distinguished Indian Buddhists like Dharmapala of Kanchi and Atisa of Bengal travelled all the way to Sumatra and remained there many years, in order to master abstruse points of doctrine as taught by learned Vijayan professors. The Buddhist kingdom of Sumatra played an important part in spreading Indian culture throughout the Malayan archipelago.

There is reason to believe that Sri Vijaya was originally a small state on the northern side of the Straits of Malacca. It began to expand, and just before I-tsing's time it had already established its capital — Vijaya, or Visaya — in eastern Sumatra. The site is believed to be the modern oil port of Palembang. From this neighbourhood came two of the earliest Sri Vijayan inscriptions. They are written in the Malay language but have dates recorded in the Saka era, corresponding to A.D. 684 and 688. The rise of Sri Vijaya was mainly due to its strategic position astride the Straits of Malacca, which gave it control over the trade of China, India and Arabia, all passing through the Straits.

But Sumatra did not satisfy the growing appetite for empire of the Sri Vijaya kings. In 686, their army invaded and conquered western Java and a good part of the Malay peninsula. All the little Hindu states in Malaya were now caught within the Sri Vijayan net. Sri Vijayan colonies were even planted in distant places like Borneo and the Philippine Islands. The Philippine settlements were not direct conquests, but offshoots of the settlements already established in Borneo. The people of the central Philippines still call themselves Visayans. Manuscripts written in Indian syllabic alphabets have been found in the islands of Panay and Luzon, and one of these describes how settlers with very Indian-sounding names arrived from Brunei, in northern Borneo, bringing with them a knowledge of metals, a code of law and their own peculiar system of writing. The ill-advised zeal of Spanish priests and friars of later times led them to destroy all vestiges of what seemed to them only pagan superstitions. A priest of Legaspi's time boasted that he had burned more than three hundred manuscripts from southern Luzon. Had such senseless destruction not taken place, much more might be known of early Indian influences in the Philippines.

From Ligor in northern Malaya, close to the old Buddhist colony of Nakhon Sri-Thammarat, a Sanskrit inscription of A.D. 775 refers to Sri Maharaja, a lord of the Sailendra dynasty. Like the Sri Vijayan rulers whom they conquered toward the end of the eighth century, all the Sailendra kings were ardent Mahayana Buddhists. Known to the Chinese as San-fo-tsi and to the Arabs as Zabag, the Sailendra kingdom now became the dominant power in Malaya and had soon expanded into a vast Pacific empire, over which Sailendra kings ruled for the next four centuries. Of their origin, three theories are held. One is that they came from Kalinga, the second, that they were related to the Indian rulers of Funan, and the third, that they first arose in Java. At any rate, they chose Kataha, or Kadara, a port on the western coast of the Malay peninsula as yet not identified, as their official seat of government.

Sailendra supremacy, resting principally on the navy, was finally challenged by the Cholas of south India, who had also developed a strong navy. At one time relations between the two powers had been more than friendly. An interesting Chola inscription on twenty-one copperplates, engraved partly in Sanskrit and partly in Tamil, records that in A.D. 1005 the Chola king Rajaraja the Great made a grant of the revenues of a certain Chola village for the support of a Buddhist monastery at Negapatam, built by the Sailendra king of Kataha. Rajaraja's son and successor broke off these friendly relations. He sent his fleet into Malayan waters, captured Kataha and took possession of many of its tributary states, including Sri Vijaya in Sumatra. Kataha soon regained its freedom, but another Chola inscription of the second half of the same century says that the Chola king, after again reconquering Kataha, was pleased to give it back to its own king — a roundabout way of acknowledging that Chola authority could not be maintained in Malaya.

The Chinese of this period were under the impression that the Chola king had actually become a vassal of the Sailendra ruler of Kataha. Hence the Chinese " board of rites " solemnly concluded that it was good enough to write to the Chola king " on strong paper with an envelope of plain silk ", instead of employing the silk-and-brocade stationery officially required for rulers of the first rank.

A long-drawn-out century of war between Hindu Cholas and Buddhist Sailendras ended in the mortal weakening of both. Meanwhile, Java had already managed to regain its freedom by the middle or end of the ninth century. About the same time, the old kingdom of Malayu, originally subdued by Sri Vijaya, came back to life and embarked on aggressive expansion in western Malaya. The end of Sailendra power came in the thirteenth century, when the Sailendra king Chandrabhanu undertook two ill-advised campaigns against Ceylon and lost his life in the second of them. With Malayu now steadily pushing north and the Thais vigorously pushing south, the remnant of Sailendra power was crushed out of existence.

It seems strange that just as the most magnificent Hindu monument is found, not in India, but in Cambodia, the greatest Buddhist monument belongs to Java, not to India. The famous stupa of Borobudur lies in the Kedu plain of central Java. Though no dedicatory inscription has ever been found, and not a single reference to this stupendous monument occurs in contemporary Javanese records, Borobudur almost certainly dates from the latter half of the eighth century, and must therefore have been built during the time when central Java formed part of the Sailendra empire, or at least was subservient to Sailendra kings.

Sailendra-Javanese genius also produced many other important Buddhist temples in central Java, such as the Chandi Sevu and Chandi Plaosan groups in the Prambanan valley, and Chandi Mendut in the Kedu plain. Sevu has a main sanctuary surrounded by 249 smaller temples. Inscriptions from Prambanan associate Sailendra kings with the erection of Buddhist temples and images in their region. One, with a date corresponding to A.D. 778, refers to an image of the goddess Tara and a temple and monastery built by a Sailendra king in honour of his religious preceptor. The image has disappeared, but the small finely carved stone temple of Kalasan still remains. Another, the Kelurak inscription of 782, records the dedication of an image of the Bodhi-sattva Manjusri by a royal priest from Gauda, who is said to have purified the Sailendra king " by the dust of his feet ". Both inscriptions are engraved in a northern Indian alphabet.

The Sailendra relationship with Bengal is further substantiated by a copperplate grant of Nalanda, issued by Devapala (815-855), the most powerful of the Pala kings of Bengal and Bihar. Devapala granted the revenue of five villages for the perpetual upkeep of a monastery built at Nalanda by the Sailendra king Balaputra. Borobudur itself, though unlike other stupas, has its nearest affinities with the great Pala temple and monastery of Paharpur.

The world-renowned Buddhist monument of Java is really a mountaintop which has been carved into nine stone terraces, each rising in height and diminishing in size, the whole crowned by a simple stupa surmounted by an octagonal pinnacle. After the work was started, it appears that the builders began to doubt whether the foundations would prove strong enough to bear the immense weight of the contemplated monument. The part of the plinth already carved and the lowest terrace were then covered over with a broad stone embankment, or pavement. The five terraces rising above this embankment are square in plan, with lacelike projections on the sides, and the upper three terraces are circular. From terrace to terrace, up the centre of each side, are staircases with covered gateways. Balustrades and narrow galleries surrounded the four lower terraces. The outer sides of the balustrades contain niches with images of the Dhyani Buddhas, altogether 432 of them — Akshobhya on the east, Ratnasambhava on the south, Amitabha on the west, Amoghasiddhi on the north. All the images in the niches of the fifth balustrade represent the fifth Dhyani Buddha, Vairochana. The three round terraces have bell-shaped latticed stupas along their outer rims, enshrining identical Buddha images. At the summit, rising from a lotus pedestal, is the stupa. It has no visible opening, but inside is a small round relic chamber, now empty.

Borobudur owes its fame to the fifteen hundred sculptured panels adorning the four galleries of the lower terraces. The Buddhist texts they illustrate have now been fully identified, and are found to be popular Sanskrit Mahayana works from India. The reliefs on the buried basement plinth, originally intended to form part of the general scheme of decoration, were inspired by the *Karmavibhaga*, a well-known Buddhist treatise on karma, the law of reward and punishment, known in Sanskrit, Pali, Chinese, Tibetan and Kuchan versions. The main sources for the reliefs of the first gallery, depicting scenes from the life of the historical Buddha and legends of his previous lives, were the *Lalita-vistara* and Aryasura's *Jataka-mala*. The principal text of Borobudur, however, which was used for the entire series of sculptured panels of the second, third and fourth galleries, was the *Gandavyuha*, recounting the story of the youth Sudhana, his 110 travels all over India in search of enlightenment, his final attainment of the quest with the help of Maitreya, the Future Buddha. The story of Sudhana was immensely popular with Buddhists in this period from Nepal all the way to Java.

The sculptured galleries of Borobudur were intended to be circumambulated in regular order by the devotee. On the lowest plane, he was to absorb the lesson of good and evil. He would then gain inspiration from the moving and noble example of the Buddha's own life. Then, mentally making the "great vow" of Renunciation, he would try to identify himself with Sudhana in the quest for spiritual knowledge. At last, with the divine help of the Bodhisattvas, he would reach the goal of Nirvana, symbolized by the stupa of the uppermost terrace.

The Borobudur bas-reliefs have many features in common with classic Gupta sculptures. As in the Indian sculpture, one finds the same youthful princes and princesses, in the same charming poses, the same chaste nudity, the same fervent spirit of adoration. But the Javanese sculpture has a remarkable simplicity, possibly imposed by the coarse volcanic stone, full of holes and granulations, which was used for the panels. Javanese atmosphere is also unmistakably created by the details of steeply gabled houses on heavy stakes, ships with outriggers, the foliage, the birds and the animals, all typically Javanese.

After Java ceased to be a part of the Buddhist Sailendra empire, about the middle of the ninth century, the Hindu dynasty whose kings had previously ruled over central Java regained power. Small Javanese bronzes of both Buddhist and Hindu deities are characteristic of this period, and the great Hindu temple of Lara-Jongrang, at Prambanan, represents the last flowering of Indo-Javanese art in central Java. On a great paved terrace surrounded by rows of smaller shrines are eight large temples, of which the three principal ones are dedicated to Brahma, Shiva and Vishnu, with Shiva's temple occupying the central position. The balustrade of this temple is decorated with forty-two sculptured panels similar to those of Borobudur, but depicting the story of the *Ramayana*, up to the point where the army of Rama enters Lanka. The sculptured story was originally continued and finished on the adjoining Brahma temple, but only broken fragments remain. Episodes from the life of Krishna formed the subject for the corresponding panels on the Vishnu temple. The Ramayana sculptures of Lara-Jongrang are vital and dramatic, superior in their plastic sense to the immense flat bas-reliefs of Angkor Wat, which are more like tapestry than sculpture.

At the beginning of the tenth century, the political and cultural centre of Java shifted eastward, and for the next five hundred years it was eastern Java that kept alight the culture and civilization transplanted from India. New Javanese kingdoms now arose — Jangala and Kadiri in the eleventh and twelfth centuries, Singhasari in the thirteenth, Majapahit in the fourteenth. The eastern Javanese kings were Hindu by faith or adopted Tantrik Buddhism, or both, like the Majapahit king Kritanagara, who assumed the title of Shiva-Buddha. Many Hindu temples were erected in eastern Java, but wars and devastating earthquakes have reduced them to a worse condition of ruin than the older monuments of central Java. Notable sculptures were also produced, including remarkable royal portrait statues, in which Javanese kings identified themselves, after the fashion of the Khmer kings, with their favourite deities.

Throughout the long period of Indian influence in Javanese history, Sanskrit literature played a significant part. In the first and earliest period, Sanskrit works brought from India supplied the inspiration for the temple sculptures, Javanese law codes were directly borrowed from those of India and Javanese society even adopted a caste structure resembling that of India, though less rigid. The second period was characterized by a brilliant outburst of literary activity associated mainly with the court of Kadiri, in eastern Java. Condensed versions of Indian works and translations in Old Javanese now appeared side by side. These were followed by Javanese metrical poems on subjects selected from the Sanskrit epics and composed on the model of Sanskrit kavyas, but the Indian heroes were successfully transformed into national Javanese heroes, who still play the chief roles in the typical Javanese dance dramas and puppet shadow plays, the *wayang purwo.*

Not until the fourteenth century did Java break away from Indian traditions and strike out along independent lines of creative endeavour. Then, as the old Indian ideals receded into the background, Indonesian elements, long held in check, rose suddenly to the surface. The *Ramayana* was still an appropriate subject for temple sculpture in eastern Java in the fourteenth century as the bas-reliefs at Panataran indicate, but these reliefs have lost the dignity and beauty of the older series of Ramayana sculptures at Lara-Jongrang, in central Java. The eastern Javanese figures are like fantastic *wayang* puppets, cut out of leather. Faces and feet are shown only in profile, noses are grotesquely long. Spiritual content and simplicity have been sacrificed for bizarre decoration.

In this much fought over part of the world, the tides of power were ever shifting, as they again seem to be doing today. By the fifteenth century, the old Indian traditions were dead or dying, and two new political forces were emerging on the horizon. The Chinese and Arabs had long been glancing jealously at the rich spice lands of Indonesia. For a brief moment, it seemed that the Chinese would win, and that the archipelago would be swallowed up in the mighty expanding empire of the Mings, but the tide unexpectedly turned the other way.

Arab trading colonies gradually sprang up all along the coast-lines, and though territorial conquest was not seriously attempted, Arab merchant princes frequently married into the old royal Indonesian families, and Arab influence grew stronger. When the last Hindu kingdom of Majapahit finally collapsed, a vacuum was created, and Islam filled it. The island inhabitants enthusiastically adopted the new faith, and the local rulers began to call themselves Sultans.

Then the European adventurers arrived, at the beginning of the sixteenth century, armed with guns and charters of trade, and the struggle continued among the new contestants, the Portuguese, the English, and the Dutch. The latter established their trade monopoly in Java and some of the adjacent islands before the end of the century, and when the Dutch East India Company went bankrupt about 1800, the Netherlands Government stepped in, remaining in control until Indonesia became independent just a few years ago. Only the little island of Bali, sometimes forming part of the various Javanese empires, sometimes asserting virtual independence for itself (the final losing battle against the Dutch was fought as late as 1908), maintained much of the ancient Indo-Javanese culture it had imbibed from the seventh century. Its rulers long resisted Islam, favouring a strange combination and fusion of Tantrik Buddhism, Shaivite Hinduism, and the cult of royal incarnations like the Khmers. Here in Bali, the fragments of dance, music and drama, temple rituals, and the four caste social order, originated in India long ago, were preserved till yesterday. So India had made her bequest to Southeast Asia — two great religions, a vast literature, well defined art traditions, legal codes and systems, and something of its peculiar social organization. These took root in the new lands and flowered with hybrid vigour for a thousand years.

Now the Indian, the Arab and the European are gone, and Malaysia and Indonesia prepare once again to renew their ancient struggle, while China probes her way relentlessly forward, for mastery of the whole of Southeast Asia.

16

CHAPTER XV

Indian Culture Beyond the Mountains

THE NORTHWESTERN FRONTIERS of India converge upon Pakistan, with Afghanistan, Tibet (now part of China), and the central Asian Soviet Republics beyond. Immense mountains separate most of these areas from India, but difficult passes lead over the Hindu Kush and by way of the famous " Iron Gates " to Samarkand. Still more difficult passes lead from Kashmir over the Pamirs and the Karakorum Mountains, which eventually join the Kunlun, or " Tiger-Dragon Mountains " forming the inhospitable boundary between Tibet and Chinese Sinkiang. North of Sinkiang, beyond the Taklamakan desert — more than a thousand miles from west to east — are other mighty mountain chains, the Altai and the Tien Shan, or " Celestial Mountains," then come the rolling grasslands of the Siberian Steppes. On its China and Mongolia side, the Taklamakan merges insensibly into the dismal Gobi, another vast stretch of sand and loess. Lifting itself spasmodically from time to time, like a heaving brown shroud, fine Gobi dust settles down at long last on the yellow-tiled roofs of distant Peking. Forbidding as the way thither seems, from whatever direction or approach, this long desiccated region of central Asia, today inhabited chiefly by Turkish-speaking Muslims, was a thriving centre of Buddhist culture for nine or ten centuries.

Down into the Tarim basin, a vague region known as Kashgaria, rivers carry melted snow from the surrounding mountains, thus creating a belt of fertile land, though the fickle waters soon lose themselves in salt marshes or the sandy wastes of the central desert. Whitened, long-dead poplars and willows are witnesses that once Kashgaria was not as arid as it is today. Two old caravan roads, strung with halting places, link the cultivated oases. Along the more northerly route lie such ancient towns as Kucha, Turfan and Hami. Yarkand, Khotan and Tun-huang are the punctuation marks on the southern road. Dividing at Kashgar in the west, both roads meet again at Ansi, on the Chinese border, a thousand miles to the east. Less well-defined tracks also crisscross the desert between the northern and southern oases, but the bold traveller who would choose one of these

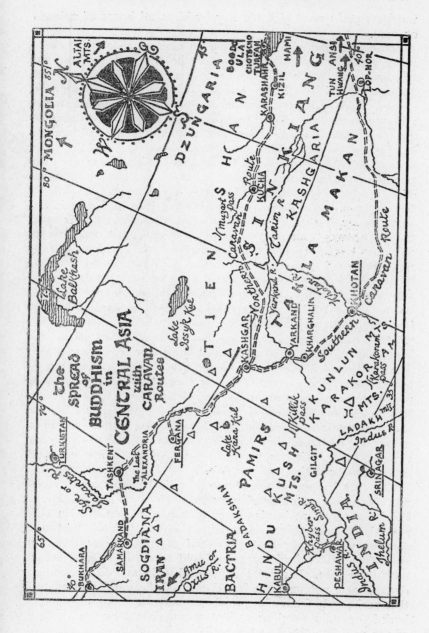

waterless paths must pick his way by bleached bones of animals or men.

During the Han and Tang periods of Chinese history, the oases came within the political sphere of the Celestial Empire, but Kushans and White Huns also fought resounding battles in Kashgaria, and about the middle of the eighth century, the Uigurs, then perhaps the most civilized of the Turkish tribes roaming about Asia, slipped into some of the northern settlements. At the beginning of the thirteenth century, the Mongol hordes, led by Jenghis Khan, bore down hard upon them.

In spite of their chequered history, there was always a settled population in the oases, and some of the early inhabitants spoke Indo-European languages or dialects — varieties of Tokharian in the northern oases, Sogdian and an eastern Iranian dialect in the southern settlements. Under aristocratic dynasties of their own, the settlements generally managed to retain their integrity as more or less independent and separate little kingdoms. If at times they had to send annual tribute of horses, borax, jade or felt to the Chinese imperial court at Loyang (Honan-fu) or Chang-an (Sian-fu), they still retained independence.

The Great Wall of China extended three hundred miles out into the desert, and along it were planted Chinese military posts, whose principal duty was to see that the famous Silk Road was kept open. Long camel caravans continuously passed westward, laden with precious Chinese silks. Long camel caravans continuously plodded eastward, led by rough Sogdians, laden with products from Bactria, India and Iran, perhaps even from Roman Syria. The central Asian oases profited greatly by the two-way traffic in merchandise. Most of the settlements, as a matter of fact, owed their existence to the epochal discovery by General Chang Kien in about 130 B.C. of a possible overland route between China and the West.

The first European actually to travel the ancient Silk Road was that prince of medieval wanderers, Marco Polo. But Marco Polo's eyes were roving in search of the mythical Christian king of Asia, Prester John, about whom Europe, in the thirteenth century, was naïvely agog. He had probably never heard of Buddhism, and ruined stupas and old monastic remains meant nothing to him. His notes on central Asia are disappointingly dry. It was not until the last decade of the nineteenth century that accidental discoveries of minor antiquities and some birch-bark leaves of mysterious ancient manuscripts drew the attention of the world to the desert oases.

Once again it was found that in the forgotten centuries the

civilizing influences of India had spread over the entire region. The court life and dress were mainly Iranian. The commercial life was controlled by China. But religion, art and learning were predominantly Indian.

The discovery of two birch-bark and palm-leaf manuscripts from Khotan and Kucha set off the archaeological investigations. They were found to be written in Indian languages and scripts, the first belonging to the second century A.D., the second to the fourth. The Khotan manuscript turned out to be the end portion of a Prakrit version in Kharoshthi writing of the well-known Buddhist *Dhammapada*, an anthology of the sayings of the Buddha forming part of the sacred Buddhist canon. The first portion of the same manuscript was found later by another scholar and taken to Russia. Previously known only in its Pali and Sanskrit versions, this Prakrit copy of the *Dhammapada* came as a complete surprise. It was the first Buddhist work in Kharoshthi to be discovered in northwest India. The Kucha manuscript turned out to be a medical treatise in Sanskrit verse, with a few Prakrit passages introduced. Complete in seven parts, it contained abstracts of ancient Indian medical works and a number of direct quotations from Indian authors, including twenty-eight extracts from Charaka and six from Susruta. India possesses only a very few manuscripts going back earlier than the tenth or eleventh century and it had long been supposed that the oldest Sanskrit manuscript actually in existence was a fragment carried away from China to Japan in the seventh century, and carefully preserved at the Buddhist temple of Horyuji, in Nara. The new finds in central Asia opened an entirely new chapter of history.

International archaeological competitors were soon reaping a harvest far exceeding their wildest dreams. Incredible numbers of written documents, in many languages and scripts, on birch-bark, palm leaves, bamboo tablets, wood, leather, silk and paper were recovered from ruined stupas and shrines, from floors and basements of buried wood-and-wattle houses, from ancient rubbish heaps left in the open, from grave pits and from the old Chinese military stations along the desert extension of the Great Wall. Wood-block prints and beautiful paintings came to light, and in deserted monasteries cut into the hills splendid Buddhist frescos, almost perfectly preserved on account of the dry desert air, were rediscovered. Thousands of sculptures, most of them of stucco, clay or wood, were dug out from the ruined sites. Architectural carvings, fragments of textiles including figured silks and brocades, remnants of woollen carpets, little embroidered shoes, lacquered furniture, engraved seals, glassware and coins — even little funeral cakes in a variety of designs and patterns, in a perfect state of preservation — were collected and sent on their way to the great museums of the world testifying to the high degree of civilization enjoyed by the inhabitants of the oases of central Asia hundreds of years ago.

The most exciting discovery went to the veteran explorer Sir Aurel Stein. Russian explorers had first discovered at the eastern end of the Taklamakan desert, eight miles from Tun-huang, an important group of 182 frescoed caves, now popularly known as the " Caves of the Thousand Buddhas ". A Chinese stone inscription gave the consecration date of the monastery as A.D. 366. Sir Aurel Stein, during a second visit in 1908, learned from a pious Taoist recluse who had taken up his habitation in the deserted caves of a secret chamber in one of the larger halls, containing a deposit of old manuscripts. After a good deal of persuasion, he was shown the hiding place into which, for safe-keeping — probably on the approach of some wild, destructive enemy — the Tun-huang monks nine hundred years ago had hastily thrust the manuscripts and religious paintings of their monastery. Afterwards the opening had been concealed by mud plaster and painted over with a decoration. The monks fled away, never to return, and the old library was completely forgotten, until its chance rediscovery in the present century.

Here, if ever, was the archaeologist's dream come true. It took three weeks merely to make a rough list of the contents of the wonderful chamber — more than 20,000 manuscripts and documents, 554 separate paintings ! Of the manuscripts, 9,000 were in Chinese, nearly as many in Tibetan, 3,000 more in Sanskrit, or in the central Asian varieties of Brahmi used for Kuchan and Khotanese, and the rest were in Sogdian, Uigur and Turkish. The collection contained 500 complete Buddhist canonical works, as well as varied assortments of geographical, historical and literary fragments, and sheaves of monastic accounts and records. In general, the material covered the period from the fifth to the end of the tenth century, the greater part belonging to the seventh and eighth centuries.

Other ruined sites in the oases also yielded quantities of manuscripts. Among them were Sanskrit originals and translations of long-lost Buddhist works. A unique find from Turfan consisted of the fragments of three ancient Buddhist dramas, written in Sanskrit characters of about the second century A.D. At least one of them was by Asvaghosha, the Mahayanist poet of Kanishka's court at Peshawar, who lived about A.D. 100.

A good many of the documents have proved to be secular in substance. They are in Prakrit, in the Kharoshthi script, which was apparently employed for administrative and business purposes in Central Asia, up to as late as the fifth century. The documents mainly consist of official or semiofficial orders, deeds, bonds and letters. A great many are written in ink on wooden tablets, and some on leather. The wooden tablets, wedge-shaped, rectangular or oblong, range in size from seven inches to seven and a half feet. Often they have been found in pairs, the name and address written on the upper half, or cover.

The oldest Chinese records are in the nature of orders for troop movements or lists of military supplies and accounts, and date back to the first and second century B.C., in the Early Han period. They are the oldest documents so far picked up in central Asia. They are written on small tablets of bamboo. The next earliest are on silk, and still later ones on coarse, primitive paper, which was a Chinese invention at the beginning of the second century A.D. Since the Chinese methodically dated their records, and these dates are often supplemented by the find of Chinese coins, accidentally dropped or perhaps offered before images in shrines, the chronology of many discoveries at the ancient sites has been easily established.

An extraordinary literary and artistic activity seems to have characterized the little oases kingdoms of central Asia, thirteen or fourteen hundred years ago, inspired by the polyglot Buddhist monks — Indian, Kuchan, Sogdian, Chinese — who crowded into the central Asian monasteries by tens of thousands. The most pressing task confronting the converts was to obtain proper texts, and since they were to be had only by laborious copying and still more laborious translation, the monasteries became busy hives of scholastic industry.

In the year 2 B.C., the first Buddhist text was taken to China by a Chinese ambassador returning from a mission either to the Yuechi or to the Kuchan court. Several decades passed, and then Ming-ti, emperor of China in the Later Han dynasty, had his famous dream, in A.D. 65, in which he saw a Golden Person standing in the West. Buddha, said the interpreters! Ming-ti promptly sent out emissaries to search for teachers, and two Indian Buddhist monks of Khotan were persuaded to return with them to China. Their names were Kasyapa Matanga and Gobharana. They arrived at Loyang, leading a white horse loaded with manuscripts and images. So Ming-ti built the " White Horse Monastery " for them, and there Matanga translated the " Forty-two Sayings of the Buddha ". The text still survives. the oldest of all Chinese Buddhist texts.

Monks from central Asia were soon going to China in ever-increasing numbers. Several Kuchan, Parthian and Sogdian monks made the journey in the second century A.D. and were responsible for some of the earliest Chinese translations of Buddhist texts. One of them was Dharmaraksha, a Kuchan monk who had settled at Tun-huang, and who was supposed to know thirty-six languages. He went to China in the year 284 and remained for thirty years. During this time he translated some two hundred Sanskrit texts into Chinese, of which ninety have survived.

Another well-known translator was Kumarajiva, who lived between 344 and 413. Kumarajiva was the son of an Indian minister of Kucha, and his mother was the daughter of the Kuchan king. The Kucha dynasty cherished a tradition of its descent from Kunala, Asoka's son. According to this tradition, Kunala was not blinded at his stepmother's order, but was banished to Kucha. There he converted the people to Buddhism of the Lesser Vehicle. As a young man, Kumarajiva went to Kashmir, mastered Sanskrit and became a monk. He then returned to Kucha, where he was suddenly converted to Mahayana Buddhism by a prince of Yarkand. After this event, he devoted himself to making translations into Kuchan of the principal Mahayanist writings, until during a political disturbance he was carried off as a prize prisoner to northern China with a retreating Chinese army. He at once began to study Chinese, and within ten years had translated many texts into Chinese, among them the *Saddharma-pundarika*, or " Lotus of the True Law ", which was destined to become the chief text of Mahayana Buddhism throughout the Far East.

Chinese monks were now beginning to feel an irresistible urge to visit India. The first of them got as far as Khotan, in A.D. 259, but a more famous successor was Fa Hian, who set out for India in A.D. 399.

Fa Hian took careful note of the kind of Buddhism and the number of monks to be found in each locality he passed through. His record includes such items as : Lop-nor, " some four thousand and more priests, all belonging to the Lesser Vehicle " ; Kara-shahr, " over four thousand, all belonging to the Lesser Vehicle " ; Khotan, " several tens of thousands, most of them belonging to the Greater Vehicle " ; Karghalik, " more than one thousand priests, mostly belonging to the Lesser Vehicle ", Kashgar, " over one thousand priests, all belonging to the Lesser Vehicle." The Gomati monastery was chief of the fourteen

monasteries in Khotan. The correct behaviour of its three thousand resident monks particularly impressed him. " When they
enter the refectory, their demeanour is grave and ceremonious ;
they sit down in regular order ; they all keep silence ; they make
no clatter with bowls ; and for the attendants to serve more food,
they do not call out to them, but only make signs with their
hands." He was also greatly impressed by the King's New Monastery west of the town whose central pagoda, so he maintains,
was 250 feet high. Yet even ordinary people at Khotan, it seems,
all had their private little pagodas — " the smallest of which
would be about twenty feet in height."

It was at Khotan that Fa Hian witnessed the great annual
Buddhist festival of the image-cars. On successive days, each
of the fourteen monasteries formed a procession, with its own
towering image-car. The procession started from a point a mile
outside the town and proceeded to the main gate of the city,
where they were met by the king, walking bareheaded and bare-
foot, scattering flowers and burning incense. A special pavilion
on top of the gate accommodated the ladies of the Khotanese
court, who showered flowers on the images as they passed below.
At Kashgar, Fa Hian witnessed the traditional five-year assembly
for the distribution of royal alms, originated by Asoka. There he
found that the monks had collected " like clouds."

When Yuan Chwang set out to travel the same road two and
a quarter centuries later, the two-way journeys of monks across
Asia had considerably swelled. Buddhism had now received
recognition throughout the Far East. Under the Northern Wei
dynasty, it had been made the State religion of northern China,
in A.D. 453. The Weis, of Tatar origin, had been converted
before they conquered China, and it was in the monastic cave
monastery of Yung-kang, their earliest capital inside the Great
Wall, that Chinese Buddhist sculpture was born. It was a direct
imitation of the Kushan Greco-Buddhist art of Bactria and Gandhara, as this was passed on to northern China through
central Asia.

During the fifth century, Buddhism had also come into high
favour in southern China under the Liang dynasty. At the close
of the first quarter of the sixth century, the Indian royal monk
Bodhidharma, coming by the sea route from India, reached
Canton. He was the real founder of the powerful Dhyana sect
of Buddhism, afterwards known as Chan in China and Zen in
Japan. Picturesque legends about Bodhidharma have to make
up for the historical vagueness surrounding his figure. He was
blunt, rough and rude, a scant respecter of persons. For nine

years he is said to have shut himself up in a mountain retreat in southern China, practising Dhyana. Popularly called " wall-gazing ", this was really a strenuous effort at mind-concentration, the purpose of which was to realize nothing less than one's own Buddha-nature. At last he opened his mouth. " I have come to teach you only that Buddha is thought," he said. " I have no interest in rules, nor ascetic practices, nor miraculous powers, nor mere placid sitting in meditation." Generally weary of the cold proprieties of Confucianism and the Quietist doctrine of Taoism, which too easily degenerated into " do-nothingness ", Chinese in ever increasing numbers began to abandon the world and flock into Buddhist monsteries.

As early as A.D. 372, Chinese Buddhist monks had gone on to Korea, where Buddhism was formally recognized in the Silla kingdom of Korea in A.D. 528. From Korea, it made its official entry into Japan in 538, the year in which the Korean king of Pekche sent copies of Buddhist scriptures, Buddhist banners and a beautiful Buddhist image to the Japanese ruler, with the following earnest message : " This teaching is the most excellent of all teachings ; it brings endless and immeasurable blessings to all believers, even unto the attainment of the Enlightenment without comparison. Moreover, it has come to Korea from the far-off India, and the people of the countries lying between are now zealous followers of it, and none is outside the pale." When a Japanese constitution was issued by the prince regent Shotoku in 604, it declared that henceforth faith in the Three Treasures of the Buddhist religion should be the foundation of national and individual life in Japan. Within another century, Indian missionaries were already landing on the distant shores of Japan.

Two centuries of turmoil in China finally ended with the restoration of peace in the great Tang period (618-907), but it appeared for a time that the popularity of Buddhism might lead to additional trouble. The old Confucian scholar Fu I, bitterly hostile, was convinced that Buddhism was rapidly undermining the loyalty of the subjects for their emperor and filial respect of children for their parents. He composed a memorial to the throne, in which he pointed out the insidious danger to the State, making his own recommendation to meet it. " This sect numbers at the present time more than a hundred thousand monks and as many nuns, who live in celibacy," he wrote. " It would be to the interest of the State to oblige them to marry one another. They would then form one hundred thousand families, and would provide subjects to swell the numbers of the armies for the coming wars." When Tai Tsung became emperor in

626, he took the old minister's advice to heart. " Emperor Liang Wu-ti preached Buddhism so successfully to his officers that they were unable to mount their horses to defend him against the rebels," he remarked one day. So saying, he passed a decree breaking up the religious orders and ruling that only one monastery should be permitted in a city, except three in the capital, Chang-an.

It was just three years later that Yuan Chwang petitioned the emperor to be allowed to go to India, to find out the truth among all the conflicting Buddhist doctrines and sects. It is not surprising that Tai Tsung refused, but Yuan Chwang went anyway, and after his return the emperor had a change of heart. Taking up his " divine pen," he himself wrote a preface to Yuan Chwang's scholarly translation of the Yogachara texts.

Riding alone across Asia in the early part of the seventh century, Yuan Chwang was deeply impressed by the piety of the people in central Asia, the atmosphere of overwhelming seriousness pervading the monasteries and the strange blend of the three different civilizations he encountered — Indian, Iranian and Chinese. The flattering but embarrassing eagerness to receive spiritual instruction on the part of the pious king of Turfan almost ended Yuan Chwang's journey before it began. The Chinese Master of the Law arrived at Turfan after dark, but the king was waiting to welcome him and kept him talking the rest of the night. He then decided that Yuan Chwang must remain at Turfan. In vain did the Master of the Law explain the purpose for which he had set out on his long and difficult journey. " The king will only be able to keep my bones, he has no power over my spirit or will," he insisted resolutely. When all argument failed, he went on a hunger strike. After three days, the penitent king at last gave him permission to depart.

Yuan Chwang even before he left China was already a follower of the Mahayanist school of the Yogachara, and he regretted that the Hinayanists of central Asia had not been converted. At Kucha, he was drawn into an acrimonious quarrel with the venerable Mokshagupta, head of five thousand Hinayanist monks in residence there. " Commonplace and superficial," sharply remarked Yuan Chwang, of the texts quoted by Mokshagupta. " Erroneous and contrary to the precepts of Sakyamuni ! " hotly retorted Mokshagupta, of the Yogachara texts. " Do you not fear to be hurled into a bottomless abyss ? " Yuan Chwang exclaimed sternly.

Beyond Kucha, Yuan Chwang had to pass through territory just recently brought under control of the Western Turks. Fortunately, his patron the king of Turfan had given him a letter to the Turkish *khan* and a handsome present of five hundred pieces of silk to hand over. The khan, encamped for the winter near a lake north of the Tien Shan, invited the Master of the Law to a great feast. Dishes piled high with mutton and endless cups of raisin wine were passed among the guests, to the accompaniment of clashing music. Yuan Chwang, seated on an iron chair, was served with his own special food. When the drinking bout was at its height, the khan then requested the Master of the Law to expound the Buddhist doctrine. Yuan Chwang did his best to comply. When the discourse was ended, the khan prostrated himself at the Master's feet, declaring that he had received the teaching with faith. He, too, wished to keep Yuan Chwang by his side. " You must not go to India," he insisted. " It is such a hot country I fear your face might melt when you arrive there !" Not long after Yuan Chwang's visit, the Turkish khan was assassinated. This was a fateful event. Subsequent history of central Asia might have taken a different course had this not happened.

The Turks were soon galloping in all directions. None of their leaders now cared to listen to any Buddhist doctrine of peace. Little armies of the oases, Tang horsemen from China, wild Tibetan soldiery, nomad Turks, met and slaughtered one another without mercy. The caravan roads were blocked, and Chinese pilgrims who still wanted to go to India preferred to face the unknown hazards of the sea, rather than the certain dangers of the overland route. Central Asia was unable to withstand the Turkish pressure, and soon Buddhist central Asia had become Muslim central Asia, and so it has remained.

With borders adjoining India's over long stretches, Nepal and Tibet also naturally received the deep impress of Indian culture, and both were also influenced by their great neighbour China, now the master in full political authority over Tibet. Nepal, roughly five hundred miles long and one hundred miles wide, takes a large bite out of northern India, between Kashmir and Bengal. Its religions, art and literature, as well as the language of its ruling class, reflect the contacts with India, going back many centuries.

The modern village of Rummindei, fourteen miles inside the present border of Nepal, is the ancient Lumbini, where Gotama Buddha was born. A pillar marking the site bears an Asokan inscription, saying that in the twentieth year after his consecration Asoka came in person and worshipped at this place, " because here the Sakya sage, Buddha, was born." The taxes of Lumbini were cancelled or reduced by reason of this fortunate circumstance. The border clans or tribes of the Buddha's time, such as the Sakyas, the Lichavis and the Mallas, must have had intimate relations with the people in the Valley of Nepal, less than a hundred miles away. Tradition says that Buddhism was introduced into Nepal by Asoka himself, who went there from Lumbini, accompanied by his daughter Charumati and his son-in-law Devapala. In Nepal, he founded the city of Patan a mile from Kathmandu and built many stupas and monasteries. Four ancient stupas of Patan, attributed to Asoka, are typically Mauryan in style, and others have an archaic simplicity which betokens great antiquity.

In the fourth-century Allahabad pillar inscription of Samudragupta, Nepal is named as a frontier state whose king " gratified his imperious commands by paying all kinds of taxes, obeying his orders and coming to do homage " to the Gupta emperor. Gupta political control, however, seems to have lain lightly on Nepal, but its proximity to ancient Magadha meant that Gupta culture inevitably penetrated Nepal. Intermarriages also took place, and dynasties tracing their descent from India held sway at Kathmandu, the Nepalese capital. Two Indian eras, Samvat (beginning 57 B.C.) and Saka (beginning A.D. 78) were adopted by Nepal though a Nepalese Samvat was inaugurated in A.D. 880. A steady stream of religious teachers, scholars and artists began moving back and forth between Bihar and Nepal, and Nepal reacted sensitively to all the principal currents of ideas arising in India. Vasubandhu, the great teacher of Mahayana Buddhism, is said to have gone to Nepal with 500 followers to preach the Greater Vehicle. Nepal adopted Mahayana Buddhism, and also the Tantrik doctrines which from the eighth or ninth centuries began to spread out in all directions from Bengal.

With the Muslim invasions of northern India in the eleventh century, an exodus of orthodox Brahmin scholars occurred, and many of them fled to Nepal, taking their Sanskrit manuscripts with them. Tantrik Buddhism, with its emphasis on Shakti worship, had already made a firm bridge between the two great ancient Indian religions, and Hindu cults and sects from this time flourished side by side with Buddhist sects, but the arrival of Rajput refugees in the wake of further conquests by Muslims strengthened the trend towards Hinduism in Nepal.

The Gurkhas, who conquered Nepal only some two hundred years ago, claim descent from these same Rajputs of Rajputana, and retain a reputation for high military valour. Some of them made their way to the hilly tracts of Kumaon and entered Nepal from the west. In the early part of the sixteenth century they conquered the little Nepalese state of Gurkha and began to call themselves Gurkhas. Expanding eastward, they reached the central Valley of Nepal, and in 1769 established their authority over the whole country. The Gurkhas of today are doubtless a mixture of Rajputs, hill Brahmins and Tibeto-Mongolians, with the latter strain predominating, but they consider themselves as a distinct racial group. Their language, Khas, is a Rajasthani dialect of Sanskritic origin, but has naturally been influenced by the Tibeto-Burman languages generally spoken in this area. The Gurkhas observe the rules and practices of a Hindu caste, and under the dynasty founded by Prittvi Narain Sah, Hinduism became the state religion of Nepal.

It is in the little central Valley, some twenty miles long and ten miles broad, with its three old capitals of Kathmandu, Patan and Bhatgaon lying within a radius of seven miles of one another, that India's religious and artistic influence upon Nepal is most strongly felt. The Valley boasts nearly three thousand temples and shrines. Apart from a few old stupas, most of its sanctuaries belong to the late medieval period of the Malla rajas. Some of them have come to be regarded as sacred places of pilgrimage for Tibetans and Indians, as well as Nepalese. The ancient Buddhist stupa of Bodhnath is especially venerated by Tibetans. Almost equally holy is the Svayambhunath, crowning a high hill above Kathmandu. Like Bodhnath, it possibly dates back to Asoka's time. Above a plain rough whitewashed stupa is a later addition consisting of a square stone tower, with four pairs of large mysterious eyes painted in red, black and white on the four sides. They are the eyes of the Adi-Buddha, or Primordial Buddha — the self-existing, all-seeing, all-knowing deity of Mahayana Buddhism. The most famous place of Hindu pilgrimage is Pashupatinath, where Shiva reigns supreme. This is a temple city spread out along the Bhagmati river, like a miniature Banaras. Innumerable shrines and temples and pilgrim's hostels line the ghats. To live at Pashupatinath, say the Hindus of Nepal, brings virtue, and to die there insures eternal bliss.

The Buddhist-Hindu Newars of central Nepal are the chief artisans, craftsmen and traders. It is they who have been largely responsible for the artistic achievements in building and image-making for which Nepal is famous. Like the Kashmiris, the Newars are born craftsmen. They have developed two characteristic types of religious architecture, used indiscriminately for both Buddhist and Hindu sanctuaries. One is the Indian stone temple type, with a massive tower rising above a comparatively small shrine. The other is the multiple-roofed pagoda, associated particularly with China, though its place of origin is still not certain. Nepalese pagodas are largely constructed of wood, but have roofs of copper. Pala art traditions were also bodily transposed from Bengal and Bihar to Nepal in the ninth and tenth centuries, and dictated the conventional types of Nepalese religious images, painted banners, illustrated manuscripts and decorated wooden covers of manuscript boxes. The three cities of the Valley, with neatly paved squares, picturesque temples and palaces, and three- and four-storeyed houses with little projecting carved balcony windows reminiscent of Ajanta sculpture and painting have a delightfully medieval and old-world look, contrasting sharply with the modern buildings now coming up.

In the past, before the age of planes, Tibet was effectively isolated on practically every side by its mountain barriers or the great Tsang-po on the south (which becomes the Brahmaputra after it enters India), and remained sealed off by the intense winter cold of its high plateau, averaging 16,000 feet. It was not until the seventh century A.D., almost a hundred years after Buddhism had already reached Japan, that Indian religious ideas penetrated to the " roof of the world ". Tibet, indeed, was the last but one of the countries of Asia to come under the spell of Indian civilization.

Tibetan Sacred Mantra

Before the seventh century, the country was divided into numerous poor little chieftainships, and the Tibetans lived in a rude state. The valley of the Tsang-po was inhabited by primitive

agriculturists, and nomad herdsmen roamed the lake region and
the desolate plateau in the north. At the beginning of the seventh
century, however, one of the petty kings or chieftains of southern
Tibet began the task of uniting the various Tibetan tribes. His
son and successor, Srong-tsan-Gampo, carried on and completed
the work of unification and became the founder of a new imperial
line of Tibetan kings, who ruled the country for 275 years.
Srong-tsan-Gampo also brought under his control parts of Kashmir, central Asia, China, Nepal and even India. The Tibetan
conquest of a substantial slice of India in the middle of the
seventh century, after the death of Harsha, is an incident not
even mentioned in Indian historical records, though it is referred
to in contemporary Chinese chronicles. According to the latter,
the Tibetans maintained their hold over northeastern India for
half a century.

As ruler of united Tibet, Srong-tsan-Gampo realized the need
for keeping in close touch with generals and officials stationed in
remote parts of his empire. He was greatly handicapped by the
fact that Tibet had as yet no form of writing, and he decided
to send one of his ministers, Thon-mi Sambhota, to study the
art of reading and writing in India and to find, or devise, an
alphabet suitable to represent the sounds of the Tibetan language.
Thon-mi Sambhota journeyed to Kashmir, where, with the help
of a Khotanese Brahmin, he learned Sanskrit and worked out
the principles of Tibetan grammar. Afterwards he invented a new
Tibetan alphabet based on the model of the Khotanese alphabet,
which was itself derived from a form of Gupta Sanskrit. The
Tibetan emperor is said to have retired for four years to a cave,
in order to perfect himself in the new art of writing, brought back
from Kashmir by Sambhota.

It was during Srong-tsan-Gampo's time that Buddhism was
introduced into Tibet, and for this the emperor's two foreign
wives were traditionally responsible. One was the princess Bhri-
kuti, daughter of Amsuvarman, king of Nepal. She arrived in
Tibet some time between 630 and 640, bringing as part of her
dowry three precious Buddhist images. The other queen of
Srong-tsan-Gampo was the Chinese princess Konjo, a daughter
of the house of Tai Tsung, who brought a highly treasured Indian
sandalwood image of Buddha, which had originally reached China
by way of central Asia. The two queens simultaneously conceived the desire to erect in Lhasa, the new Tibetan capital founded
by Srong-tsan-Gampo, temples worthy of their respective images.
In the northern part of the city, the Chinese queen built the
temple of Ramo-che. The Nepalese queen, coming from a poorer

country, lacked adequate means, but the emperor himself built a temple for her images, the famous Jo-khang, in the very heart of Lhasa. After Srong-tsan-Gampo, his immediate successors apostatized to the old native Tibetan religion, Bon-po, until after ninety years king Thi-Srong Detsan reestablished Buddhism on a firm basis. Other Tibetan kings remained ardent Buddhists, with the exception of the last, under whom, in the early part of the tenth century, the Tibetan empire toppled to its fall. Then a long period of political chaos resulted in the division of Tibet into eastern and western kingdoms, followed by a redivision into still smaller states.

In spite of royal favour, Buddhism in Tibet long had to contend with its very powerful rival, Bon-po, a strange mixture of nature worship and necromancy, of oracle-mongering and propitiation of evil spirits by sorcery and magic. The Bon priests, dressed in sombre black, exercised a strong hold over the common people of Tibet, and eventually succeeded in creating their own influential party at court. Whenever they felt themselves strong enough, they instigated severe persecutions of the Buddhists. In the ninth century, during the minority of the emperor Khri-srong, they turned the great Jo-khang of Lhasa into a slaughterhouse and removed the famous sandalwood image of Buddha, installed there after the death of Srong-tsan-Gampo.

Khri-srong's son Muni, undaunted by the powerful clique opposed to him, went farther than any previous king of Tibet in his effort to embody the Buddhist ideals in administrative reforms. He embarked on a socio-economic experiment, which sounds quite modern. By royal decree, he confiscated the entire wealth of the country, and then proceeded to redistribute it on a basis of perfect equality. The result was that the poor, no longer under any immediate compulsion to work, grew lazy and poorer than before, while the discontented rich, by incessant scheming, managed to recover all their former wealth and more. The Bons used this opportunity to foment a serious rebellion, and the king was eventually poisoned at the instigation of his own mother. At the end of the same ninth century, king Ralpachan showed such excessive devotion to Buddhism that he handed over all the important state offices to monks. This scarcely improved the factional jealousies. He was succeeded by his brother Lang-darma.

Lang-darma favoured the Bons, and at once ordered all Buddhist monks to return to lay life, put many of them to death, and ruthlessly destroyed monasteries and sacred books. But his orgy of persecution was short-lived. One day a certain monk,

17

disguised as a Bon priest, rode into Lhasa on a black horse. He found the king in the open square in front of the Jo-khang, and with the words, " If a tyrannous king is to be disposed of, this is the way to do it," shot him through the heart with an iron-tipped arrow. This famous episode of Tibetan history became the basic theme of popular mystery plays, wrongly called " devil dances ", formerly performed annually in many Tibetan monasteries. The theme represents the perennial struggle between good and evil and the final triumph of good. In Lhasa, the dance pantomime was performed to music by masked Tibetan monks on the very spot where Lang-darma met his end.

Tibetan Buddhism with the passage of time began to assume its own distinctive shape. Among the manuscripts recovered from the monastic caves of Tun-huang, in central Asia, are two authentic early Tibetan chronicles, perhaps the oldest manuscripts existing in the Tibetan language. They appear to date from the ninth century, but they deal with a considerably earlier period. One covers the reigns of eleven early Tibetan kings, seven of them antedating Srong-tsan-Gampo. The other is a diary of historical events recorded year by year, from A.D. 650 to 747. When translations of these remarkable manuscripts become available, more information will certainly be brought to light on the introduction and development of Buddhism in Tibet. All the traditional Tibetan accounts, however, agree in naming Padma Sambhava, the " Lotus-born ", as the real founder of Tibetan Buddhism, or Lamaism, his particular school being known as Nyingma.

This enigmatic person is supposed to have arrived in Tibet in A.D. 747, about a century after Buddhism had first become known in Tibet. Legend has conveniently supplied him with a miraculous early life, having some features in common with the life of Gotama Buddha. He was born " of a lotus " in Udayana, the borderland region between Kashmir and Afghanistan, from whence he derived his popular Tibetan name of Urgyen. After renouncing worldly life, Padma Sambhava studied under many teachers, acquiring knowledge of all scriptures, as well as mystic powers. He is said to have studied at Nalanda also. At the special invitation of king Thi-Srong-Detsan he finally set out for Tibet, and consecrated the first Buddhist monastery of Sam-ye, some thirty miles southeast of Lhasa. Burning with missionary zeal, he remained in Tibet for fifty years (or a hundred, according to some accounts), all the while tirelessly preaching and performing miracles to confound the enemies of Buddhism. At last promising to return to his beloved Tibet at some future time, he mounted a blue horse and—so the legend runs—rose up into the air and vanished from the sight of men. The statue or portrait of Padma Sambhava, the great Buddhist saint, can always be identified by the skull drinking-cup and thunderbolt sceptre he invariably carries.

The particular type of Buddhism which Padma Sambhava encouraged in Tibet was the Buddhism prevalent in northern India in his time — Mahayana Buddhism, strongly coloured with Tantrik ideas and practices. It had its trinities of spiritual Buddhas, Bodhisattvas and earthly Buddhas, to which were added female Bodhisattvas, or Taras, innumerable tutelary deities and many varieties of supernatural beings. Padma Sambhava chose the Bodhisattva Avalokitesvara as the patron saint of Tibet, but Maitreya the Future Buddha and Manjusri the Bodhisattva of Divine Wisdom also gained special favour in the eyes of the Tibetans. Already Hindu deities — in particular Shiva and his consort, in their twofold mild and terrible aspects (the latter for the destruction of evil as well as the salvation of the unenlightened) were included within the all-embracing Buddhist pantheon as protectors of the faith. Tantrik rituals were adopted, such as the recitation of sacred syllables, the use of mystic diagrams and the performance of secret-rites in the names of particular deities by joint assemblies of men and women devotees (*mandalas*). To secure the triumph of Buddhism in Tibet, Padma Sambhava is said to have outdone even the Bonists in the display of miracles and magic, as a result of which magic and miracles came to be considered as an integral part of Tibetan Buddhism. Some Bonist deities and demons were also admitted in course of time to a place among the humbler ranks of servitors in the Buddhist heavens, as a means of placating the opposition.

Buddhist texts in Sanskrit and Buddhist images and paintings found their way to Tibet in ever-increasing quantities, inspiring a new Tibetan religious art. The people of northern Nepal were closely affiliated to the Tibetans, and Nepalese craftsmen tutored the first Buddhist Tibetan craftsmen. Chinese art conventions impressed themselves upon Tibetan art at the same time, though this influence was less marked than the Indian and Nepalese influences. In the end, however, Tibetan genius, thus stimulated and guided, produced its own distinctive styles.

In spite of the zeal and ardour of Padma Sambhava, Tibetan Buddhism, with its complicated background, remained in a highly confused state for the better part of a century. On this account Khri-srong, father of the social experimenter Muni, invited the Indian scholar-monk Santa Rakshita of Nalanda to come to

Lhasa in the early part of the ninth century and reorganize Buddhism on a sound basis. There was still no Buddhist Church in Tibet. Santa Rakshita took up his residence at Sam-ye and twelve Nalanda monks arrived to ordain the first seven Tibetan monks. Manuscripts were collected, and Indian and Tibetan scholars set to work with great industry to make Tibetan translations of the Sanskrit Buddhist texts.

Though monasticism was now established in Tibet, sinister forces constantly worked to drag it down into a state of corruption. Reformers were constantly needed to purge Tibetan Buddhism of its preoccupation with magic and omens, astrology and sorcery, and to check the love of pomp and luxury, and worse vices. Subsequently a king who had become a monk and who was greatly troubled by the impurities with which he found Buddhism defiled, felt that better translations of the sacred texts and commentaries might help to remove mistaken ideas, and he arranged to send twenty-one young Tibetans to Kashmir for study early in the eleventh century. Nineteen of them died within a short time, but Rinchen-stan-po, one of two survivors, returned to Tibet after many years, with important new translations. He also brought back with him thirty-two Indian artists to beautify Tibetan temples and monasteries. Frescos belonging to this period were discovered not very long ago in some monasteries of western Tibet by the Italian explorer, Tucci.

Of the great reformers of Tibetan Buddhism, the first was Atisa, the famous Indian from Vikramasila monastery of Bengal. He went to Tibet in the middle of the eleventh century. Another was the Tibetan poet and mystic Milarepa, of the same century. The third, Tsong-khapa, was born about two hundred years later, on the spot where Kunbum monastery now stands, in the eastern Tibetan province of Amdo.

After repeated invitations, Atisa finally set out for Tibet and first went to Tholing monastery, not far from Lake Manasarovar. Here his Tibetan followers, under his best-known disciple, Bromston, formed a new Tibetan sect, the Kadampa. From Tholing, Atisa went on to Sam-ye, and eventually died there after thirteen years of strenuous work. At this time Atisa was considered the most distinguished of all Indian Buddhist scholars. After pursuing his earlier studies in all the chief Buddhist centres of northern India, he had gone to Sumatra to study under the distinguished Dharmakirti, then teaching there. Later on he had become the chief professor at Vikramasila university. In Tibet, he did much to suppress magical practices and to re-establish Buddhism on a higher plane. He preached a purer form of

Mahayana Buddhism, and placed great emphasis on true learning and scholarship.

Nineteen years after Atisa's death, a Tibetan noble founded Sakya monastery, in the southern province of Tsang, on the road from Nepal to Shigatse, about fifty miles northeast of Mt. Everest. Its original inmates described themselves as the "Old Ones," claiming to be followers of Padma Sambhava. In time, however, Sakya came to be the recognized headquarters of the Dukpa sect, or "Red Caps." Sakya abbots could marry and the abbot-ship was established on hereditary lines. This monastery rendered a great service to the cause of Tibetan Buddhism by promoting the translation of Indian religious literature, and the Sakya library became widely known for its valuable collection of manuscripts. Its temples and the palaces of its abbots were repositories of the finest works of art, both Indian and Tibetan. One of the Indian scholar-monks who added special lustre to Sakya was Sri Bhadra, one time head of Vikramasila and preceptor of the contemporary Pala king. When Vikramasila was destroyed at the beginning of the thirteenth century, Sri Bhadra and several companions sought refuge at Sakya.

As late as the fourteenth century, the scholarly reputation of the Sakya monks was still undimmed. Bu-ston, before founding his own monastery at Shalu, close to Shigatse, was for a time a teacher at Sakya. Access to the great Sakya library made it possible for Bu-ston to undertake the gigantic task of compiling the first authoritative edition of the Tibetan Buddhist canon. He began by getting copies made of all the existing Tibetan translations of Buddhist texts. He then rearranged these in chronological order and divided them into the two vast collections, the *Kanjur* and *Tanjur*. The *Kanjur*, in some 108 volumes, comprises more than a thousand texts, all traditionally representing the actual words of the Buddha. About a dozen are Hinayana texts and three hundred are Tantrik texts. The rest are Mahayana works. The *Tanjur*, in 225 volumes, is made up of works on philosophy and mysticism, grammar and logic, medicine, a few purely literary compositions, and all the innumerable commentaries on the *Kanjur*. The original copies of the *Kanjur* and *Tanjur* as prepared by Bu-ston were carefully preserved in Shalu monastery. Both collections were cut on wood blocks at the beginning of the eighteenth century, and printed editions have since been made from these identical blocks. Shorter versions of the *Kanjur* and *Tanjur* have also been brought out.

Love of magic being deeply rooted in the Tibetan nature, the cult of the mystical powers of the Yogi, rather than his spiritual realization, had a compelling attraction for ordinary Tibetans. The Eighty-four Great Sorcerers, or Siddhas, soon had devotees all over Tibet, as well as in Bengal, central Asia and China.

Atisa was still alive in Tibet when the charming figure of Mila-repa appeared upon the scene. It was his life's effort to lift magic to the plane of true Yoga, or mystic union with God. As a child, Milarepa suffered bitter poverty because an uncle had cheated his widowed mother out of the family property. The mother apprenticed her young son to a magician, in order that he might learn Black Magic, punish the wicked uncle and restore the family fortunes. But Milarepa was at heart a mystic, not a magician. Recognizing as his Guru the great master Marpa, once a disciple of Atisa's in India, he joined Marpa and under-went years of severe discipline, never faltering in his determination to obtain spiritual liberation in this life. There followed years of hermit life, during which he lived in inaccessible mountain caves and subsisted on nettles. At last, emerging from his cave, he adopted the life of a wandering monk.

Milarepa was not only a mystic but perhaps the greatest of Tibetan poets. He chose to instruct the people through song, and his " Hundred Thousand Songs " appealed directly to the heart. In these songs he describes the mystic beauty of the vast solitudes and the ineffable joy of the contemplative life. The Tibetan hermit sect of Marpa and Milarepa, the Kargyutpa, gave rise to several great monastic institutions, which became powerful rivals of Sakya. Milarepa himself was in due time canonized, and Tibetan paintings show him with his right hand cupped behind his ear, as if listening to nature's distant echo answering back his own song.

As monasteries in Tibet grew richer and more powerful, worldliness and indifference to monastic rules also increased exactly as they had in India. Scholars became fewer, and once more religion tended toward superstition and questionable prac-tices. It was at such a psychological moment, in the middle of the fourteenth century, that Tsong-khapa, the greatest of Tibetan religious reformers, was born. His father was a poor herdsman of the village of Tsong-khapa, in Amdo, from which he acquired his name. After receiving his early schooling at the nearest monas-tery, Tsong-khapa left Amdo at fifteen for Sakya to receive his higher training there. One of his teachers at Sakya was a disciple of Bu-ston. Tsong-khapa was deeply impressed by Bu-ston's achievements. He became convinced that people could be weaned from their ghost worship and fear only by right education and right example of stern self-discipline, set before them by the monks. When he felt ready to begin his great mission, he went to Lhasa. This was in the year 1390.

Tsong-khapa's reforms were thorough-going. He insisted first and foremost on strict celibacy for monks. He also denounced the Tantrik use of intoxicating liquor, and demanded extreme simplicity in dress. He advocated the reintroduction of the old Buddhist rule of fortnightly confession in open assembly, and also the observance of the annual retreat. He introduced, as a new measure, an annual week of prayer and fasting, for both laymen and monks. Tsong-khapa was not opposed to Tantrik Buddhism of the right path, properly followed by initiates of the inner circle, and his greatest literary work was his codification of Tantrik writings, but he strongly opposed sorcery, magical practices and humbug. The new sect which embodied Tsong-khapa's reforms was the Gelugpa, " Virtuous." It is also referred to as the " Yellow Caps," from the yellow hoods worn by the monks of this order, in contrast to the red hoods of the older, " unreformed " sects, and the black hats of the Bons.

Before Tsong-khapa's death, in 1414, three huge monastic seminaries of this Gelugpa sect had been founded in Lhasa, and thirty thousand followers had swarmed into them. Tsong-khapa himself founded Galdan monastery, some twenty-five miles outside the capital and this monastery became the highest educational centre of Tibet. Its monks preserved their reputation for piety and strict discipline. Within five miles of Lhasa two other important " Yellow Cap " monasteries, Depun and Sera, were also built. They were built in Tsong-khapa's lifetime by two of his disciples. Still another Gelugpa monastery, Tashi-lhumpo, was founded at Shigatse, in southern Tibet, by Tsong-khapa's nephew, who afterwards became the second Chief Lama of the Order.

Tibetan monastic wars and internal disorders, as also the greed of those in power, often resulted in long periods of chaos and ruin in the country, but in the past there was always the chance for some reformer to arise and re-establish order once more. An entirely new situation has been created by the expansionist policy of Communist China. The military conquest of Tibet by the Chinese, and the flight of the Dalai Lama and many thousands of Tibetan refugees to India in 1959 have left the country paralyzed. No other country was willing or able to attempt a rescue. It is now the open policy of the Chinese, in the name of political and economic conquest, to destroy Lamaism, to wipe out or suppress the monasteries as centres of learning, to degrade the Lamas, and to reduce the Tibetans themselves to a helpless minority in their own former country, by bringing in

ever increasing numbers of Chinese to colonize Tibet. Will
enough vitality remain for the people ever to reassert themselves
and win back their freedom? In any case, Tibet can never be
the same again. The contribution in the field of religion, learning and art has been made, and scholars of the future will have
to be content with salvaging what they can of Tibet's distinctive
genius.

It was the Tibetan form of Buddhism that was finally adopted
by Mongolia and Manchuria, after the Great Khans had established the Mongol empire. As early as the eighth century,
some of the Buddhist scriptures were translated into the Mongol
language and written down in the Syriac-Uigur script of the
Naimans, one of the principal Mongolian tribes. A Chinese work
records that an Indian monk named Prajna came to China in
A.D. 780, to search for the Bodhisattva Manjusri, whom he was
convinced was actually living there. Prajna failed to find Manjusri, but he seems to have made the acquaintance of Adam,
Bishop of the Nestorian Christian Church in China, whose name
is mentioned in the inscription of the famous Nestorian monument erected about this time in the old city of Chang-an, or
Sian-fu. Prajna and Adam set to work to translate from Mongolian into Chinese seven volumes of an unnamed Buddhist sutra.
When the result was examined by the Chinese emperor, he
condemned the translation as "rough and obscure." The obvious
reason was that Prajna knew neither Mongolian nor Chinese, and
Adam neither Sanskrit nor anything whatever about Buddhism!

Jenghis Khan, before his death in 1227, had achieved the unity
of all the Mongol tribes in Asia, and the vast Mongol empire
he created was the greatest empire the world had known up to
this time. It stretched from the Balkans in Europe across
southern Russia and Siberia to the Pacific Ocean, and it extended
southward to the borders of China, Tibet and India. Under
the fifth Great Khan, Jenghis Khan's grandson Kublai Khan,
eastern Tibet and the whole of China were added to the Mongol
domain, and Kublai's brother Hulagu conquered Persia.

The Mongols in general were omen-loving Shamanists, but
were surprisingly tolerant of all religions. In the thirteenth
century, they appeared always eager to listen to religious discussions. Jenghis Khan, whose religion was a somewhat vague
worship of the Everlasting Blue Sky, took time off on his way
back from a victorious battle on the banks of the Indus to hold
three protracted interviews with a famous Taoist monk, Chang
Chun, who had come all the way to Samarkand at his invitation,
just to talk philosophy. Nestorian Christianity had spread across

Asia several centuries earlier, and the Nestorians were active propagandists for their faith. The first two Catholic friars from Europe, Carpini and Rubruquis, were a bit late on the scene, arriving at the camps only of the third and fourth successors of Jenghis, his grandsons, Kuyuk, son of Oggatai (second Great Khan), and Mangu, son of Tului. Buddhists and Muslims were also eagerly engaged in seeking converts to their respective creeds in distant Mongolia in the thirteenth century. At Kara-korum, on the River Orkhon, the northern Mongol capital, Rubruquis was astonished to find twelve Buddhist temples, two mosques and one Nestorian church already established.

The two grandsons of Jenghis Khan just referred to were both converted to Buddhism by Tibetan missionaries. As a result, Buddhism spread rapidly among the Mongols, and through them also reached the Manchus. The scholarly abbot of Sakya monas-tery, Sakya Pundit, who was a disciple of the former abbot, Sri Bhadra, visited the court of Kuyuk, third of the Great Khans of the Mongol tribes, and was accepted by Kuyuk as his spiritual teacher. Another Tibetan monk, who claimed great mystic powers and who belonged to the Kargyut sect of Milarepa, was chosen as spiritual adviser by the fourth Great Khan, Mangu. Sakya Pundit sent two of his nephews to Mongolia to carry on the work of Buddhist propaganda, and one of them, Phags-pa, became the teacher and guide of Mangu's youngest brother Prince Kublai, afterwards the fifth Great Khan and emperor of China.

Interesting accounts of at least four religious parliaments held under Mangu and Kublai have been preserved. Two assemblies were summoned at Karakorum. Another was held at the nearby Mongol summer camp of Syra Ordu, and still another at Chang-du, the first Mongol capital in China, a hundred miles inside the Great Wall. In the religious debates presided over by these Mongol princes of the thirteenth century, Muslims, Christians, Taoists and Buddhists strenuously competed against one another to prove the truth of their respective doctrines. Apparently the Buddhists came out on top, for Mangu announced in final judg-ment, " Just as the fingers come out of the palm of the hand, the Buddhist doctrine is likewise the palm, the other religions are the fingers." At the Chang-du assembly, several hundred Buddhists and Taoists were pitted against each other, and on this occasion Kublai Khan appointed neutral Confucian scholars to act as judges. Phags-pa was present, and thanks to his bril-liant oratory, the Buddhists were again pronounced victors. The defeated Taoist monks, according to the custom of the day, were compelled to shave their heads and become Buddhists.

It must have been just about this time that the elder Polos, father and uncle of Marco, reached Chang-du. Kublai Khan, whose mind was still open on the subject of religion, invited the Polos to act as his personal ambassadors to the Pope, and sent a letter by them on their return journey, asking for one hundred educated Christian priests to be dispatched to China. If they could convince him that Christianity was the best religion, he said, he and his subjects would immediately accept it. The Polos returned to China for the second time, in 1275, bringing along young Marco, but they had not been able to persuade any priests to accompany them. In any event, Kublai Khan had meanwhile made up his mind that Tibetan Buddhism was the religion best suited to the Mongols.

Phags-pa remained near the Great Khan for twelve years, and it was at the request of the emperor that he devised a phonetic system of writing for the Mongolian language, based on the Tibetan script. By an imperial decree, issued in 1269, this new script was declared to be the official Mongolian script, for adoption throughout Kublai Khan's empire. Though it appeared in some of Kublai Khan's inscriptions and on his coins, in less than a century it had altogether disappeared from both China and Mongolia. The Mongol people preferred a reversion to the old Uigur script, previously used by them. Phags-pa remained in great favour with Kublai Khan, who appointed him head of the Tibetan Buddhist Church and also nominated him to be his viceroy in Tibet, with full powers of civil administration. Phags-pa, on his part, performed the ceremony of consecrating Kublai Khan as emperor of China. The Sakya abbots, from the time of Phags-pa's elevation to the headship of the Buddhist Church and his nomination as viceroy, became virtual rulers of a great part of Tibet. Twenty-one Sakya abbots in succession ruled the country through regents directly appointed by them.

In the latter half of the fifteenth century, and through the whole of the sixteenth, monastic wars raged all over Tibet. Since the monasteries obtained their main support from the lands they owned, armed guards became necessary to administer and protect the monastic properties. The guards, however, soon transformed themselves into monastic armies, and the formidable army of Sakya monastery gained control of the whole of Tsang province in southern Tibet. Violent battles continued, monasteries were burned down, the inmates were ruthlessly slaughtered. Early in the seventeenth century, the Gelugpa monks of Depun monastery at Lhasa suffered a particularly horrible massacre, and the Head Lama appealed to a Mongolian chief, who had recently occupied northeastern Tibet, to help him in the fight against Tsang. The Mongolian army defeated the Tsang army, and in 1642, with Mongolian support, the abbot of the reformed " Yellow Cap " sect of Tsong-khapa assumed the position of Grand Lama and supreme ruler of Tibet, henceforth known by his Mongolian title of Dalai Lama, meaning " Ocean of Wisdom ". At the same time, the reformed sect of Tsong-khapa was declared to be the official religion of Tibet.

Ties with Mongolia were cemented still more firmly when a Mongol actually became the fourth Dalai Lama, and when the fifth Dalai Lama assumed the supreme rulership of Tibet with Mongol intervention. It was he who, in 1645, undertook to build the great Potala Palace, overlooking Lhasa. The fifth Dalai Lama was also declared to be an incarnation of the Bodhisattva Avalokitesvara, while the abbot of Tashi-lhumpo monastery (the successor of the Dalai Lama's spiritual teacher) was declared to be an incarnation of the Dhyani Buddha Amitabha. The old Indian concept of rebirth and incarnation took on this new form in Tibet, of incarnated Lamas, just as it had led to the deification of the kings in Cambodia and Java. All the abbots of the leading monasteries were soon looked upon as incarnations, now popularly called " Living Buddhas ", and the idea spread with Tibetan Buddhism to China, Mongolia and Manchuria. Today there are innumerable incarnated Lama abbots presiding over Buddhist monasteries in northern Asia. Even Srong-tsan-Gampo's Nepalese and Chinese wives were retroactively declared to have been incarnations of Tara, and Tara was thought to have reincarnated herself in the Abbess of Samding monastery, over which she presided.

And so the long story of India's cultural expansion in Asia, over a period of a thousand years and more, comes to an end. The relationship, with only a few exceptions, was always one of co-operative inspiration. Having obtained her own political emancipation in recent years, India would like to see all her Asiatic neighbours equally free to direct their future development according to their particular national genius with a renewed strengthening of the old ties of friendship among them.

Bibliography of Principal Sources

GENERAL

The Cambridge History of India. Vol. 1. Ed. by E. J. Rapson, and Vol. 3. Ed. by Sir Wolseley Haig

The History and Culture of the Indian People. Vols. 1-6. Ed. by R. C. Majumdar

History of India. Vols. 1-3. Ed. by A. V. William Jackson

Chand, Tara : *A Short History of the Indian People.*

Dunbar, Sir George : *A History of India.*

Hoernle, A. F. R. and Stark, H. A. : *A History of India.*

Hunter, Sir William Wilson : *A Brief History of the Indian Peoples.*

Moreland, W. H. and Chatterjee, Atul Chandra : *A Short History of India.*

Nehru, Jawaharlal : *Discovery of India.*

————— *Glimpses of World History.* 2 vols.

Panikkar, K. M. : *Geographical Factors in Indian History.*

————— *A Survey of Indian History.*

Saunders, Kenneth : *A Pageant of India.*

Smith, Vincent A. : *The Oxford History of India.*

Waley, Adolf : *A Pageant of India.*

RELIGION, ART AND CULTURE

The Cultural Heritage of India. 3 vols. Sri Ramakrishna Centenary Memorial publication.

The Legacy of India. Ed. by G. T. Garratt.

A Source Book in Indian Philosophy. Ed. by Sarvepalli Radhakrishnan and Charles A. Moore

Altekar, A. S. : *The Position of Women in Hindu Civilization.*

Anesaki, M. : *Buddhist Art.*

Sri Aurobindo : *Essays on the Gita.* 2 vols.

Grousset, René : *The Civilizations of the East.* 4 vols.

Brown, C. J. : *The Coins of India.*

Brown, Percy : *Indian Architecture (Buddhist and Hindu).*

Bournouf, Eugène : *Legends of Indian Buddhism.* Tr. by Winifred Stephens

Carus, Paul : *The Gospel of Buddha according to old Records.*

Chandrasekharan, K., and V. H. Subramania Sastri : *Sanskrit Literature.*

Chatterji, J. C. : *India's Outlook on Life.*

Coomaraswamy, A. K. : *The Dance of Shiva.*
———————— *A History of Indian and Indonesian Art.*
Cousins, James H. : *The Cultural Unity of Asia.*
Dasgupta, Surendranath : *A History of Indian Philosophy.* 3 vols.
Datta, B., and Singh, A. N. : *History of Hindu Mathematics.*
Davids, T. W. Rhys : *Early Buddhism.*
Davids, Mrs. C. A. F. Rhys : *Buddhist Psychology.*
Dickinson, G. Lowes : *An Essay on the Civilizations of India, China and Japan.*
Farquhar, J. M. : *A Primer of Hinduism.*
Foucher, A. : *L'Art grèco-bouddhique du Gandhara.*
———————— *The Beginnings of Buddhist Art and Other Essays.* Tr. by L. A. Thomas and F. W. Thomas
Fox-Strangways, A. H. : *The Music of Hindosthan.*
Govinda, Lama Anagarika. : *Foundations of Tibetan Mysticism.*
———————— *The Psychological Attitude of Early Buddhist Philosophy.*
Gowen, Herbert H. : *A History of Indian Literature.*
Hackin, J. : *Les Collections bouddhiques.*
———————— Siren, Warner, Langdon and Pelliot : *Studies in Chinese Art and Some Indian Influences.*
Havell, E. B. : *The Ideals of Indian Art.*
Jayaswal, K. P. : *Hindu Polity.*
Kabir, Humayun : *Our Heritage.*
Keith, A. Berriedale : *The Samkhya System.*
Kramrisch, Stella : *Indian Sculpture.*
———————— *The Hindu Temple.* 2 vols.
Krishnamachariar, M. : *Classical Sanskrit Literature.*
Dr. S. Krishnaswami Aiyangar Commemoration Volume.
Macdonell, Arthur A. : *A History of Sanskrit Literature.*
Maitra, H. : *Hinduism : The World Ideal.*
McGovern, Wm. Montgomery : *An Introduction to Mahayana Buddhism.*
Sister Nivedita and Coomaraswamy, A. K. : *Myths of Hindus and Buddhists.*
Popley, H. A. : *The Music of India.*
Swami Prabhavananda : *Vedic Religion and Philosophy.*
Radhakrishnan, S. : *Eastern Religion and Western Thought.*
———————— *The Hindu View of Life.*
———————— *The Vedanta according to Samkara and Ramanuja.*
Raju, P. T. : *Telugu Literature.*
Rao, T. A. Gopinatha : *Elements of Hindu Iconography.* 2 vols.
Renou, Louis et Filliozat, Jean : *L'Inde Classique.*
Rice, Stanley : *Hindu Customs and Their Origins.*
Sharma, Chandradhar : *A Critical Survey of Indian Philosophy.*

Stcherbatsky, Th. : *Buddhist Logic.* 2 vols.
Winternitz, M. : *A History of Indian Literature.* 2 vols.
Woodroffe, Sir John : *Shakti and Shakta.*
——————— *The Garland of Letters, Studies in the Mantra-Shastra.*
Vivekananda, Swami : *Complete Works,* 8 vols.
Zimmer, Heinrich : *Myths and Symbols in Indian Art and Civilization.*
——————— *Philosophies of India.*

HISTORICAL PERIODS AND BIOGRAPHIES

Altekar, A. S. : *Education in Ancient India.*
Bader, Clarisse : *Women in Ancient India.*
Bhandarkar, D. R. : *Asoka.*
——————— *Inscriptions of Asoka.*
——————— *Some Aspects of Ancient Hindu Polity.*
Bose, P. : *The Indian Colony of Champa.*
——————— *The Hindu Colony of Cambodia.*
Brewster, E. H. : *The Life of Gotama the Buddha.*
Chakravarti, N. P. : *India and Central Asia.*
Chatterji, B. R. : *Indian Culture in Java and Sumatra.*
——————— *Indian Cultural Influence in Cambodia.*
Cumming, Sir John : *Revealing India's Past.*
De Beerski, Jeannerat P. : *Angkor Ruins in Cambodia.*
Dikshit, K. N. : *Prehistoric Civilization of the Indus Valley.*
Fick, Richard : *The Social Organization in North-East India in Buddha's Time.*
Ghoshal, U. K. : *Progress of Greater Indian Research.*
Goddard, Dwight : *A Buddhist Bible.*
Grousset, René : *In the Footsteps of the Buddha.*
Havell, E. B. : *Aryan Rule in India.*
Hawkridge, Emma : *Indian Gods and Kings.*
Laufer, Berthold : *Sino-Iranica.*
MacKay, Ernest : *The Indus Civilization.*
Majumdar, R. C. : *Ancient Indian Colonies in the Far East — Champa, and Suvarnadvipa.* 2 vols.
——————— *Corporate Life in Ancient India.*
Marshall, Sir John : *A Guide to Sanchi.*
——————— *A Guide to Taxila.*
——————— *Mohenjo-daro and the Indus Civilization.* 3 vols.
Mehta, R. N. : *Pre-Buddhist India.*
Mookerji, Radhakumud : *Harsha.*
——————— *A History of Indian Shipping and Maritime Activity.*
Pargiter, F. E. : *Indian Historical Tradition.*

Pillai, V. K. : *The Tamils Eighteen Hundred Years Ago.*
Prasad, Beni : *The State in Ancient India.*
Radhakrishnan, S. : *Gautama the Buddha.*
Rao, R. R. : *The Aryan Marriage.*
Rawlinson, H. G. : *Intercourse between India and the Western World.*
Sastri, S. S. : *Sankaracharya.*
Smith, V. A. : *Asoka.*
Stein, Sir Aurel : *On Ancient Asian Tracks.*
———— *Serindia.*
Sykes, Brig. Gen. Sir Percy : *The Quest for Cathay.*
Thomas, E. J. : *The Life of Buddha.*
Vats, M. S. : *Excavations at Harappa.* 2 vols.
Wales, H. G. Quaritch : *Towards Angkor.*

SANSKRIT AND PALI LITERATURE IN TRANSLATION

Bana's Harsacharita, tr. by E. B. Cowell
The Bhagavad Gita, tr. by Charles Johnson
The Brahma-Sutras, tr. by Swami Vireswarananda
Buddhism in Translation, by Henry Clarke Warren
Buddhist Birth-Stories, tr. by T. W. Rhys Davids
Buddhist Legends, 3 vols., tr. by Eugene Watson Burlingame
Buddhist Parables, tr. by Eugene Watson Burlingame
Buddhist Texts through the Ages, ed. by Edward Conze
The Culavamsa, tr. by Wilhelm Geiger and Mrs. C. Mabel Rickners
Hymns of the Rigveda, tr. by R. T. H. Griffith
The Kama Sutra of Vatsyayana, tr. by H. S. Gambers
Kautilya's Artha Sastra, tr. by R. Shamasastry
The Little Clay Cart (Mricchakatika), tr. by Arthur W. Ryder
The Mahabharata, 11 vols., tr. by P. C. Roy
The Mahavamsa, tr. by Wilhelm Geiger
Manava Dharmasastra, tr. by J. Jolly
Mudrarakshasa or *the Signet Ring of Visakha-Datta,* tr. by R. S. Pandit
The Panchatantra, tr. by Arthur W. Ryder
Panchatantra and Hitopadesa, tr. by A. S. P. Ayyar
The Psalms of the Early Buddhists, 2 vols., tr. by Mrs. T. W. Rhys Davids
Rajatarangini or *the River of Kings* of Kalhana, tr. by R. S. Pandit
Ritusamhara or *the Pageant of the Seasons* of Kalidasa, tr. by R. S. Pandit

Sankhya Karika of Iswara Krishna, tr. by Henry Thomas Cole-
brooke and *Bhashya* of Gaudapada, tr. by Horace Hayman
Wilson
The Upanishads, tr. by Max Muller
The Thirteen Principal Upanishads, tr. by Robert Ernest Hume
Sources of Indian Tradition, ed. by Wm. Theodore de Bary
The Vairagya-Satakam or *the Hundred Verses on Renunciation*
of Bhartrihari, tr. by Swami Madhavananda
Valmiki Ramayana, tr. by P. P. S. Asatri

EARLY TRAVEL RECORDS IN TRANSLATION

Ancient India as Described in Classical Literature, tr. by J. W.
M'Crindle
I-Tsing : Records of the Buddhist Religion, tr. by J. Takakusu
Carpini and Rubruquis, Hakluyt version, ed. by C. Raymond
Beazley
Chau Ju-kua, tr. by Friedrich Hirth and W. W. Rockhill
Kitab-ul-Hind of Alberuni, tr. by E. C. Sachau
Periplus Maris Erythraei, tr. by W. H. Schoff
Si-yu-ki or Buddhist Records of the Western World of Hiuen
Tsiang, tr. by S. Beal
The Travels of Fa-hsien, tr. by H. A. Giles
Travels of Marco Polo, by Sir Henry Yule, revised by Henri
Cordier

INDIAN PERIODICALS

Annual Reports, *The Archeological Survey of India*
Bharatiya Vidya
Journal of the Greater India Society
Journal of the Indian Society of Oriental Art
Marg
The Modern Review
Prabuddha Bharat
Proceedings of the Indian History Congress
Science and Culture
The Visvabharati Quarterly

Index

18